You too can make a shooter

Can one person make a first-person shooter? The size, scope, and sheer detail of a typical triple-A game – the *Call of Duty*s, *Battlefield*s and *Halo*s of this world – might leave you thinking that the answer's a resounding no. But beneath all the polish and modes, the basic elements that underpin the shooter genre haven't changed all that much since *Doom* and *Quake* defined it way back in the 1990s.

In fact, with a bit of help and guidance, even a relative newcomer can put together a simple shooter with most of the trappings you'd expect: a level to navigate around, keys that unlock doors and, most importantly, hordes of enemies to blast.

That's where this guide comes in – it'll take you step by step through the process of making your very own first-person shooter. From downloading the free software you'll need, to setting up a player character and waves of zombies, it'll show you how to get a basic shooting game up and running. Once that's in place, you'll be taken through the process of building level assets and 3D models, and shown how to add lighting, sound, and other effects.

"Follow our guide through to the end and you'll have a shooter that you can customise further"

Follow our guide through to the end and you'll have a shooter that you can customise further with optional mechanics and even a boss fight. So if you've always wanted to make your own first-person action game, or simply wanted an approachable means of getting started in Unity, this is the book for you.

Turn the page, and let's get started.

Ryan Lambie
Editor

Sub-Editors
David Higgs, Vel Ilic, Nicola King

Design

criticalmedia.co.uk

Head of Design
Lee Allen

Designer
Harriet Knight

Contributors

Stuart Fraser, Patrick Gordon, Steve Lee, Andrew Palmer, Ryan Shah, Mark Vanstone

Publishing

Publishing Director
Russell Barnes
Email russell@raspberrypi.org

Director of Communications
Liz Upton

CEO
Eben Upton

Advertising

Commercial Manager
Charlie Milligan
Email charlotte.milligan@raspberrypi.org
Tel +44 (0)7725 368887

Distribution

Seymour Distribution Ltd
2 East Poultry Ave, London EC1A 9PT
Tel +44 (0)207 429 4000

Subscriptions

Unit 6, The Enterprise Centre, Kelvin Lane, Manor Royal, Crawley, West Sussex, RH10 9PE

To subscribe
Call 01293 312192 or visit wfmag.cc/subscribe

Subscription queries
wireframe@subscriptionhelpline.co.uk

ISSN: 2631-6722 (print), 2631-6730 (online).

Wireframe

Build Your Own
FIRST-PERSON SHOOTER
in Unity

Contents

Levels, models, and more

Building the basic engine

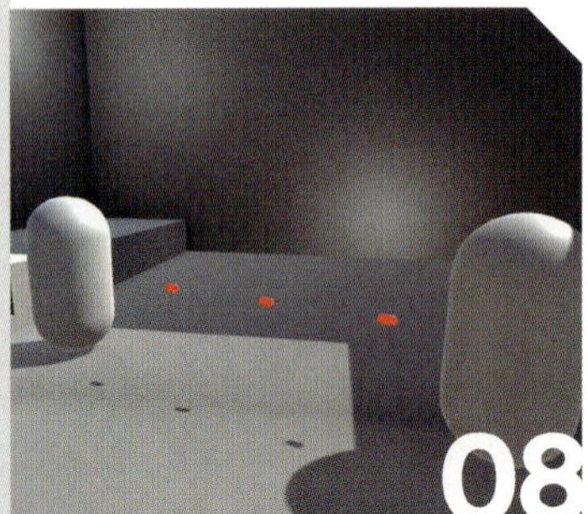

WHERE TO FIND ASSETS

You'll find all the files, models, and other assets you need for this book at **wfmag.cc/fps-guide**

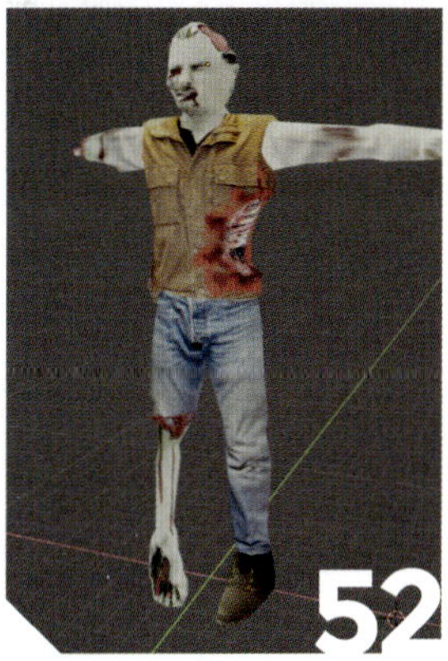

Additional mechanics

Level design and inspiration

Building the basic engine

From downloading the Unity engine to creating a player character, here's everything you need to get your shooter started

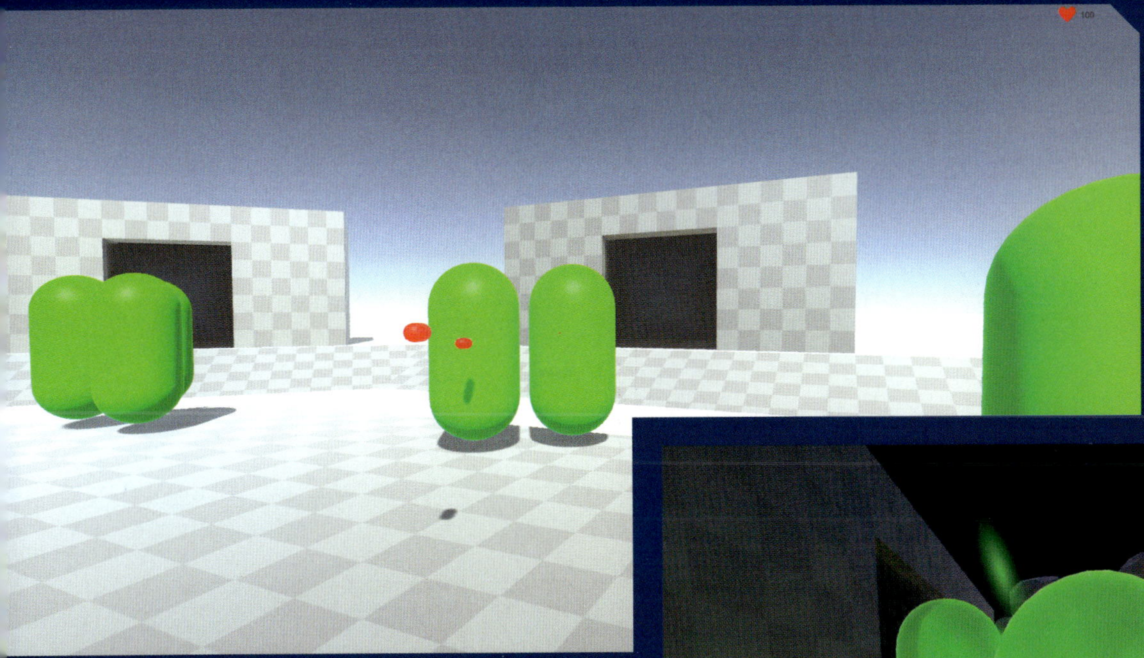

Follow the tutorials in this section and you'll have the basics for your shooter down, including simple enemies that attack the player.

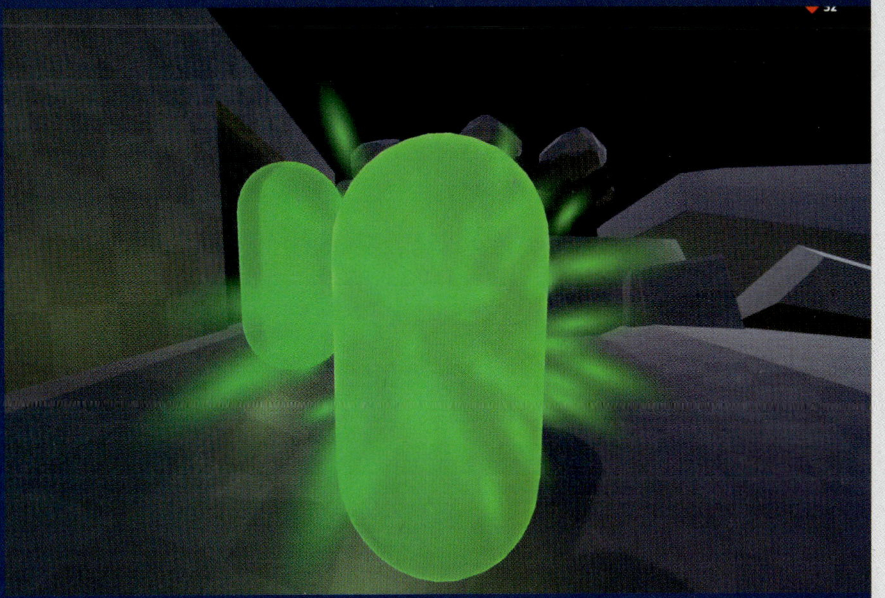

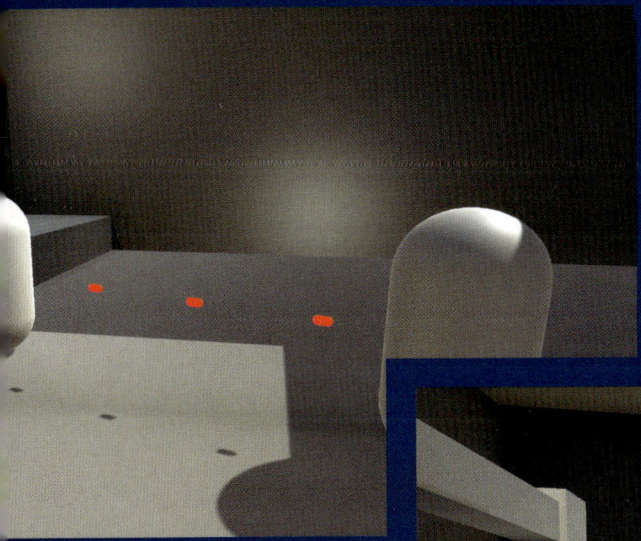

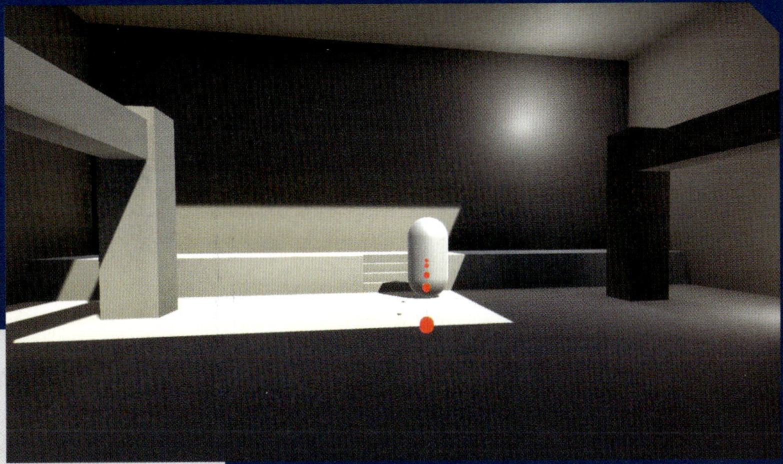

Taking your first steps in Unity

From setting up Unity to creating a moving, firing character, here's how to lay the foundations for your shooter

AUTHOR
STUART FRASER
Stuart is a former designer and developer of high-profile games such as *RollerCoaster Tycoon 3*, and has also worked as a lecturer of games development.

Tools such as Unity and Unreal Engine have opened the way for just about anyone to make high-quality video games. In this guide, we're going to look at Unity, and how we can develop a basic first-person shooter. The great thing about the Unity engine is that it works well on multiple platforms, and the documentation is really clear, with a suite of easy-to-follow tutorials available for beginners and also experts.

GETTING HOLD OF UNITY

First, then, we need to get our hands on the Unity software itself and get it installed on your PC or Mac. The maker has made it easy to get hold of any supported version of Unity by using a tool called Unity Hub. This is essentially a program launcher and still in beta, but it's simple, reliable, and will give you fast access to what you need. First, open up a web browser and navigate to the downloads page: **wfmag.cc/get-unity**. Then you need to select Download Unity Hub, run the UnityHubSetup to continue, and select a suitable install location.

INSTALLING UNITY USING THE HUB

Once you open the Hub, you'll be presented with some choices in the launcher. They're pretty self-explanatory, with the headings Projects, Learn, and Installs. I'll touch on Projects later, but this is where your games will live. As mentioned earlier, the Learn section has some great resources. Finally, we'll choose the heading Installs, and on the top right-hand side, click on Add. Next, choose the 2019.2 version of Unity and select Next. Once it's complete, you'll be able to launch Unity and your projects from the Hub.

TAKE CONTROL OF THE EDITOR

Now you have the Unity Hub, it's a simple process of selecting New from the top-right set of icons, and then giving your project a name and set a location for it to live on your drive; by default, the version of Unity we downloaded is selected. We'll leave the Templates options

Under the official releases window, we can see the various available versions of Unity.

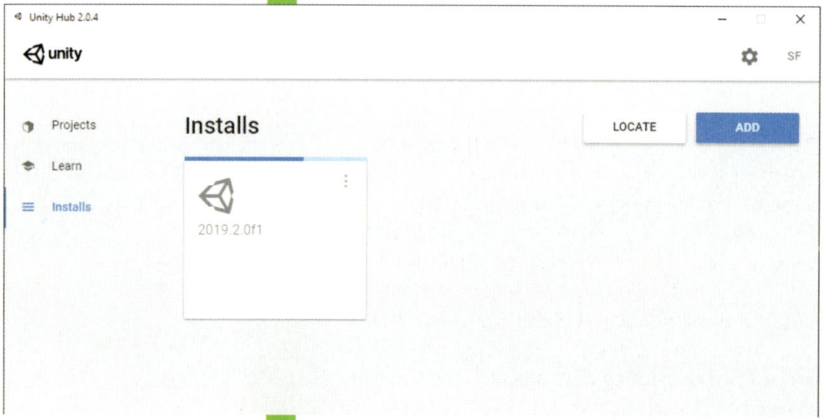

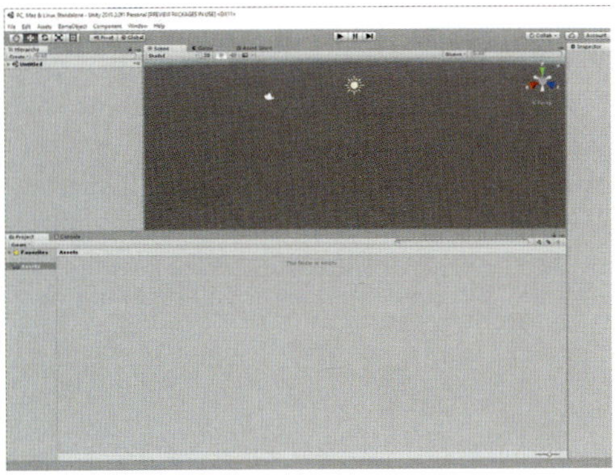

The default view from the Unity editor. We can easily customise the layout to suit your needs as a developer.

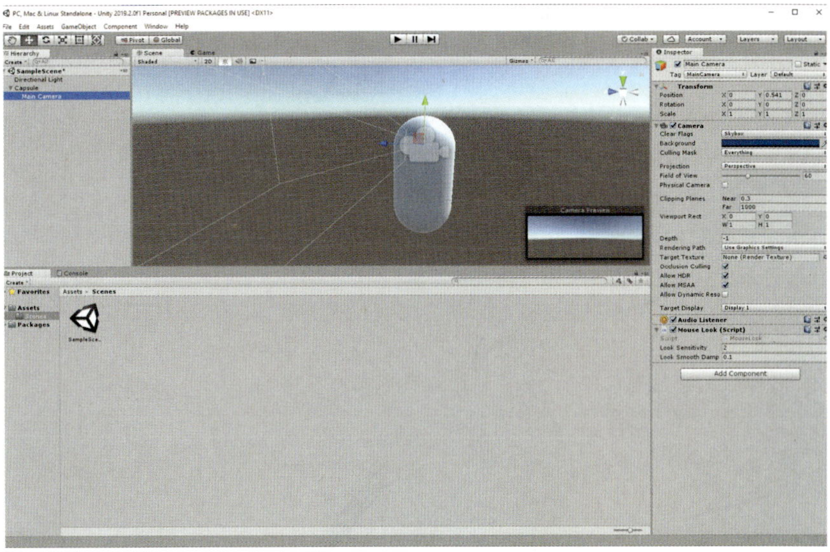

This is my setup for our representation of the character. I have moved up the camera, and you can see the positional difference for the Y value in the Inspector.

set to 3D, and then complete the process by selecting Create. When you start up into the Unity Editor, you'll see a bunch of windows – this can be daunting to someone who hasn't used a games editor before. Again, Unity has some brilliant starter guides at **wfmag.cc/unity-tut**, but I'll take you through the process anyway.

The first thing we need to do is think about a typical first-person shooter: you generally can't see the character you're playing, but you have a viewport onto the world via a camera.

The first viewport is in the Scene tab, in the centre of the default layout. This is where we see the entire game world and build our levels. Next to the Scene tab in the same window is the Game tab; click this and preview what our players will see when they start our game. Unity has given us a starting point of a camera and a light in its default startup scene. This provides us with the building blocks to get started – and if you hit the play button, you'll start the game running. You might be unimpressed with the result, though: there's no ability to move, and pressing the keyboard will have no effect. Press Play again to exit out of the preview mode, and let's make the game do something more interesting.

SETTING UP OUR FIRST-PERSON CHARACTER

We want to add the ability to move our camera around and have it behave like a first-person character. The first step is to allow the camera to be controlled by the player. First, we need to do some setup in the Unity editor, then we'll be doing some very basic game programming. This is sometimes referred to as game scripting, and allows rapid development of the gameplay mechanics in a programming language that is easy to understand. So let's get going and make our first-person character.

We'll use a capsule object to represent the player. From the toolbar, select GameObject > 3D Object > Capsule. While we won't see this in the game, it gives us a reference point in our editor, and it will allow our player to collide with objects in the game world. Reset this capsule back to the origin, i.e. (0,0,0) – this can be achieved simply by using the Inspector, which is the panel on the right-hand side.

"The great thing about Unity is that it works well on multiple platforms"

Look for the panel labelled Transform. If you don't see the values (0,0,0) for X,Y,Z, then select the cog icon to the right of the pane and select Reset Position. Now, select the Main Camera in the Hierarchy tab and set this back to the origin (0,0,0) using the above method. Finally, use the Hierarchy window and drag the Main Camera onto the Capsule game object. You should see that the camera is now parented to the capsule. In other words, the camera is attached to and placed below the capsule in the Hierarchy.

We're going to do some more setup to the viewing position of our character. Select the camera that we parented and you'll see a camera preview in the lower right of the Scene viewport. You should also see a transform gizmo with three arrows (red, green, blue) extending out of the camera object. Select the arrow that's pointing up and coloured green. Use the left mouse button to drag it up slightly so it's in the upper area of the capsule. Think about →

› The Project window will show all the assets you are using for your game and which can be placed in your levels. This could be scripts, audio, textures, models, and much more.

TIP

It's best practice to set your game world and game objects to the world origin – position 0,0,0 – when you import them into Unity or any other game engine. It makes things easier when implementing script logic or building your levels, as you aren't applying additional transforms to your objects.

the capsule being your character: you want the camera to be its eyes. If you want to adjust your viewing angle within the Scene viewport, you can move the view angle by clicking and dragging the right mouse button within the viewport, and you can use **WASD** or arrow keys to move around.

ADDING THE BASE MOVEMENT

We're now going to add our script to move the character. Unity is mostly object driven, so we essentially attach our scripts to the game objects that we want to affect. In this case, we need to select our capsule object in the editor. Go to your Inspector window on the right and click the Add Component button at the bottom. In the new pop-up window, scroll to the very bottom and select New Script. You need to set a name for your script – I suggest CharacterMovement – and then click the Create and Add button. This method is great, as it attaches the script to the object and saves it to your game project automatically.

The only thing we have to do now is open the script. This can be opened from the bottom Project window by double-clicking. You'll be provided with some sort of scripting environment – this will be either MonoDevelop or Visual Studio. Now all we need to do is replace our code with the template script that Unity provides. Don't forget to save.

```
using UnityEngine;

public class CharacterMovement : MonoBehaviour
{
    public float speed = 5;

    // Use this for initialization
    void Start()
    {
        Cursor.lockState = CursorLockMode.
Locked;
    }

    // Update is called once per frame
    void Update()
    {
        float Horizontal = Input.
GetAxis("Horizontal") * speed;
        float Vertical = Input.
GetAxis("Vertical") * speed;
        Horizontal *= Time.deltaTime;
        Vertical *= Time.deltaTime;
        transform.Translate(Horizontal, 0,
Vertical);

        if (Input.GetKeyDown("escape"))
            Cursor.lockState = CursorLockMode.
None;
    }
}
```

⌄ It isn't exactly *Crysis*, but it's still a solid basis for your own shooter in Unity.

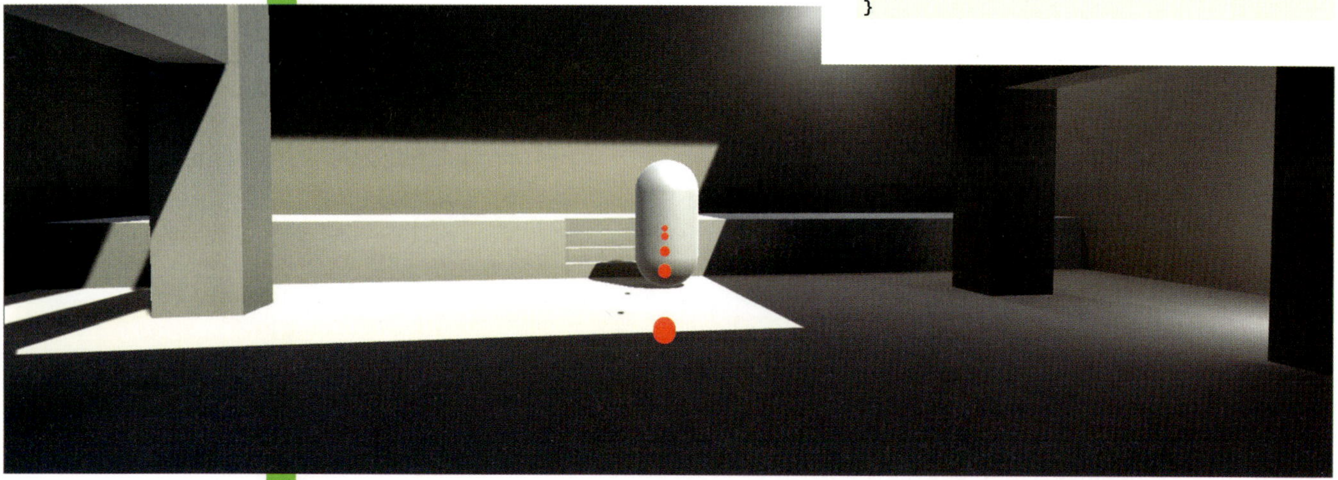

We should have our movement script ready to go. I'd suggest changing your viewport setting before pressing Play so you can easily see the effect in your Scene view. Select the Game tab with your mouse, then drag the window and it will undock. Drag it towards the Inspector and it will expand, then release. You should now have two easy-to-access viewports for the Scene and the Game. Press Play and use **WASD**, arrow keys, or a controller to apply movement. While it's difficult to see in the Game viewport, it's easy to see the applied motion in the Scene viewport. Again, when you finish, you need to press the Play button to exit this game preview.

> **"I suggest adding a floor object, otherwise your character will fall forever"**

ADDING GRAVITY AND JUMP ABILITY

What we have is pretty limited, so we want to expand the range of motion and apply gravity limitations to our character. We're going to expand the code we created earlier, but we first need to expand our character so it understands that it has physics rules. First, we're going to add another component called a rigidbody – this is from a physics term that describes any solid object, and is used in the mathematical understanding of applying forces like velocity and acceleration. We'll select our capsule and then, in the Inspector, select Add Component. We can then use the search box at the very top of this window to search for Rigidbody.

I suggest adding a floor object to the scene, otherwise your character will fall forever. It also helps you to have a reference point when moving around your level. From the toolbar, select GameObject > 3D Object > Plane.

You can use the transform gizmo to move the object around; the arrows dictate the direction you'll move the object in. Move this under the player capsule. We're going to expand the code we have already, so we need to open up the same code editor we had before. Select the **CharacterMovement.cs** file and then simply replace the original example with the following code:

```
using UnityEngine;

public class CharacterMovement : MonoBehaviour
{
    public float speed = 5;
    public float jumpPower = 4;
```

TIP

Make sure you are careful with your script file name and the name of the public class in your C# script. These have to be identical to each other, else the script will fail to compile.

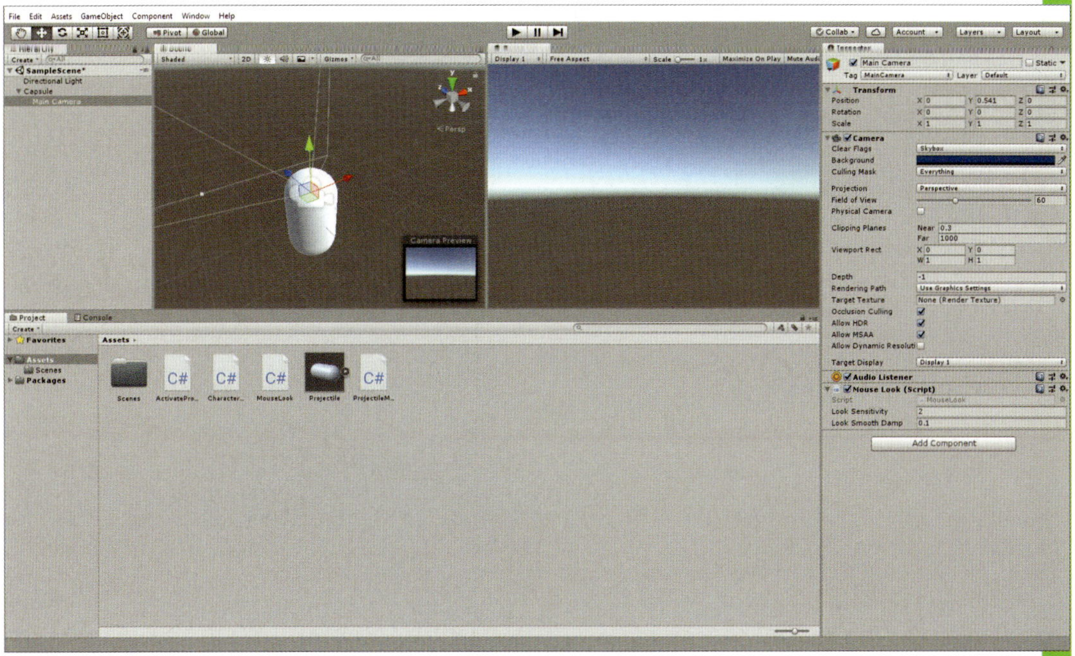

With this layout, you can clearly view the world you're editing and preview your gameplay at the same time.

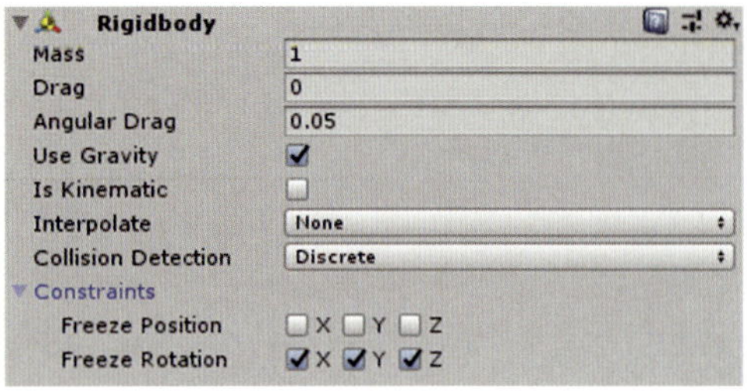

› Components often have properties that you can override to change how they behave. In this case, we're stopping the object from rotating in an undesirable direction.

```
    Rigidbody rb;
    CapsuleCollider col;

    // Use this for initialization
    void Start()
    {
        Cursor.lockState = CursorLockMode.
Locked;
        rb = GetComponent<Rigidbody>();
        col = GetComponent<CapsuleCollider>();
    }

    // Update is called once per frame
    void Update()
    {
        //Get the input value from the
controllers
        float Horizontal = Input.
GetAxis("Horizontal") * speed;
        float Vertical = Input.
GetAxis("Vertical") * speed;
        Horizontal *= Time.deltaTime;
        Vertical *= Time.deltaTime;
        //Translate our character via our
inputs.
        transform.Translate(Horizontal, 0,
Vertical);

        if (isGrounded() && Input.
GetButtonDown("Jump"))
        {
            //Add upward force to the rigid
body when we press jump.
            rb.AddForce(Vector3.up *
jumpPower, ForceMode.Impulse);
        }

        if (Input.GetKeyDown("escape"))
            Cursor.lockState = CursorLockMode.
None;
    }

    private bool isGrounded()
    {
        //Test that we are grounded by drawing
an invisible line (raycast)
        //If this hits a solid object e.g.
floor then we are grounded.
        return Physics.Raycast(transform.
position, Vector3.down, col.bounds.extents.y
+ 0.1f);
    }
}
```

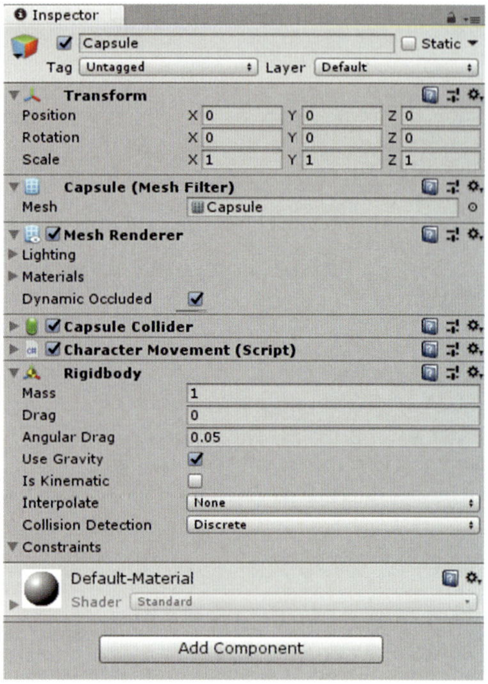

^ You can view what components are on a game object in the Inspector. You can add multiple components to change the behaviour of these objects.

Again, select to play your game and use the SPACE bar or buttons on the controller to try to jump as your character. You may notice some odd behaviour, as the character may topple over. We can fix this by selecting the capsule object; in the options for the Rigidbody, you'll see the word Constraints and a small down arrow. If you click this, it will expand and show Freeze Position and Freeze Rotation. Activate the checkboxes for X, Y, and Z for the Freeze Rotation only. If you play the game again, it should be impossible to make the character topple.

LOOKING AROUND THE ENVIRONMENT

One element of a first-person shooter is that you can look around the environment or level by using your mouse or the controller sticks to effectively move the head of the character. We are going to add another script to our player, but this time to our camera and not the capsule.

First, we need to select the camera, and repeat the process of selecting Add Component and then making a new script. I would name the script MouseLook, and then you can open the code editor and add the code provided.

```
using UnityEngine;

public class MouseLook : MonoBehaviour
{
    private GameObject player;
    private float minClamp = -45;
    private float maxClamp = 45;
    [HideInInspector]
    public Vector2 rotation;
    private Vector2 currentLookRot;
    private Vector2 rotationV = new Vector2(0,
0);
    public float lookSensitivity = 2;
    public float lookSmoothDamp = 0.1f;

    void Start()
    {
        //Access the player GameObject.
        player = transform.parent.gameObject;
    }

    // Update is called once per frame
    void Update()
    {
        //Player input from the mouse
        rotation.y += Input.GetAxis("Mouse Y")
* lookSensitivity;
        //Limit ability look up and down.
        rotation.y = Mathf.Clamp(rotation.y,
minClamp, maxClamp);
        //Rotate the character around based on
the mouse X position.
        player.transform.
RotateAround(transform.position, Vector3.up,
Input.GetAxis("Mouse X") * lookSensitivity);
        //Smooth the current Y rotation for
looking up and down.
        currentLookRot.y = Mathf.
SmoothDamp(currentLookRot.y, rotation.y, ref
rotationV.y, lookSmoothDamp);
        //Update the camera X rotation based
on the values generated.
        transform.localEulerAngles = new
Vector3(-currentLookRot.y, 0, 0);
    }
}
```

TIP

You can build out your level by using the basic 3D objects that are available in Unity, or you can explore the Unity Store. The Unity Store has both free and paid items that can help expand the quality of your projects, such as meshes, effects, sounds, and even scripts. You can access the store at any time by selecting Window > General > Asset Store within the taskbar or by using the key combination **CTRL+9**.

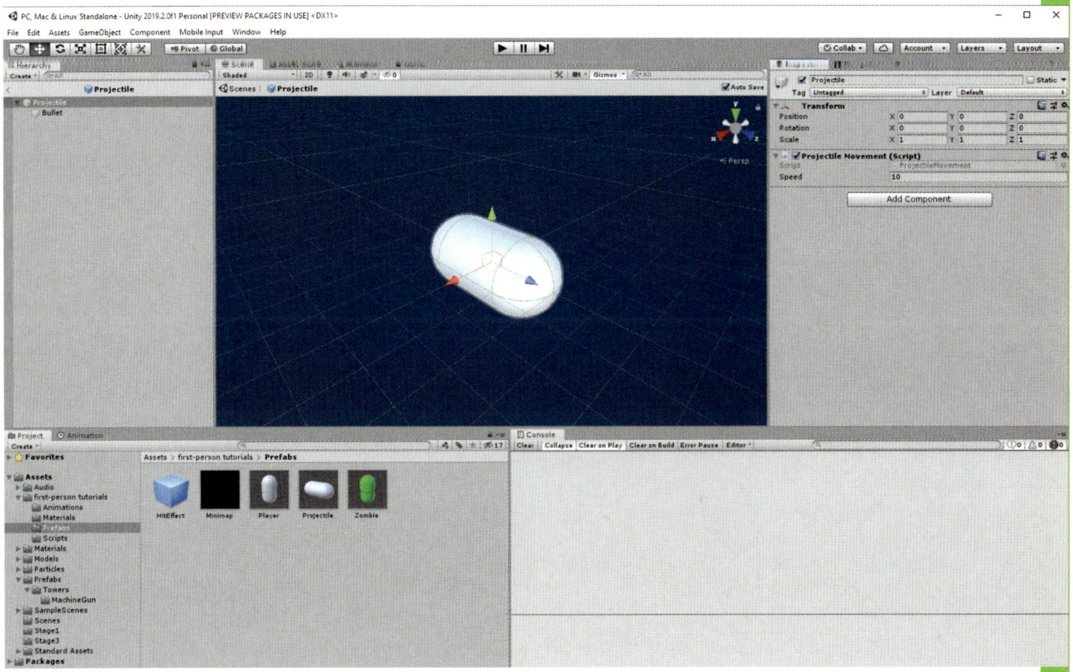

I've parented my second capsule object, which has been rotated to an empty game object. You'll notice that it has a default rotation and no other components attached.

Our prefab in our Project window is ready to go. Prefabs are extremely useful as they can be used multiple times in the project and will always have the same behaviours we set.

TIP

You can better visualise an empty object by adding an icon to it. In the top-left of the Inspector is a small cube with a down arrow. Select this and you can set one of several icon looks. This won't show in the game, but it's great as a guideline when moving objects in the viewport.

You may notice that this works as a mouse look only, and that it doesn't work on a controller. Unfortunately, creating controls like these is beyond the scope of this tutorial, but you can always try to implement this yourself if it's something you want to add.

MAKING A PROJECTILE WEAPON

Of course, this wouldn't be much of a first-person shooter without being able to shoot. There are many ways to implement a weapon mechanic, and a game like *Quake Champions* has several ways to handle weapon types, from projectile to beam weapons. We're going to add ours in the most basic way and have a projectile that we can fire in the direction we face.

"You've created the basis for your very own first-person shooter"

First, we need to select the capsule. This time, we're going to use a shortcut to parent a new object to it. We now need to right-click on Capsule in the Hierarchy and select Create Empty. We're going to use this to spawn our projectile on. This is a quite common practice in games, where you have an empty or dummy object for positioning or spawning. I would also advise renaming the game object by typing in the text box at the top of the Inspector with this object highlighted. I would suggest calling this 'Weapon' or something meaningful.

We also need an object to use as a projectile, so we'll quickly create this from two objects: another dummy and another capsule. On the taskbar, select GameObject > Create Empty. We're going to use this to help us make sure the bullet moves in the correct direction even when we rotate the capsule object. I'd rename this object to 'Projectile' so we can find it later on. Now we need to select the new object in the Hierarchy, then right-click and choose 3D Object > Capsule.

I'd rename this 'Bullet' in the Inspector window. Now we want to make some size and rotation adjustments. Just underneath the left-hand side of the upper-left taskbar, you have six to seven icons. You'll notice that one is highlighted (a cross shape of arrows); this means you're using the Move tool. Select the icon to the right of this ( ); a tooltip will tell you it's the Rotate tool. You'll notice the gizmo is now a sphere with overlapped circles. Select the red circle, and then drag until the capsule faces forward or the Inspector shows approximately 90 degrees in the rotation box labelled X.

Finally, we need to rescale the dummy object. First, you need to select this dummy object in the Hierarchy. To the right of the rotation icon is the Scale tool icon ( ); select this, and the gizmo will change again. This time the gizmo will be similar to transform, but instead of arrows we have cubes. We're going to select the bigger white cube at the centre of the gizmo; this will let us rescale all directions at the same time. If you drag downwards you'll see that the capsule object will shrink. We need to make this about one-tenth the scale of the character.

The final step for the projectile is to centre it to the world. In the Inspector you can select the cog on the Transform for your dummy object, and then select Reset Position.

FIRING THE WEAPON

We're going to add two new scripts. The good news is that these are really simple and comprise only a few lines of code. We need one to make the projectile spawn, and one to make the projectile move in a constant direction. We'll deal with the movement first, as we should still be highlighting the projectile object. As with the other scripts, we add them via Add Component and then giving the script a name. You should set the name to ProjectileMovement for your script.

```
using UnityEngine;

public class ProjectileMovement : MonoBehaviour
{
    public float speed = 10f;

    // Update is called once per frame
```

```
    void Update()
    {
        transform.Translate(Vector3.forward * 
speed * Time.deltaTime);
    }
}
```

Before we work on the next script, we're actually going to remove this initial projectile game object from the scene. However, we still want to use it in the project, so we're going to make a special type of object called a prefab. We can make this a prefab by selecting it in the Hierarchy and dragging it into the Project window at the bottom of the screen. You then need to make sure you've now selected the version in the Hierarchy and hit **DELETE**.

Now for the second half of this scripting adventure: select the Weapon game object and then, as before, you can select Add Component and follow the flow. Name your script ActivateProjectile and then open the script to add the final part of the code:

```
using UnityEngine;

public class ActivateProjectile : MonoBehaviour
{
    public GameObject projectile;

    // Update is called once per frame
    void Update()
    {
        if (Input.GetButtonDown("Fire1"))
        {
            var clone = Instantiate(projectile, 
gameObject.transform.position, gameObject.
transform.rotation);
            //Destroy after 2 seconds to stop 
clutter.
            Destroy(clone, 5.0f);
        }
    }
}
```

There is one issue we currently have: if we spawn our bullet, it will collide with the player as we spawn this inside our player collider. There is a very simple fix for this by telling the player to ignore collisions from our bullet. To do this, we are going to create two layers; this is simply done by selecting the Layer drop-down in the Inspector and choosing Add Layer. You should see the expanded list of Layers and some that are inaccessible. We will choose an empty user layer slot and type the word Player into that field. We will then type the word Projectile in the entry below that, so we should have two additional entries. Next, we need to select Edit > Project Settings... and we need to select Physics from the new window that appears. In this window, you will see the Layer Collision Matrix and our entries; we want to untick the checkbox for Player in the first column.

With that set up, we will need to select the player capsule and make sure that we have set the Layer drop-down to Player in the Inspector panel. It will ask you about applying the changes to the children; we want to say Yes, change children. We then need to select the Projectile in the Project panel and, in the Inspector, change the drop-down to Projectile, and repeat the selection for the message about applying to all children.

We have one last thing to do. We have our prefab, but our spawn script doesn't know to use it yet. In our Weapon object we can see the script we added, called ActivateProjectile. You'll also see the words Projectile and a slot that says 'empty' or 'none'. We need to add our prefab here by selecting the circle to the right of the slot. A window will appear, which has Assets and Scene tabs. Select the Assets tab and you'll see our Projectile prefab.

Make sure you've selected it, then press Play to see the result. You should be able to fire using the left mouse button, and see multiple projectiles when you click. Congratulations: you've created the mechanical basis for your very own first-person shooter.

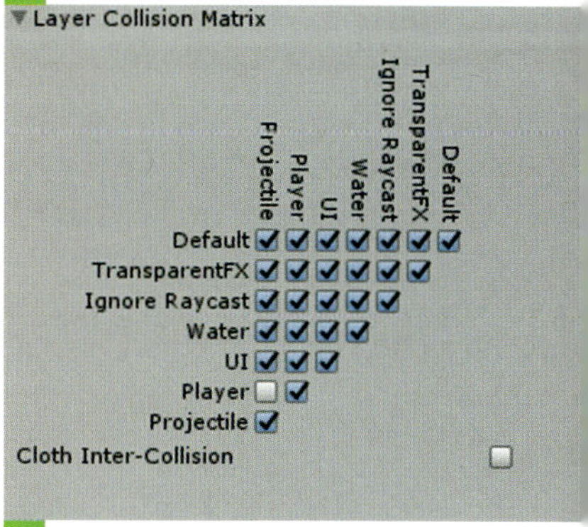

We can easily make sure that the fired bullet never hits the player by changing the physics matrix to ignore it.

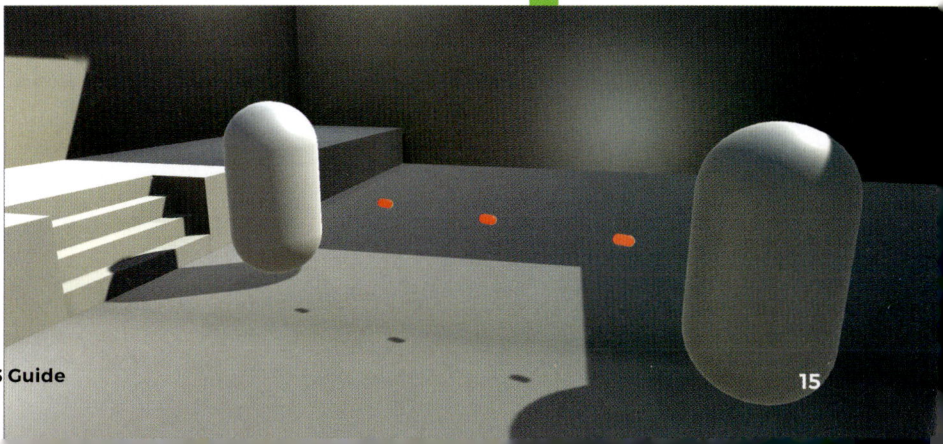

It may look rough right now, but we'll be adding character models and lots more soon.

Add enemies and make improvements

With the basics for our shooter now in place, here's how to add enemies and more

AUTHOR
STUART FRASER

Stuart is a former designer and developer of high-profile games such as *RollerCoaster Tycoon 3*, and has also worked as a lecturer of games development.

In this second Unity tutorial, we're going to look at advancing the simple shooting mechanics. In the first part, we focused on getting our player character in motion and adding the ability to shoot a basic projectile. Now we're going to add some basic AI, have a way to detect damage to them, and have points displayed. In addition to this, we'll add some basic 'quality of life' elements to the experience.

IMPROVING THE FIRST-PERSON AIMING

First, we're going to add a crosshair to the first-person camera – this will help the player with their aiming as they move and fire. We'll also make it so that the player can aim up and down. The first thing to do is to open the project; if you are using the Unity Hub then you should see a list of all the projects as soon as you load into the launcher. Select the applicable project, and then this should load the Unity Editor and the last scene you worked on.

Select the Hierarchy window to the left-hand side of the screen, and then right-click in an empty space and select UI > Canvas. Next, select the Canvas object in the Hierarchy, right-click, then select UI > Panel. You'll see that the Panel is linked to the Canvas game object. With the newly created Panel selected, look to the right-hand side of the editor and find the Inspector. In your Inspector, you should see the first pane is called Rect Transform. Select the icon that looks like a blue cross with arrows at each end. A new window will be shown called Anchor Presets. Select the icon in the centre that looks like a red cross with a red dot in the middle.

You should see there are now values in the Width and Height boxes; we want to type the value of 3 into both boxes. You then need to change some parameters in the Image script component. First, select the box to the right of the word Color. This will bring up a colour selection tool similar to one in a photo manipulation package. We want to choose a bright colour – for example, a nice red. We also want to adjust the bottom slider prefixed by the

Use the Anchor Presets to set the relative positions your UI element will be anchored to. This will be unaffected by changes to the screen resolution.

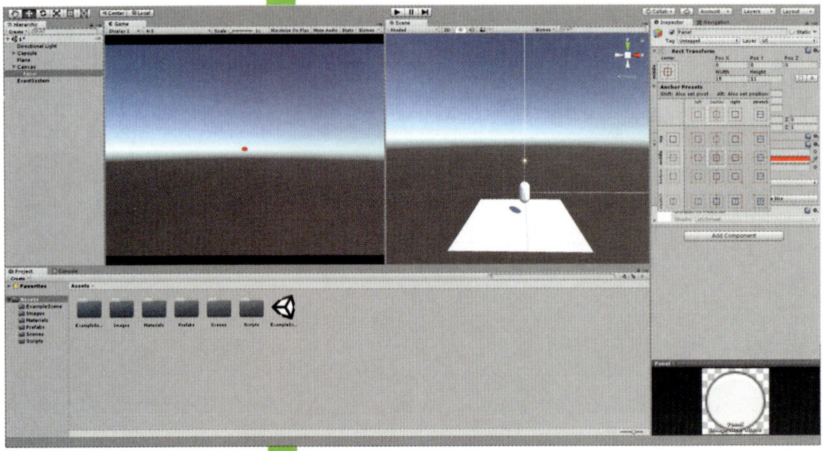

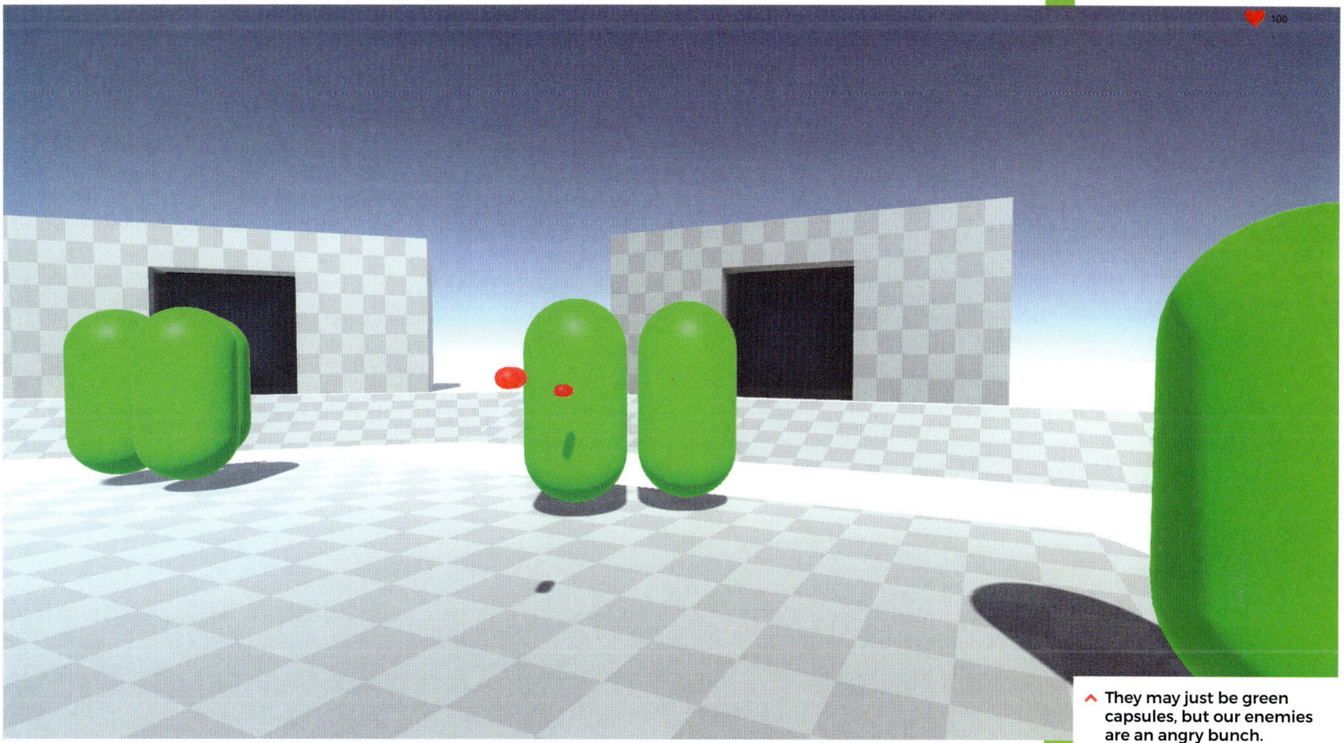

They may just be green capsules, but our enemies are an angry bunch.

letter A (for alpha) to be fully to the right-hand side. This will make the red dot be fully opaque, so you can easily see it in the centre of the screen. We now have a simple crosshair that should be rendered to the screen.

The next change is to make the projectile fire from the centre point of where we're looking. For this, go to the Hierarchy and select the Weapon game object we created last time, and drag this onto our Main Camera. If you can't see these objects, you may need to click the arrow next to your Capsule object.

The final change is to keep the Weapon game object selected, and then in the Inspector, set the Position for the X, Y, and Z to 0. This will effectively set the object to be aligned to the Camera position. Feel free to try out the current iteration of what you've done by pressing the Play button. You should see the crosshair and the projectile spawn from that point. Don't forget to exit the preview by selecting the Play button again.

SETTING UP OUR ENEMY

We're going to effectively make our shooter into a wave-based game. For simplicity, we'll have 'zombie' enemies who'll do you damage on contact. We're going to use the AI pathfinding in Unity to create this logic, so the first thing to do is create a separate capsule to represent our enemy. In the Hierarchy window, right-click and select 3D Object > Capsule. With the new capsule selected, go into the Inspector panel, and rename the Capsule to a unique name. I'd suggest Zombie.

"We're going to make our shooter into a wave-based game"

We're also going to add a unique colour to the capsule to help differentiate it. First, we select the Project window and then right-click and select Create > Material, then add a unique name to the material – for example, Zombie Skin. With this material still selected, go to the Inspector panel, and click on the box next to Albedo colour to open the Colour Palette window. You can try adjusting the colour on your material; I've gone with a bright green. Once you've set your material colour, select it from the Project window and drag onto the Zombie game object in the Hierarchy window.

The final thing we need to do is to use a component on our enemy to make it navigate to the player.

To do this is easy enough: select the enemy in the Hierarchy, and then in the Inspector, select Add Component and choose Navigation > Nav Mesh Agent. →

A TIP FOR PREVIEWS

If you can't tell whether you're in a preview of your game or not, then there's a great setting you can use in Unity preferences. From the taskbar, select Edit > Preferences... and from the new window, choose Colors. There are lots of customisation options for colours here, but we want to select Playmode tint. Select the colour to open the colour palette window and simply choose an obviously different colour from the standard Unity grey. From now on, you will always see this colour tint in a game preview.

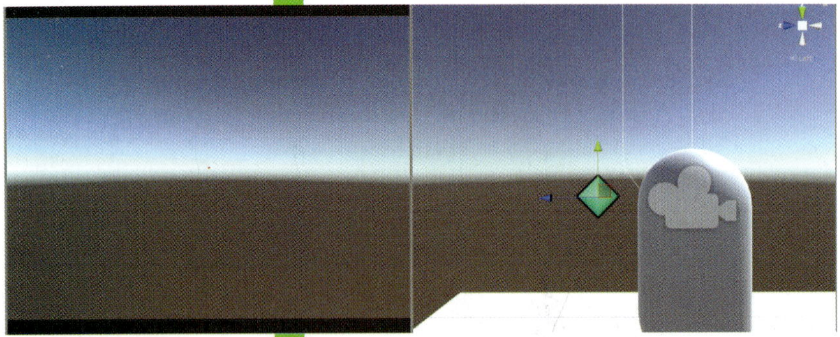

To allow for vertical movement of our projectile weapon, we need to make the Weapon game object a child of our camera.

While we now have our navigation agent, we will also need to tell it where we want it to go. It's just a case of creating a simple script to drive the AI character.

First of all, select Add Component and scroll down to the New Script entry. Then, in the next window, set the script name to MoveToPosition and select Create and Add. We can double-click the new script on the Inspector and the script editor should load. Now, simply replace the template script with the code below.

```
using UnityEngine;
using UnityEngine.AI;

public class MoveToPosition : MonoBehaviour
{


    public Transform goal;
    private NavMeshAgent agent;


    void Start()
    {
        agent = GetComponent<NavMeshAgent>();
    }
    void Update()
    {
        agent.SetDestination(goal.position);
    }
}
```

Once you've saved the script and navigated back to the Unity editor, you'll see that the script will have a slot called Goal; this was made publicly accessible in our script above. What we need to do is set the Goal as our player. This is simply a case of selecting our player capsule in the Hierarchy window and dragging it to the slot to the right-hand side of the word Goal.

The final step is to select the Zombie in the Hierarchy window, and then drag this into the Project window to create our second prefab object. The reason to do this is so we can drag in or spawn more copies of the same enemy.

GENERATING OUR ENEMY NAVIGATION

So, we have our enemy, and it has the navigation component and a script to tell it where to go. There is, however, one final and critical step that we must perform to make this all work. We need to create a navigation mesh. This is an invisible mesh that tries to contour itself to the floor of a game level. This is something that most modern games will use as a way to create AI navigation. In the example, we only have a flat plane, but let's imagine we have a sprawling level with steps, slopes, and so on. This will work out if the AI could acceptably make it to these places. To use this feature, go to the taskbar and select Window > AI > Navigation. It will open a new tab which will appear where the Inspector is usually shown.

Now the issue is that we need to have a static object to bake the navigation. So, in the Hierarchy, select the Plane we created for our floor. We actually need to select the Inspector tab, so switch away from the Navigation tab for a second. In the Inspector for the Plane game object, you need to select the checkbox to the top-right called Static. We can now move back to the Navigation tab and from the row at the top of this window, select the Bake option. Finally, select the Bake button to the bottom-right of the window. You will now see the navigation mesh in a blue colour that will render just above the Plane mesh.

We're ready to test our enemy character navigation. All we need to do is use the

Once you have created a material, selecting the Albedo will allow you to set a colour of your choice via the colour wheel, sliders, or a hex value.

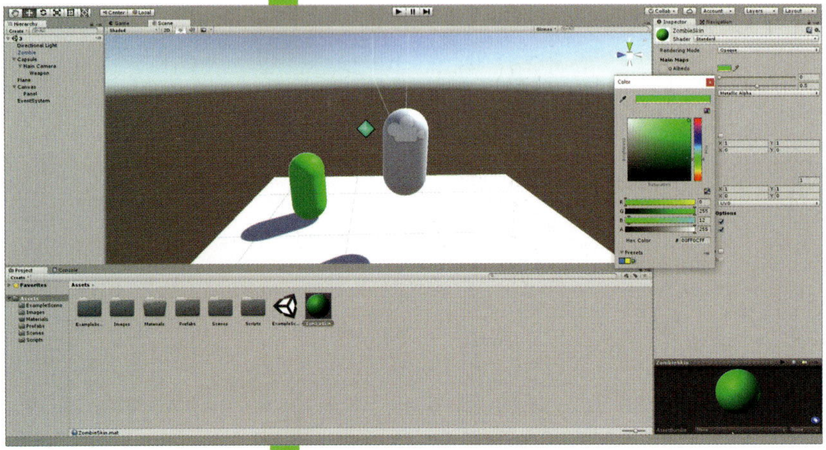

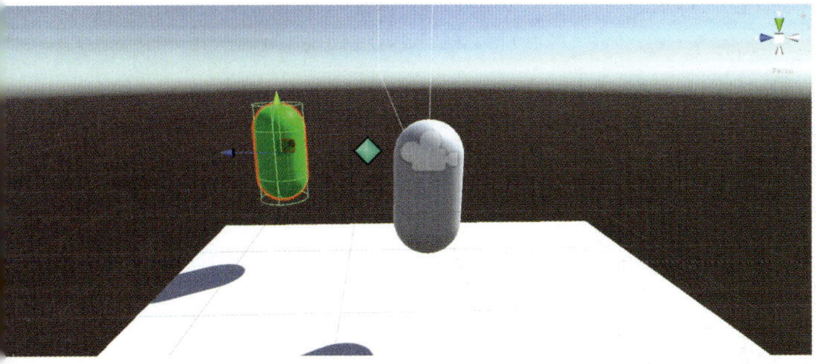

To make the AI navigate to the player, make sure that you have dragged in the appropriate game object to the entry marked Goal on the Move to Position script.

Select the Bake button to generate your navigation mesh; this will be previewed as a blue mesh above the level geometry.

transform gizmo tool to move the position so that it doesn't start on top of the player character or the ground. Simply select the red, green, or blue axis and they should highlight. Drag these until you're happy with the position. When we press Play to preview, you'll see that the AI will navigate to our player's position.

One issue we can see straight away is that the enemy navigates to the same point as the player, and we can see some odd behaviour in this interaction. To fix this, we need to stop the game from playing and then select the enemy game object. In the Inspector, look at the Nav Mesh Agent component, and then set the Stopping Distance value to around 1.5, as this will make the enemy stop just before it touches the player.

UNDERSTANDING TRIGGERS AND COLLISIONS

We now want to set up a way of testing for damage when the enemy collides with our player, and when the projectile hits the enemy. We're going to use an event trigger in both cases to achieve this. An example of a trigger in video games is when you walk into an area and this starts a cutscene. Effectively, there's an invisible box around the area, and by walking into it, the player sets off the event.

While I say we are using a trigger, we're actually going to test if we're colliding with an object, and set our events based on that. By default, in Unity, anything with a collider can be used to check if something is interacting with it. The only limitation with the event is that one of the two colliding objects needs a Rigidbody. As a rule of thumb, I would add a Rigidbody to any dynamic object.

We already added a Rigidbody to the player in the first tutorial, so let's add one to the enemy. In the Hierarchy, select the enemy game object. We then go to the Inspector and select Add Component and then select Physics > Rigidbody. I'd also expand the Rigidbody component and check the option Is Kinematic. This means while it has a Rigidbody, the Physics interactions of motions won't be applied, as we want this driven by our AI script.

Remember, we created the enemy as a prefab. To make sure all the prefabs have the same properties we need to select Apply All from the Overrides drop-down; this is to the top-right of the Inspector options, and should be below the Static checkbox and Layer drop-down.

"Our enemy has the navigation component and a script to tell it where to go"

We want to do the same with the projectile we created last time; in fact, we'll also be adding a script to this. The script will check that the bullet object has hit an object with a collider; this will then disable or 'destroy' the game object. The first thing is that we never now have our projectile in the scene. It's a prefab that is created when we are pressing the fire button.

We can still make changes to it by looking for it in the Project window. We do want to, however, expand the object by selecting Open Prefab in the Inspector when we have highlighted it. Now select the bullet mesh and you should see the capsule mesh listed in the Inspector. We want to select Add Component and repeat the process of adding a Rigidbody to the object. I recommend disabling the Use Gravity option on the Rigidbody, as while there would be some gravity applied to a real bullet, this is much larger, and we want an arcade feel to the game.

As mentioned above, we want to add a script to the object, so select Add Component and scroll down to New Script. Give this script the name BulletHit, and select Create and Add. We then open it in the script editor. We can ➜

OBJECT AVOIDANCE

While we're using static objects to generate navigation, we can do the same for dynamic objects. To set an object to have object avoidance, you need to select the game object and then use Add Component to add the Nav Mesh Obstacle component. There are various settings here, but you must remember to check the carve option to make it work with your navigation. Do remember that this is costly in terms of performance, so use it sparingly in your scenes.

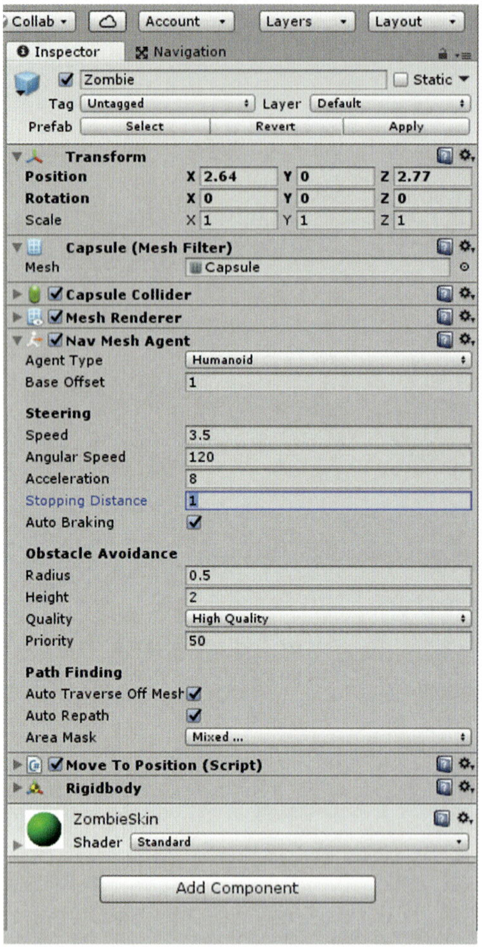

› Change the stopping distance for the Nav Mesh Agent to stop the AI character moving onto the same spot as the player.

then copy the code below over the template Unity provides.

```
using UnityEngine;

public class BulletHit : MonoBehaviour
{

    //When we touch the collider we disable
this object.
    void OnCollisionEnter()
    {
        gameObject.SetActive(false);
    }
}
```

Once you've saved the code and you're back in Unity editor, try previewing the game. You should be able to fire the projectile and it will disappear when hitting the enemy or the ground plane. If this bullet doesn't appear at all, check that it's not spawning in the player.

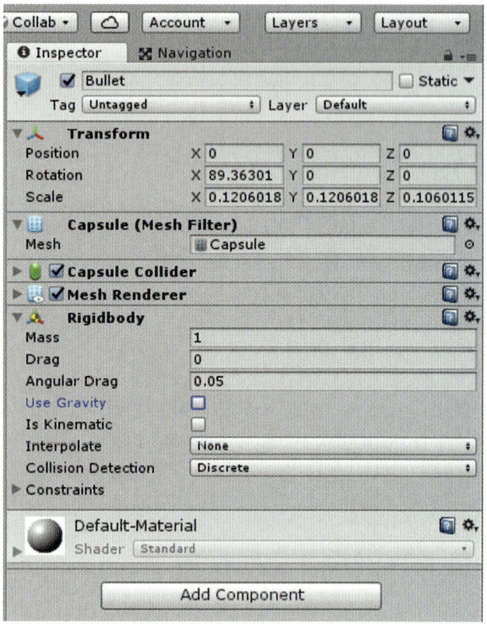

^ On the bullet prefab we want to disable the Use Gravity checkbox on the Rigidbody component.

HANDLING OUR ENEMY DAMAGE

We now have our bullet understanding that if it collides with an object, we want it to be removed from the scene. Let's say we want to apply this logic to the enemy, but we want it only to be damaged by the bullet, and we only want it to be destroyed after three bullets have hit it.

The first challenge is to work out if the projectile has hit the enemy. Unity has provided us with a way of marking up certain game objects to help us identify them. This feature is known as a tag, and we're going to add it to our projectile prefab. We need to go back to the Project window and find our Projectile prefab; if you need to expand it then do so. You should then select the Bullet mesh that we added the script to earlier.

Look at the top-left of the Inspector, and you should see the words Tag, and in the drop-down, it will show Untagged. Select the drop-down and then select Add Tag... and the Inspector will change to show Tags & Layers. We want to expand the Tags element by clicking the down arrow, and then you should see a + icon to the bottom-right of this element. Click the + icon and add your tag name, and then Save. I would type in 'bullet' for the name, but do note that this is case-sensitive, so it must be exactly the same in the code.

We need to reselect the Bullet mesh in the Project window to get back to our original Inspector view. You'll notice that, annoyingly, the

COLLIDERS AND TRIGGERS

Games engines like Unity all have a concept of a collider, which is often an invisible, simplified version of the more detailed visual mesh you see in-game. The reason we use a collider is that it's processor-intensive to do collisions, so a simplified mesh – for example, a box – is less costly to calculate. You can find more about colliders and triggers in the Unity online documentation (**wfmag.cc/RYXD**). This also has a matrix of which components are required to create a collision event.

tag wasn't added even though we just specified it. We just need to make sure that we select the Tag drop-down and change it to our bullet tag we set up. You will need to select the back button to the left of the word Projectile in out Hierarchy to go back to the Scene view.

We now need to turn our attention to the enemy and the script to track whether it's been hit by a bullet, and how many times it's been hit. If we count enough hits, we'll destroy the enemy. As usual, select the Zombie enemy in the Hierarchy and then in Inspector, select Add Component and choose New Script. We then name the script as EnemyDamage, and then add the code below.

```
using UnityEngine;

public class EnemyDamage : MonoBehaviour
{
    //Private means only this script can
access the variable.
    private int hitNumber;

    //Unity stores the collider it hits and we
can access it via the name other.
    void OnCollisionEnter(Collision other)
    {
        //We compare the tag in the other
object to the tag name we set earlier.
        if (other.transform.
CompareTag("bullet"))
        {
            //If the comparison is true, we
increase the hit number.
            hitNumber++;
        }
        //if the hit number is equal to 3 we
destroy this object.
        if (hitNumber == 3)
        {
            Destroy(gameObject);
        }
    }
}
```

Do remember to save the code and then move back to the Unity Editor. If we play the game in preview mode now, we'll see that when we successfully hit the enemy three times, it'll be destroyed. Once you're happy that you've tested the feature, exit out of the play mode so we can continue.

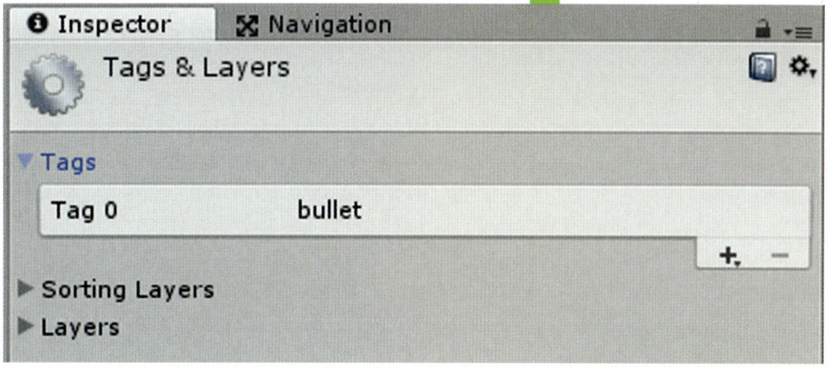

We want to add our own unique tag to our bullet by first creating a new tag in the Tags & Layers window.

DISPLAYING DAMAGE TO THE PLAYER

We want our zombies to do damage when they touch the player game object, but we need a way of expressing the damage to our player. We're going to expand our canvas that we created for the crosshair and add the player's health to the interface. We're also going to communicate between the enemy and the player. Effectively, we'll send a message from a script on the zombie that they're biting the player. This means that if we have multiple zombies, each one will apply damage at the appropriate times.

> "We want our zombies to do damage when they touch the player game object"

We're also going to reuse the tag functionality, but this time we don't need to create a new tag. First, select the player capsule in the Hierarchy window, and then in the Inspector, select the Tag drop-down, and select Player from the list. While we're in here, rename this object from Capsule to Player. It'll make it easier for us as we expand the game and make it clear to us which is our Player object.

Now we've done those changes, let's go back to our enemy object and add a new script to send a message from the zombie to our player. We use a command called SendMessage that Unity created to talk between game objects. It is by no means the only way to do this and, arguably, not the best way. However, it's ➜

THE POWER OF TAGS

Tags are a powerful tool in Unity and help to improve performance. They allow you to quickly look for all objects with a tag and perform an operation on those objects. You could find all the objects individually, but this is an inefficient way of working and will slow performance of your game.

The SendDamage script will let our angry capsule zombies injure the player.

simple to understand and effective enough for our needs.

So, select the Zombie game object in the Hierarchy, and then in the Inspector, select Add Component, and then New Script. We will call our new script SendDamage, and then we can open the script in our code editor and replace with the script shown below. Do also remember to apply the prefab changes.

```
using UnityEngine;

public class SendDamage : MonoBehaviour
{

    void OnCollisionStay(Collision other)
    {
        //We compare the tag in the other
object to the tag name we set earlier.
        if (other.transform.
CompareTag("Player"))
        {
            //If the above matches, then send
a message to the other object.
            //This will also pass a value of 1
for our damage.
            other.transform.
SendMessage("ApplyDamage", 1);
        }
    }
}
```

As I said above, we want to add some sort of output to the Canvas object we created to show the player health. We'll keep this really simple for now, and just display a health value of 100 to 0. In the Hierarchy we need to find the Canvas, and then right-click and select UI > Text.

You should see the default text string that says New Text in the viewport. We don't need to change the text as we will overwrite it in code, but we do need to reposition it. We'll use the Anchor Presets we used when setting up our crosshair. With the Text object selected, go over to the Inspector and once again select the anchor presets icon.

We need to look for, but not select, the icon that is on the second row down and has a red dot on the top-right outer box. As we select this, hold the **SHIFT** key, and this will set the pivot rather than moving the position of the text. Now, back in the RectTransform, replace Pos X and Pos Y values with 0. Also, you need to set the Paragraph Alignment option for the Text component by clicking the right-hand icon on the first row. The text is now neatly positioned in the top-right corner.

The final steps are to add some code to the player, and then link our Canvas to it so it correctly updates. Find the newly renamed Player object and select it in the Hierarchy. Move to the Inspector and select Add Component, and then select New Script. We'll call this new script PlayerDamage, and then open it ready for editing with our code.

```
using UnityEngine;
using UnityEngine.UI;
public class PlayerDamage : MonoBehaviour
{
    //Use this to reference the text in the
canvas
    public Text healthPanel;
    //Sets default health to 100
    public int health = 100;
    private void Start()
    {
        //Sets the health text at the start,
we pass 0 as we don't want to remove health.
        ApplyDamage(0);
    }
    void ApplyDamage(int damage)
    {
```

WHY NOT TRY...

You may want to tweak things like the player health or number of Zombies to make for a better-balanced game. This is now in a stage that you can go to town on the level layout, too; feel free to expand the plane or even build in additional structures to the Unity scene using 3D Objects. Don't forget to bake your navigation and set the geometry to be static if you do modify the level structure.

```
        //Checks we has attached a health
panel and out health is greater than 0
        if (healthPanel != null && health > 0)
        {
            //Stores the current health and
subtracts the damage value
            health = health - damage;
            //Sets the text on our panel.
            healthPanel.text = health.
ToString();
        }
    }
}
```

As usual, you'll want to save and return to the Unity Editor. We still, however, need to link our Canvas. Select the Player object and look in the Inspector – you'll see the script has two entries, one called Health Panel and one called Health. The Health entry is self-explanatory and has a default value of 100.

The other is where we need to drag in our Text object, so go ahead and do that. Just for completeness, and to make it easier to reuse our Player game object, we should select it in the Hierarchy and drag it into the Project panel to make it into a prefab.

We should be ready for a test, but you may want to duplicate your Zombie enemy a few times and move them around. Once you're happy with the setup, hit Play and start your new zombie-blasting challenge.

We should use the Anchor Presets again, but we want to align the pivot for the text in the top-right corner.

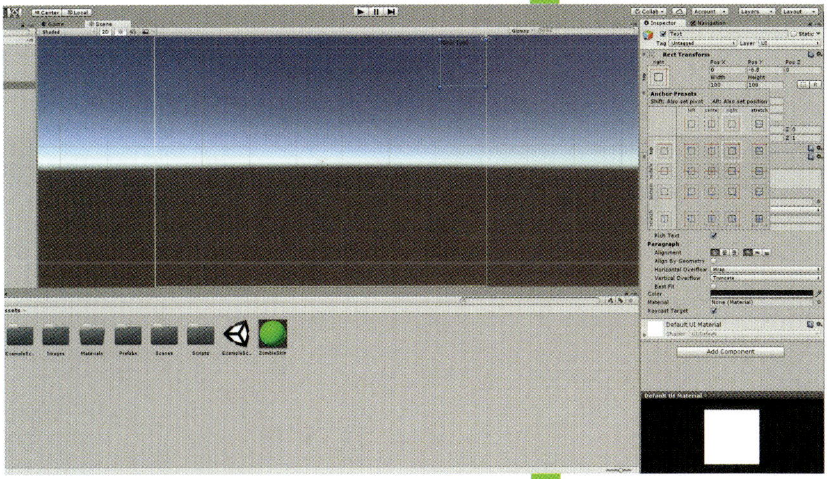

If everything's working correctly, a collision with a capsule zombie will now damage the player's health.

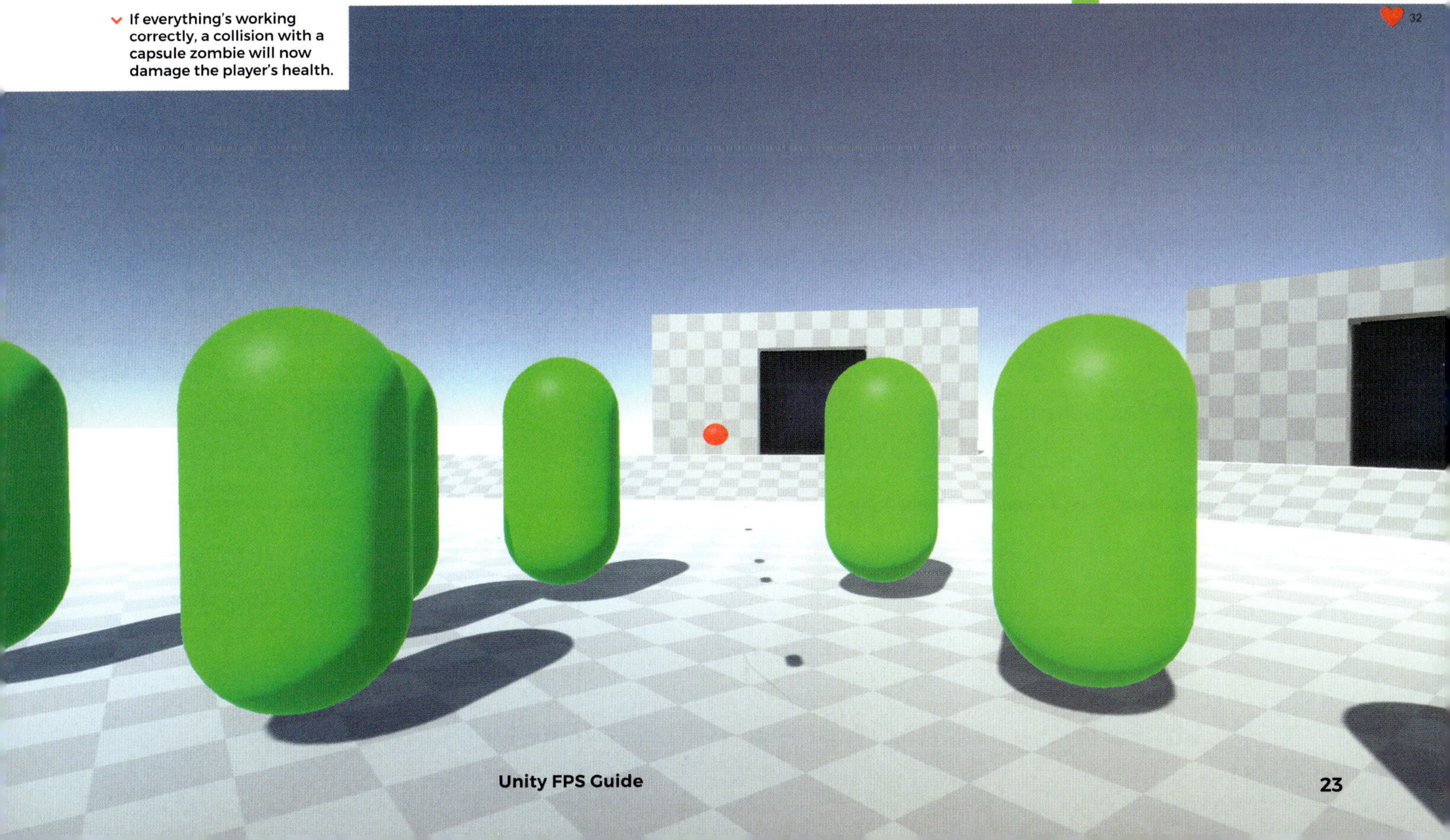

Expanding your first-person shooter

With our foundations in place, we'll expand our shooter with visual effects, menus and more

AUTHOR
STUART FRASER
Stuart is a former designer and developer of high-profile games such as *RollerCoaster Tycoon 3*, and has also worked as a lecturer of games development.

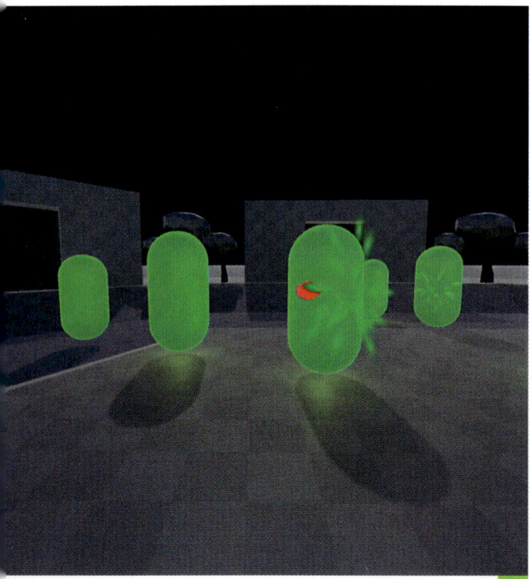

With the addition of rounds, menus, and effects, our project is really starting to feel like a proper game.

In our earlier tutorials, we looked at building the foundations of our first-person shooter, and worked through adding gameplay elements and mechanics, such as firing a projectile and creating a simple enemy type. We also added a wave-based survival mode, which we'll now expand on further by adding an enemy spawner and rounds. We'll also polish the game, adding a menu system and visual effects to our projectile hits.

CREATING AN OBJECT SPAWNER

First, let's create a spawner that we can use to spawn multiple enemies. This is going to be very simple, and we've already used some of this logic to spawn our bullet object. We'll also expose some variables or values so that we can expand the idea of a wave-based survival mode.

To do this, we need to create a game object to be our spawner object. You can simply right-click in the Hierarchy and select Create Empty. In the Inspector window for this object, rename it to Spawner. We'll add a script that allows us to choose the object to spawn, the number of spawned objects, and a delay between spawns. In Inspector, select Add Component and then select New Script and set the name to Spawner. We can then double-click the script to open the script editor of our choice, and then replace the script with our code. Remember to save and go back to Unity when you are done.

```
using System.Collections;
using System.Collections.Generic;
using UnityEngine;

public class Spawner : MonoBehaviour {
    public GameObject spawn;
    public int amount = 1;
    public float delaySpawn = 1;

    private int getAmount;
    private float timer;
    private int spawned;

    private void Start()
    {
        ResetRound();
    }

    private void ResetRound()
    {
        getAmount = amount;
    }
```

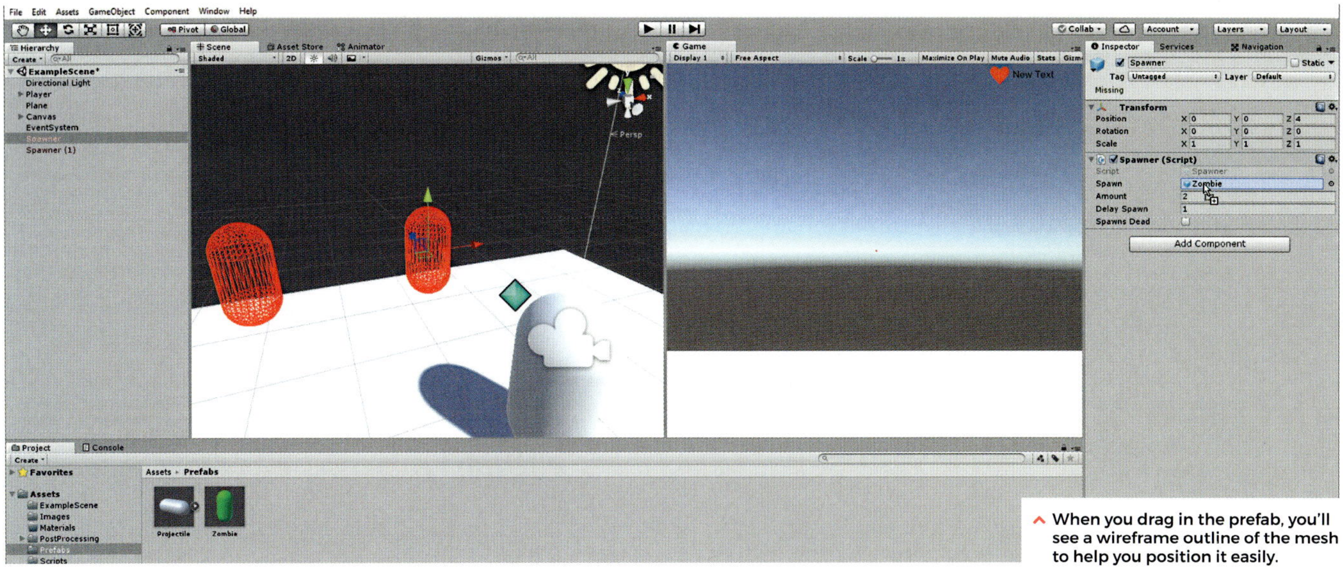

When you drag in the prefab, you'll see a wireframe outline of the mesh to help you position it easily.

```
    void Update () {
        timer += Time.deltaTime;
        if (delaySpawn < timer)
        {
            if (spawned< getAmount)
            {
                //Reset our timer.
                timer = 0;
                spawned++;
GameObject instance = Instantiate(spawn,
transform);
                instance.transform.parent
= null;
            }
        }
    }

    private void OnDrawGizmos()
    {
        //Draw the wireframe mesh of what
we intend to spawn in our editor.
        Gizmos.color = Color.red;
        if (spawn != null)
        {
            Gizmos.DrawWireMesh(spawn.
GetComponent<MeshFilter>().
sharedMesh,transform.position, spawn.
transform.rotation, Vector3.one);
        }
    }
}
```

We made our Zombie enemy a prefab in our Project in the last tutorial, so we should be able to select this and drag it onto the slot named Spawn that is shown for the Spawner object in the Inspector window. You can then delete any other Zombie objects that are in the Hierarchy, as we can now spawn them via this spawner object.

"The enemy is spawned, but it won't move"

Now test the spawner by pressing Play to preview the game. The first thing you may notice is that the enemy is spawned, but it won't move, and we have an error in the Unity log. The reason for the issue is that while we have the Player in our scene, the Zombie prefab is in the Project so the engine doesn't understand this exists. This is not a huge issue, but we need to change how we're going to set the goal for our AI script.

We need to stop the game playing, and then we need to select the MoveToPosition script. The fix is going to use the tags that we looked at in the second tutorial. We'll tell the script to set the goal to the object with the tag Player as soon as it spawns. So, open the script and you can replace the existing code with the changes below.

```
using UnityEngine;
using UnityEngine.AI;

public class MoveToPosition :
MonoBehaviour {

    private Transform goal;
    private NavMeshAgent agent;

    void Start()
    {
        goal = GameObject.
FindGameObjectWithTag("Player").
transform;
        agent =
GetComponent<NavMeshAgent>();
    }

    void Update()
    {
        agent.SetDestination(goal.
position);
    }
}
```

Save this, run the game again, and the error should be gone, and the AI will →

GET THE FILES

Remember, you can download all the project files, models, snippets of code, and other assets you'll need to follow along with this guide at our website – simply visit **wfmag.cc/fps-guide**

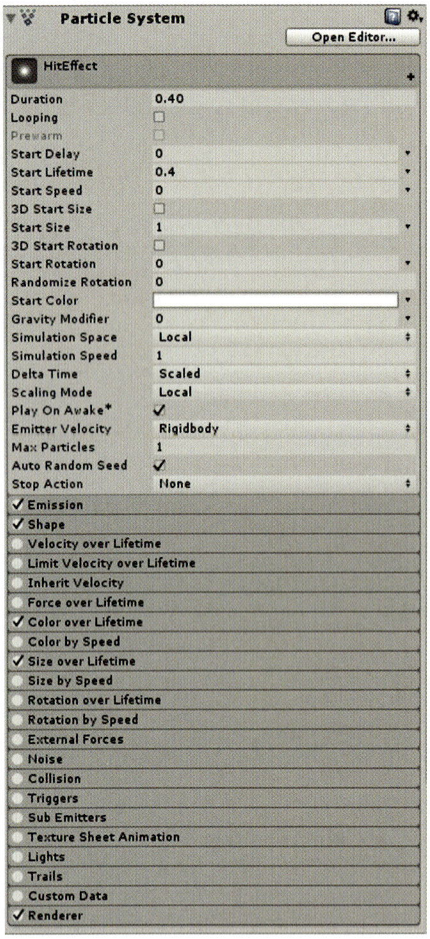

The Particle System contains a lot of useful modules that allow you to control your particle effect.

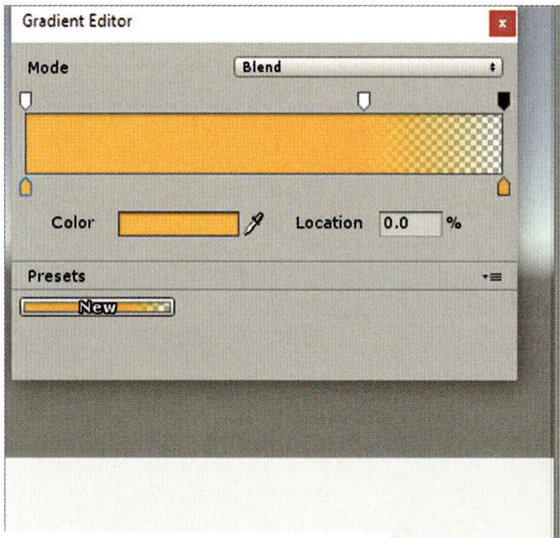

The gradient editor allows you to control the transparency and colour of the particles within a timeline.

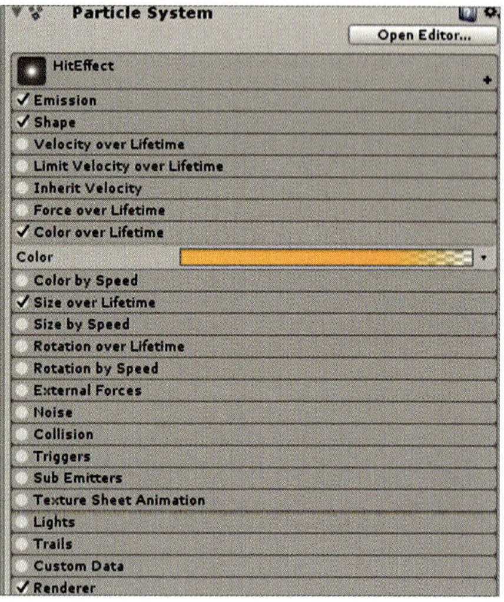

work as before. You can then exit the play mode and we will look at improving the look of our projectiles.

ADDING WEAPON PARTICLE EFFECTS

Let's add some particle effects to the action – this will make the game look more engaging. First, some setup: we're going to add another camera. We do this so the particle hit effects render before the rest of the scene – otherwise, the particle effect will clip with whatever it hits. To achieve this, select the Player in the Hierarchy and expand it until you find the Main Camera, then right-click and select Camera. We'll get a warning if we have two or more Audio Listeners on cameras, so select Audio Listener in the Inspector and then right-click to remove the component.

Check the Depth on the camera component is 0 rather than the default of -1. This is telling Unity to render this camera before the main camera. We'll also set the drop-down under Clear Flags to Depth only. Next, we select the Layer drop-down to the top-right of the Inspector window and select Add Layer. We'll now see the Tags & Layers tab we used on the last tutorial. We need to expand the Layers option and then, in an active empty layer, type WeaponFX.

Now we need to select our Main Camera in the Hierarchy. In the Inspector, select the Culling Mask drop-down and then untick our new WeaponFX layer. You'll notice that the drop-down will now say Mixed – this is the correct behaviour. Now,

"We'll add a spark effect on top to make it more dramatic"

select your new camera and select the Culling Mask drop-down and then Nothing from the options. Reselect the Culling Mask and tick just the WeaponFX layer.

We're now ready to create a particle effect and make it a prefab. To make this easier, we'll create a new level – from the Taskbar, select File > New Scene. Save the previous scene if you're prompted. In the Hierarchy, right-click and select Effects > Particle System. In the Inspector for the Particle System, reset the position to 0,0,0 and then expand the Particle System component. We need to uncheck Looping and change the parameters of Duration and Start Lifetime to 0.4, the Start Speed to 0, and Max Particles to 1. Now expand the Shape module and then change the Shape drop-down to Sphere and set the Scale for the shape to 0,0,0.

If you select Restart from the Particle Effect window that appears in the Scene viewport, you'll see a single particle appear at a fixed position, then disappear. We'll now enable the Size over Lifetime module and the Color over Lifetime module. Open the Color over Lifetime module and click the box to the right of the word Color. You'll see the Gradient editor. This has several sets of arrows that control the transparency or the colour of the particle over time.

Let's add a new arrow along the top by clicking in the same approximate area as the other down arrows. We select this arrow and drag it to be about three-quarters along the top. Now select the down-arrow to the top-right and you'll see an Alpha slider; change the value from 255 to 0. This should make a nice fade out when your particle is about to die off. Next, select the up-arrows that are along the bottom. This will let you set colours of your choice. I've selected the same orange colour for both the left and right arrow, but this is up to your own artistic choice. Finally, close the Gradient editor and try replaying your effect by restarting the playback.

We'll add an additional spark effect on top of this to make it more dramatic. With our Particle System still selected in the Hierarchy, right-click and select Effects > Particle System. Select the new Particle System and then, in the Particle System

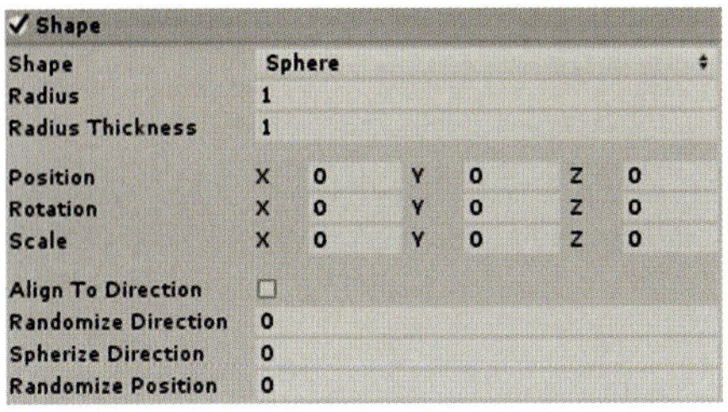

^ The shape module allows you to set the shape of the volume that the effect will be emitted from.

component, deselect Looping and change the Start Lifetime and Start Size to 0.2, and the Duration and Start Speed to 2. Select and open the Emission module and change Rate over Time to 0 and then, under the Bursts parameter, select the + to the bottom-right; the defaults are fine here.

Next, select the Shape module and change the Shape drop-down to Sphere. Select the Color over Lifetime module, and again, open the Gradient editor and set up the Alpha and Colour settings to mirror the ones for the first particle. In the Renderer module, select the Render Mode drop-down and select Stretch Billboard and then change the Speed Scale to 0.2 and the Length Scale to 1.

You can then preview the effects together; this should be quite satisfying, but feel free to tweak the settings to your preference. For ease of identification, select the first Particle System we made and, in the Inspector, name it HitEffect. One last thing is to change the Layer drop-down to WeaponFX and select Yes; choose children from the prompt.

As an addition, we'll add a script to destroy the particle effect so it won't clutter our inventory. In the Inspector, select Add Component, select New Script, and name this DestroyEffect, then open the script and replace with the code below.

```
using UnityEngine;

public class DestroyEffect :
MonoBehaviour
{
    public float maxTime = 1;
    private float timer;

    // Update is called once per frame
    void Update()
    {
        timer += Time.deltaTime;
        if (timer > maxTime)
        {
            Destroy(gameObject);
        }
    }
}
```

Save the script and then return to the Unity editor. We'll now drag this object into our Project window to make a prefab. Next, we load our original scene from the Project window – you don't need to save the current scene, as we have our prefab.

We now need to make some updates to our existing scripts. This will allow us to spawn a particle effect on the exact point our bullet hits the collider and add a knockback force to the Zombie enemy. Let's first find the BulletHit script in the Project and double-click to open it. We then replace the existing script with the modified code below.

```
using UnityEngine;
using System.Collections;

public class BulletHit : MonoBehaviour {
    public GameObject particle;

    //When we touch the collider we
disable this object.
    void OnCollisionEnter(Collision
other)
    {
        //Find the contact point on the
object we collided with.
        ContactPoint contact = other.
contacts[0];
        //Set the exact position and
rotation we hit the collider at.
        Quaternion rot = Quaternion.
FromToRotation(Vector3.up, contact.
normal);
        Vector3 pos = contact.point;
        //Spawn our particle using the
above parameters.
        Instantiate(particle, pos, rot);
        gameObject.SetActive(false);
    }
}
```

THE JOY OF LAYERS

Layers are extremely useful and can be applied to more than camera rendering. We can use them to specify which lights would cast on an object, or which objects can interact with each other. You can find out more about layers from the Unity documentation: **wfmag.cc/sWAQFT**

Save this and then we want to open and replace our MoveToPosition script in a similar fashion.

```
using UnityEngine;
using UnityEngine.AI;

public class MoveToPosition :
MonoBehaviour
{
    public float knockbackTime = 1;
    public float kick = 1.8f;
    private Transform goal;
    private NavMeshAgent agent;
    private bool hit;
    private ContactPoint contact;
    private float timer;

    void Start()
    {
        goal = GameObject
FindGameObjectWithTag("Player").
transform;
        agent =
GetComponent<NavMeshAgent>();
        //Set timer to the same a
knockback in first instance.
        timer = knockbackTime;
    }

    void Update()
    {
        if (hit)
        {
            //Allow physics to be
applied.
            gameObject.
GetComponent<Rigidbody>().isKinematic =
false;
```

```
            //Stop our AI navigation.
            gameObject.
GetComponent<NavMeshAgent>().
isStopped=true;
            //Push back our enemy with an
impulse force set via the kick value.
            gameObject.
GetComponent<Rigidbody>().
AddForceAtPosition(Camera.main.transform.
forward * kick, contact.point, ForceMode.
Impulse);
            hit = false;
            timer = 0;
        }
        else
        {
            timer += Time.deltaTime;
            //After being knocked back,
restart movement after X seconds.
            if (knockbackTime < timer)
            {
                gameObject.
GetComponent<Rigidbody>().isKinematic =
true;
                gameObject.
GetComponent<NavMeshAgent>().isStopped =
false;
                agent.
SetDestination(goal.position);
            }
        }
    }

    void OnCollisionEnter(Collision
other)
    {
        //We compare the tag in the other
object to the tag name we set earlier.
        if (other.transform.
CompareTag("bullet"))
        {
            contact = other.contacts[0];
            hit = true;
        }
    }
}
```

Save this script and move back to Unity editor, select the Projectile in the Project window and expand it by clicking the right-arrow and select the Bullet mesh. In the Inspector for the mesh, you should see our BulletHit script. Select the slot labelled Particle, click the small circle next to it, and then select our HitEffect particle prefab.

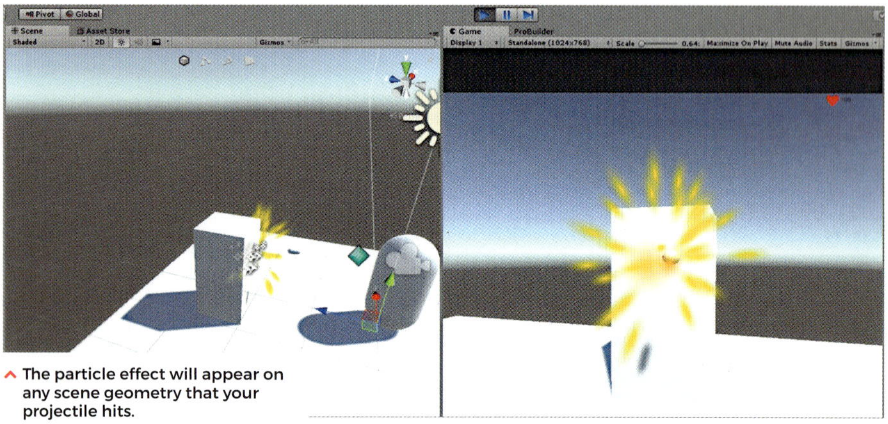

^ The particle effect will appear on any scene geometry that your projectile hits.

DEVELOPING OUR ROUNDS SYSTEM

We want to add a rounds system. For this, we'll make a new Game Object. Go to the Hierarchy, right-click in an empty space, and select Create Empty. In the Inspector, rename this object to GameManager. We then select Add Component and then New Script and call the script GameManager. Then we will open this and add the code below.

```
using System.Collections;
using System.Collections.Generic;
using UnityEngine;
using UnityEngine.UI;
using UnityEngine.SceneManagement;

public class Spawners
{
    public GameObject go;
    public bool active;
    public Spawners(GameObject newGo,
bool newBool)
    {
        go = newGo;
        active = newBool;
    }
}

public class GameManager : MonoBehaviour
{
    public GameObject panel;
    public delegate void RestartRounds();
    public static event RestartRounds
RoundComplete;

    private int health;
    private int roundsSurived;
    private int currentRound;
    private PlayerDamage playerDamage;
    private Text panelText;

    public List<Spawners> spawner = new
List<Spawners>();

    void Start () {
        Time.timeScale = 1;
        panel.SetActive(false);
        playerDamage = GameObject.
FindGameObjectWithTag("Player").
GetComponent<PlayerDamage>();
        panelText = panel.
GetComponentInChildren<Text>();
        foreach (GameObject go in
GameObject.FindObjectsOfType(typeof(Game
Object)))
        {
            if (go.name.
Contains("Spawner"))
            {
                spawner.Add(new
Spawners(go, true));
            }
        }
    }

        void Update () {
        int total = 0;
```

```
        health = playerDamage.health;
        if (health > 0)
        {
            for (int i = spawner.Count -
1; i >= 0; i--)
            {
                if (spawner[i].
go.GetComponent<Spawner>().spawnsDead)
                {
                    total++;
                }
            }

            if (total == spawner.Count &&
roundsSurived == currentRound)
            {
                roundsSurived++;
                panelText.text =
string.Format("Round {0} Completed!",
roundsSurived);
                panel.SetActive(true);
            }

            if (roundsSurived !=
currentRound && Input.GetButton("Fire2"))
            {
                currentRound =
roundsSurived;
                RoundComplete();
                panel.SetActive(false);
            }
        }
        else
        {
            if (Input.GetButton("Fire2"))
            {
                Scene current =
SceneManager.GetActiveScene();
                SceneManager.
LoadScene(current.name);
            }
            else
            {
                panel.SetActive(true);
                panelText.text =
string.Format("Survived {0} Rounds",
roundsSurived);
          Time.timeScale = 0;
  } } } }
```

We now need to update the Spawner script. This is because we want to be able to trigger the spawners to restart when we've completed a round. The manager will look at when all the spawners are marked as depleted and restart spawning when a new round initialises. So we need to open our Spawner script and replace it with our updates below.

```
using System;
using System.Collections;
using System.Collections.Generic;
using UnityEngine;

public class Enemy
{
    public GameObject go;
    public bool active;
    public Enemy (GameObject newGo, bool
newBool)
    {
        go = newGo;
        active = newBool;
    }
}

public class Spawner : MonoBehaviour
{
    public GameObject spawn;
    public int amount = 1;
    public float delaySpawn = 1;
    public bool spawnsDead;

    private int getAmount;
    private float timer;
    private int spawned;
    private int enemyDead;

    public List<Enemy> enemies = new
List<Enemy>();

    public void Start()
    {
        GameManager.RoundComplete +=
ResetRound;
        ResetRound();
        while (spawned < getAmount)
        {
            //Increment the amount
spawned count.
            spawned++;
            //Create the prefab as an
instance.
            GameObject instance =
Instantiate(spawn, transform);
            enemies.Add(new
Enemy(instance, false));
            //Removes the spawned object
from the spawner object.
            instance.transform.parent =
null;
        instance.SetActive(false);
        }
        ResetRound();
    }
    public void ResetRound()
    {
        spawnsDead = false;
        getAmount = amount;
        spawned = 0;
        timer = 0;
        enemyDead = 0;
    }

    void Update()
    {
        //Increase timer per frame.
        timer += Time.deltaTime;
        //Do the spawn if our timer is
larger than the delay spawn we set.
        if (delaySpawn < timer)
        {
            //And we haven't reached the
spawn amount.
            if (spawned < getAmount)
```

NOISES OFF

You can easily add sound effects to game objects by using the Audio Source component. By default, these will play the audio as soon as the object is active in the scene. You can import standard audio formats: MP3, WAV, and OGG. A great addition is to add a weapon firing audio effect to your bullet prefab; each shot will then play the effect on spawning.

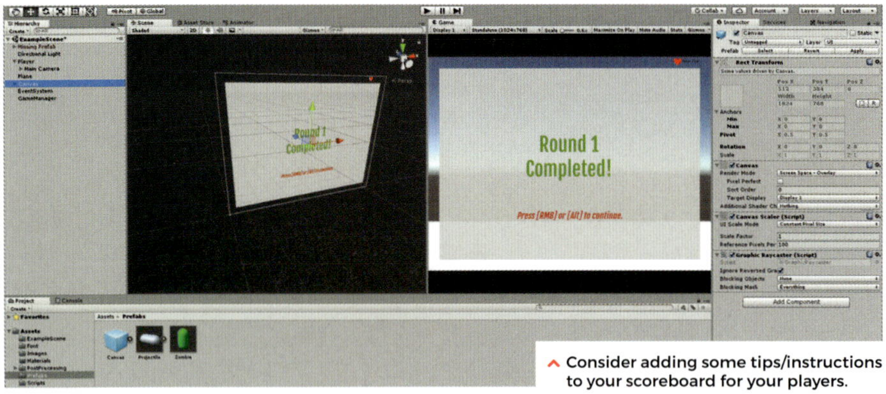

Consider adding some tips/instructions to your scoreboard for your players.

```
            {
                //Reset our timer.
                timer = 0;
                //Set our bool to track
the state of the enemy.
                enemies[spawned].active
= true;
                //Set the enemy to be
active.
                enemies[spawned].
go.SetActive(true);
                //Get ready to set
isKinematic.
                StartCoroutine(SetKinemat
ic(spawned));
                //Increment the amount
spawned count.
                spawned++;
            }

            for (int i = enemies.Count -
1; i >= 0; i--)
            {
                //If another script
disabled the object but we set them
active above.
                if (enemies[i].
go.activeSelf == false && enemies[i].
active == true)
                {
                    //Reset the spawn
position and set our tracking bool that
they are not active.
                    enemies[i].
go.transform.position = transform.
position;
                    enemies[i].active =
false;
                    enemyDead++;
                }
            }

            if (enemyDead == enemies.
Count)
            {
                spawnsDead = true;
            }
        }
    }

    IEnumerator SetKinematic(int id)
    {
        //We set isKinematic at the start
of the next frame to avoid confusion with
other commands.
        yield return null;
        enemies[id].
go.GetComponent<Rigidbody>().isKinematic
= true;
    }

    private void OnDrawGizmos()
    {
        //Draw the wireframe mesh of what
we intend to spawn in our editor.
        Gizmos.color = Color.red;
        if (spawn != null)
        {
            Gizmos.DrawWireMesh(spawn.
GetComponent<MeshFilter>().sharedMesh,
transform.position, spawn.transform.
rotation, Vector3.one);
        }
    }
}
```

AMAZING SCENES

You can create a game object with a script that is persistent in your scene (or set of scenes) and will not get disabled or deleted. Essentially, they take in input from other scripts, can control elements in other game objects, and help manage other elements of gameplay. I tend to refer to these game objects as managers, but you may see these called a slightly different name elsewhere.

We need to make one very small change to an existing script. Open the EnemyDamage script and replace this with:

```
using UnityEngine;

public class EnemyDamage : MonoBehaviour
{
    private int hitNumber;

    private void OnEnable()
    {
        hitNumber = 0;
    }

    void OnCollisionEnter(Collision
other)
    {
        if (other.transform.
CompareTag("bullet"))
        {
            //If the comparison is true,
we increase the hit number.
            hitNumber++;
        }
        if (hitNumber == 3)
        {
            gameObject.SetActive(false);
        }
    }
}
```

DISPLAYING OUR ROUNDS SCOREBOARD

We'll also set up a new Panel in our canvas; this will let us display a round scoreboard and a message when you run out of health. In the Hierarchy, right-click the Canvas and select UI > Panel. Select the new Panel and, in the Inspector, change the name

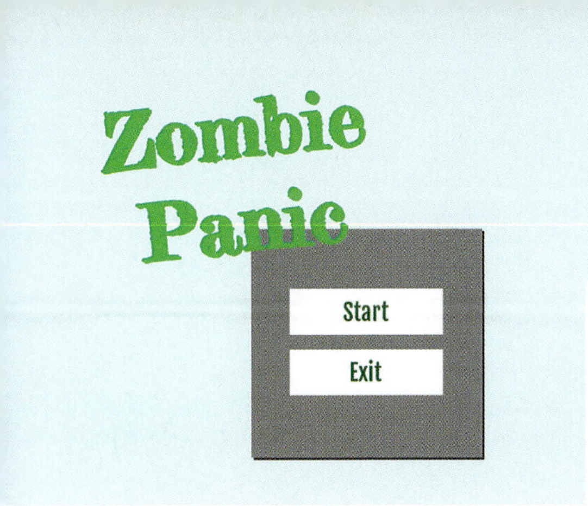

Just using the UI elements we are familiar with, we can create our title screen.

to ScorePanel. You might want to change some of the other parameters in the Image component, such as the opacity and colour of the panel image.

We now right-click in the Hierarchy with the new panel still highlighted and choose UI > Text. You can try changing the Alignment, font size, and colour of the text component in the Inspector. Once you're happy with the look of the panel, select the GameManager object and drag the ScorePanel into the slot called Panel on the Inspector window.

We now have a complete experience in terms of our game loop; we'll know when we've completed a round, and when we get down to no-health we'll see the total rounds complete and have a chance to restart the game. To progress to the next round or to restart, we can use the binding for Fire2 which equates to the right-mouse button or left **ALT** on the keyboard.

IMPLEMENTING OUR GAME FRONT-END

It would be quite cool to add a front-end menu and be able to play through the game as a standalone executable like any other PC game. Let's start with the main menu first, and create a new scene by selecting File > New Scene and saving our current work.

In the new scene, go into the Hierarchy and right-click and select UI > Canvas. Next, right-click and select UI > Panel. As with the score panel, try changing the defaults to give this a look and feel that suits your game. Again, keep the panel selected, then right-click and select UI > Text.

I'd place this at the top of the canvas by selecting the Anchor Presets from the Rect Transform in the Inspector. Remember last time, when we held the **SHIFT** key to change the behaviour of the anchor? We'll do this again and then select the icon with the blue dot at the top-middle of the inner square. You'll then need to type in the value of 0 to Pos Y.

You should also change the values for the width and height of the Rect Transform to 300 by 200. Choose a font size of about 70 and set your alignments to the centre for the Text component. You can then come up with a title for your game; I chose Zombie Panic for mine.

We'll make two buttons; one to start a new game and the other to exit. First, select the Panel from the Hierarchy, then right-click and select UI > Button. We then repeat the process to add our second button. The two buttons will be overlaid, so with the second button still selected, we can use the move tool. Select the green arrow that's pointing up in the Scene window, then drag it downwards when highlighted.

> **"We should have a complete experience in terms of our game loop"**

Next, we'll expand the Button object by selecting the right-arrow next to it in the Hierarchy. You should see another Text object attached. Select this and then in the Inspector change the text from Button to Exit. We expand the first button we created and repeat the process; however, we want to replace text with Start.

We need to make a script to start or exit the game. We can then link this to the buttons with an OnClick event. First, select the Canvas in the Hierarchy and then in the Inspector select Add Component. We then select New Script and name this MenuScript, then open it ready to replace it with the code below.

```
using UnityEngine;
using UnityEngine.SceneManagement;

public class MenuScript : MonoBehaviour {

    public void StartGame()
    {
        SceneManager.LoadScene(1);
    }

    public void ExitGame()
    {
        Application.Quit();
    }
}
```

Save the script and return to Unity editor, then we can reselect the first Button we created. In the Inspector, look for the OnClick option. To the bottom-right is a +, so click this and a new entry will appear. Select the Canvas and drop this into the slot that displays None (Object). Now select the drop-down that says No Function and then choose MenuScript > StartGame. Repeat the step with our exit button, but this time choose MenuScript > ExitGame.

We now save this scene by selecting File > Save Scene as... from the taskbar, then go back to the taskbar and select Build Settings. In the new window, select the Add Open Scenes button. Close the window and now load our game scene. Next, select Build Settings and again Add Open Scenes. We're now in the position to make an executable. All we need to do is select Build and Run, select a suitable folder and file name for the game, and Save.

We'll now be able to try our menu system and play through the entire experience from start to finish. There are still many more improvements we can make, but you can see how we're building up the layers of a complete game experience.

Having the spawns separated and in their own 'caves' increases the challenge.

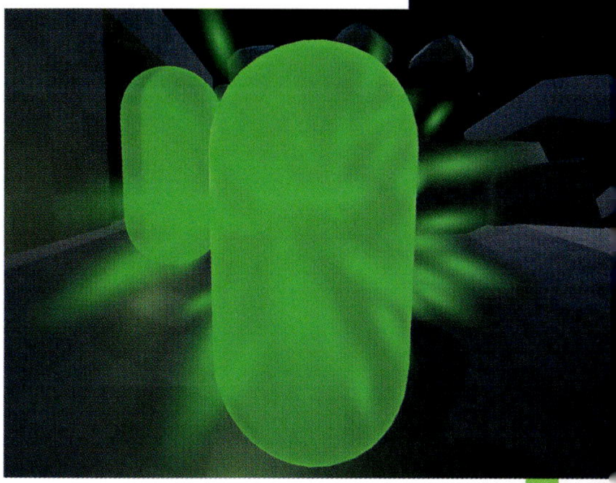

Add levels, models, and more

Let your shooter take shape with walking zombies, lighting, sound effects, and a castle to explore

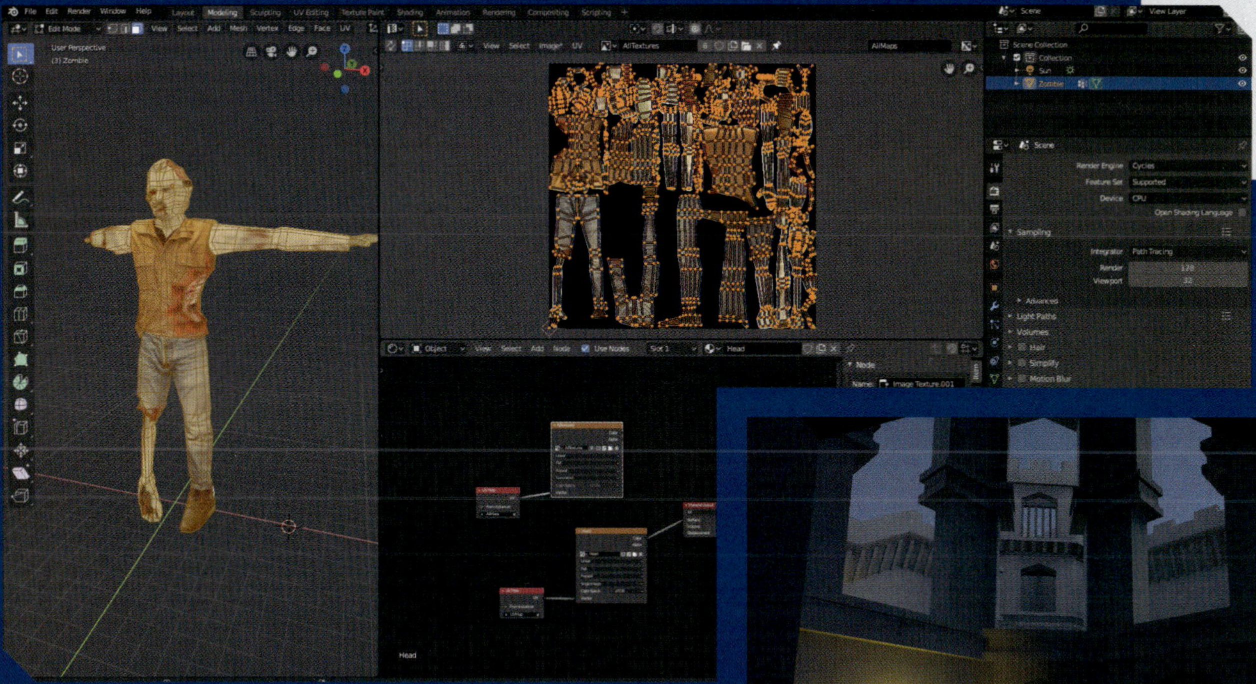

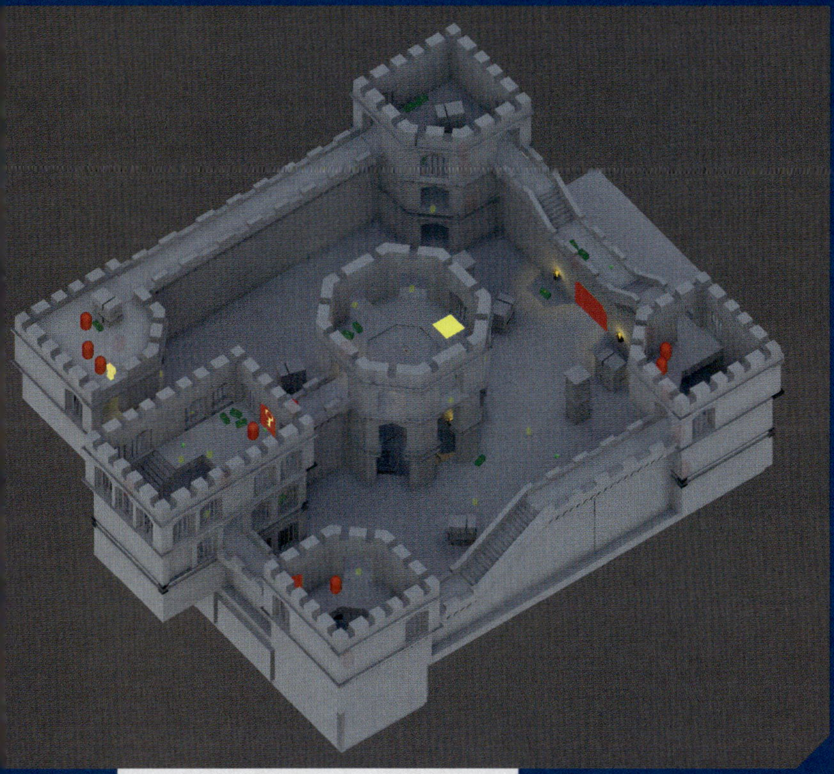

Zombie meshes, level assets and atmospheric lighting will transform your shooter's look and feel.

Prison Break: the view from the start of our castle level.

Creating a **level**

Now we have the basics in place, let's create a level that players will remember

AUTHOR
ANDREW PALMER

Starting out as a hobbyist level designer in the nineties, Andrew has contributed to a long list of published titles in design, art, and technical art roles. He currently works for indie game developer 17-BIT, in Kyoto, Japan.

Level design is where designers take all the various components of a game and piece them together into one cohesive chunk of entertainment, and doing it well – especially when creating opportunity for player creativity and including a satisfying narrative – can be extremely complicated. For a simple game design with few moving parts, though, level design doesn't need to be difficult and can be lots of fun.

LEVEL DESIGN GOALS

Before you can begin building a level, it's important to understand the game your level's for. This includes the player's abilities, enemies, and power-ups. There may be an overall narrative progression you want in your game, in which case it's important to decide where the level will fit in, and how the level will further this narrative. Even if your game has no story, you'll need to decide on what the player will face based on their experience at that point in the game, and if you're going to introduce a new mechanic, then the level will need to feature gameplay focusing on that mechanic, and perhaps how it builds upon other mechanics from previous levels.

Depending on your game, the goal of your level could be something as simple as reaching the exit, surviving for as long as possible, or something more complex, broken down into smaller objectives, like finding your way into a building, getting past the guards, and safely guiding an ally out of the building.

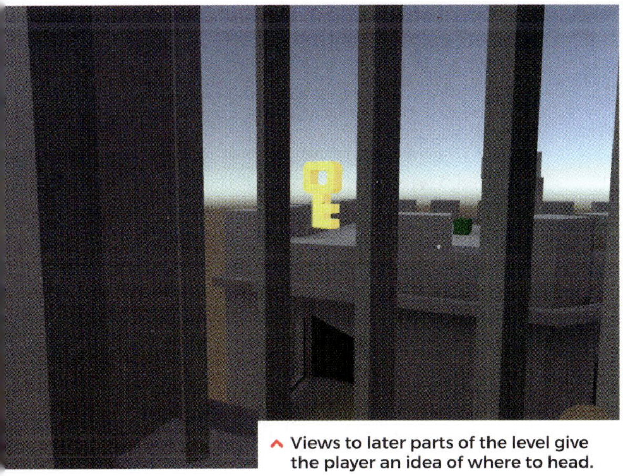

Views to later parts of the level give the player an idea of where to head.

In the original *Doom*, for example, the goal of all the levels was simply to reach the exit, maybe finding a key to open a door in order to progress. Players weren't really guided by anything other than the sound of the next group of monsters that needed to be dispatched, or the sight of the aforementioned key or other valuable item sitting in a darkened room, beckoning them inside. I personally remember exploring *Doom*'s maze-like levels, feeling lost and trying to find the route forward, but often stumbling across secret areas before I finally got back on the right path.

Most modern FPS games aren't much more complicated than this, but the keys and doors which served to guide the player along a predetermined path are replaced with other things that help drive the narrative. Levels tend to be a lot more streamlined and linear, often with elaborate set-pieces, which are usually tied into the story. These games aim to provide a memorable, focused experience, where there's no potential to get lost, or secret areas to distract from the experience the designers want to craft for the player.

There are exceptions, of course, with titles such as the open-world *Far Cry* series, and immersive sim *Deus Ex* putting the player in a world with consistent and predictable rules, and providing a set of tools that encourage experimentation, allowing missions to be solved in a variety of ways – sometimes in ways even the designers hadn't planned for.

There's also been a resurgence of the simpler FPS games of past generations that put a greater reliance on the player's navigational and combat skills, and the return of secret areas to uncover. The 2016 reimagining of *Doom* brings back some of the complex, secret-filled level design from earlier games, while upping the focus on intense combat against a bestiary of demons, with all the graphical bells and whistles that modern technology allows. Games such as *Ion Fury* and *Wrath*: *Aeon of Ruin* even use the actual game engines (from *Duke Nukem 3D* and *Quake*, respectively) used by games released in the nineties.

For *Zombie Panic*, we'll focus more on the style of level design used in older games. There's a lot to learn, and we'll mix in lessons learned since the early days of the FPS to improve the experience for our players.

LOOKING AT THE PARTS

In *Zombie Panic*, there are a small number of building blocks for our level, so it's up to us to make the most of these to create an entertaining experience. Not only do we need to think about the individual parts that make up the game, but we must think about how these parts interact with each other in order to design a level that makes the most of what we have. →

Player	Walk, Shoot, Punch, Jump
Zombie	Follow player, Attack player (drain health)
Zombie Spawner	Create more zombies
Health Pick-up	Restore the player's health
Ammo Pick-up	Allows the player to shoot instead of punch (less danger)

Our castle stage isn't huge, but its winding layout means it takes a little time to explore.

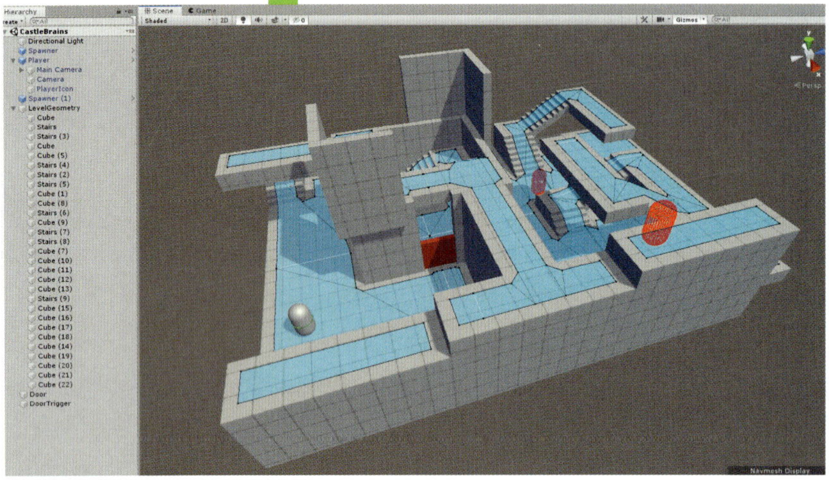

An early scale test for the castle level, with navmesh overlay.

In addition to what's already in the game, we'll create some environmental components that allow us to control the level flow and guide the player along the path we wish them to take. You'll learn about how to make these in the next chapter (page 40).

Door	Block player and zombie movement, Open, Close. Can be locked.
Key	Allows locked doors to be opened
Switch	Allows player to open or close doors
Trigger	Invisible switch we will use to spawn zombies and activate doors

Although this may seem limiting, there's a lot that can be done even with just these parts. The zombies are simple and will always move towards the player, but we can spawn them where we want at just the right time using triggers, and we can use doors to trap them or allow the player to redirect them. The key can be used to open up multiple new areas at once and give the player a choice of route. Although a key is functionally similar to a switch that opens a door, it feels fundamentally different to the player, and makes more logical sense when placed far from the door (or doors) it unlocks.

We can ration the ammo and health so that we know players are likely to need to use their punch attack at certain times, or run out of ammo during a zombie onslaught and be forced to run looking for more, urging them forward into the next horde of zombies we unleash.

The other thing we have control over is how we build spaces and where we place walls, stairs, floors, and other architectural elements. Spaces should be created to make combat with our enemies interesting, and tailored to encourage certain types of combat or situation to occur based on the level goals.

EXPLORING DESIGNS

Before you begin building a level, it's a good idea to write some notes and sketch some ideas for the shape of the environment and path you'd like the player to take. Although it's rare that the level you build will be exactly like your initial design, it helps to get an idea in your head before starting. Of course, you might prefer to skip notes and start blocking out the level in 3D, and that's fine too, but try to at least have an idea of what it is you want to create first. I find writing notes and sketches really helps to get me started with the blocking out process.

"There are a few options when it comes to turning your ideas into reality"

BUILDING THE LEVEL

There are a few options when it comes to turning your ideas into reality. You can use an external tool, such as Blender, to model the level and import it into Unity, or tools such as ProBuilder, which let you work directly inside the Unity editor. While external tools may provide more freedom, in general it's best to start with something inside Unity so that you can play with scale, forms, and spaces and quickly test the game without the extra step of importing geometry from an external program.

When you first start creating your level, it's important to get a sense of scale by building a few simple rooms, doorways, stairs, and other things you wish to incorporate into your level. Failure to do this could result in a massive amount of wasted work if you end up making a level that feels too cramped, or too large because you didn't feel out the scale before starting. Even worse, you could end up making something too small for your enemies to navigate, so make a small test environment and put some enemies in it before you start building your level. If you're making multiple levels, you

Castle level before adding doors and triggers.

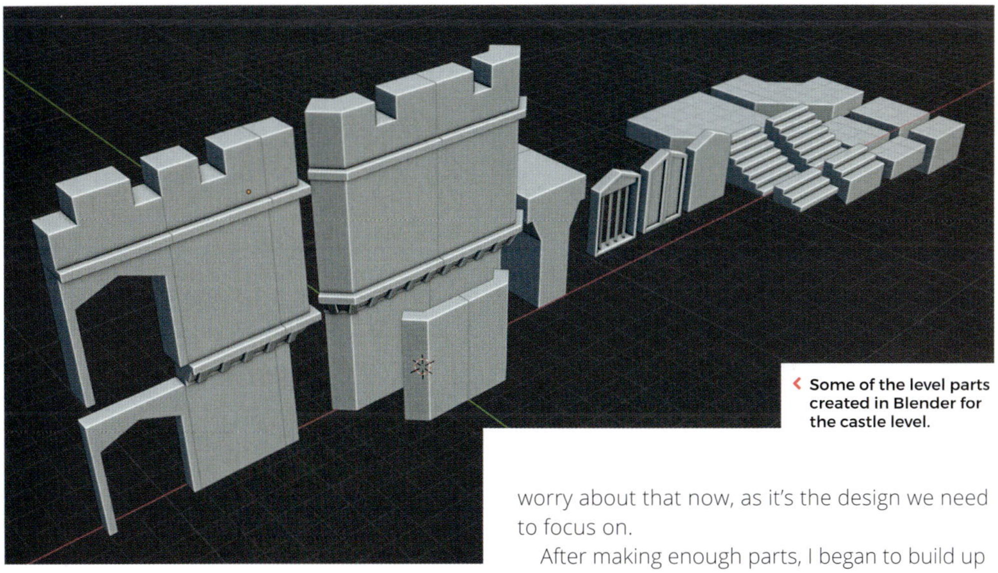

Some of the level parts created in Blender for the castle level.

only need to do this once or twice until you get a good sense for the scale things should be in your game, and you can always refer back to your tests, or add to them in order to ensure you are working at the right scale.

Likewise, it's a good idea to make combat tests. Let's say you have multiple enemy types, and different weapons that can be used to dispatch them. In order to ensure that a particular combination of enemies is fun to fight, you should test them out in a simplified environment before working it into your level. The simplified environment or test level can be used to quickly iterate on your design, and then you can copy it into your level once you've refined it.

For my castle level, I began by blocking out some simple shapes inside ProBuilder, testing the scale of doorways, staircases, and other elements I'd need to make sure they could be easily navigated by both the player and zombies. After a while, I figured out the scale I wanted, and moved into Blender, where I'm more comfortable with the modelling tools, and started to build parts that I could quickly piece together inside Unity.

The parts I made were all turned into prefabs, with collision added and set to static. Doing this meant that all my parts would work with the navmesh baker, which requires static geometry to create the navmesh. It also has the benefit of being easier to update colliders and any other components attached to the parts with changes being reflected across the entire level, just by editing a single prefab. It's also easy to pass these placeholder parts to an environment artist to turn into beautiful, finished assets, but don't worry about that now, as it's the design we need to focus on.

After making enough parts, I began to build up the level gradually until I had something similar to what I had initially imagined – even if it looked nothing like my messy sketches! Although this level was initially devoid of gameplay, save the odd zombie to check the scale was OK, I had thought about the route I wanted the player to take through the level, as well as what they would see as they passed through it. Although this route wasn't completely confirmed after making my notes, it began to solidify as I saw the level forming and spent more time looking at it in three dimensions.

CONTROLLING LEVEL FLOW

We've all had the experience of playing a game and getting lost. Sometimes we go the right way, but don't notice something and then spend ages looking for what was right under our noses all along, and sometimes the level's so complex, or its scenery so similar, that we just stay lost. In general, good level design should try to mitigate this problem as much as possible, and there are many ways to keep your players on the right path.

Players will tend to remember anything that looks important along their path through a level; the locations of locked doors, currently unreachable items, and even just unique decoration (visual markers) will be noted so that if the player finds something relevant to their discovery, such as a key or new ability, they can easily return to that point.

INSTALLING PROBUILDER

Although ProBuilder is a free and supported by Unity, it needs to be downloaded through the package manager. To install, open up the Package Manager (Window > Package Manager), and wait while it refreshes the list of available packages. Once the list of packages has been loaded, select ProBuilder and hit the 'Install' button in the bottom right corner. From there, you can create ProBuilder meshes by pressing **CTRL+K** to create a cube, or **CTRL+SHIFT+K** to open a shape menu, allowing you to create a variety of shapes, including cylinders and staircases. There will also be a new menu item in the top menu bar (under Tools > ProBuilder) with more options, and any mesh created by ProBuilder will have a special component on it, allowing you to toggle editing features easily.

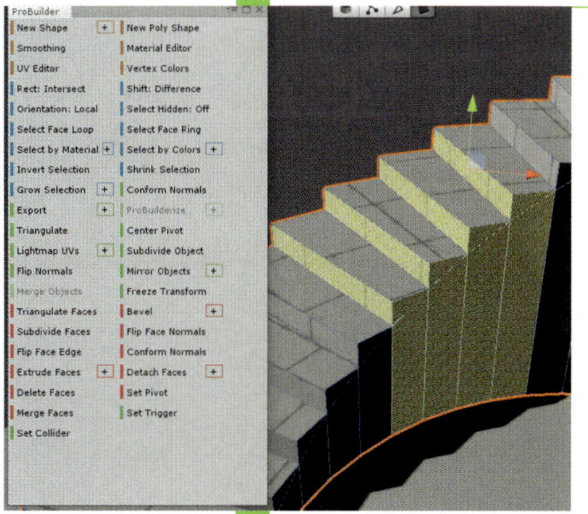

^ Finding the locked door and spotting the key in *Zombie Panic*.

Environment art can aid level design by creating strong visual markers that players remember, and gradually build a mental map around. Likewise, lighting and sound can be used to draw players toward important locations and away from others. However, there are things we can do in the design of spaces to push players forward, or aid their understanding of said space.

Just like in real life, players become more familiar with something the more they are exposed to it. Creating a space the player will revisit from several angles allows players to figure out where they are in relation to where they've already been, and build a much better mental map of their environment than if they were walking through a set of rooms and corridors. While this trick takes a bit more thought than placing lights or other markers to highlight the route, it can not only help players navigate the level, but also reinforces the sense that they're in a real place and not just walking through a movie set.

Of course, there are times when you can't design in a way that allows players to get familiar with the environment. If your game has a level where you must run out of a huge underground complex before it blows up, then you'll have to rely on clear visual markers to guide the player out.

Although *Zombie Panic* features a simple key and locked door, some games unlock new areas with abilities in place of keys. In the *Legend of Zelda* series, players will notice elements throughout the world that they're not equipped to make use of, such as mounted hooks around the environment. Later on, after defeating a tough enemy, the player receives a grappling hook which can be used with the mounted hooks to access entirely new areas. This is much more work to implement than locked doors, since it requires game design and level design to work closely together, but a great deal more rewarding and interesting for the player.

Challenge can also force players to avoid an area until they've gained a certain amount of power or experience. RPGs often do this, but it can be done in FPS games, even within the space of a single level, by putting difficult enemies near the beginning, and powerful weapons elsewhere. This also has the added benefit of providing two ways to tackle the situation: face down the enemy under-prepared, or get loaded up to tip the balance. Players who manage to defeat difficult situations without preparing are also able to glean added satisfaction from overcoming the increased challenge.

With *Zombie Panic*, there are many other ways to control how players can move through your level. For this level, I used several techniques in order to guide players through the level:

- The player can see out from the start, and back to the start from other parts of the level, allowing them to see their progress.
- Ammo packs placed in front of the player in the courtyard help pull the player forward, triggering even more zombie spawners.
- The route passes the main gate, which is a large red door. Hopefully, this tells the player that it is important.
- From the locked door, the key is visible. The player just needs to figure out how to reach it.
- Likewise, the locked door is visible and directly in front of where the key is found.
- The entire level can be seen from the battlements, helping the player understand the space.
- The main gate switch is right above the gate itself, with a window allowing the player to see down to the gate.

Of course, you may not want to guide players clearly all the time; secrets and alternative routes should be hinted more subtly, allowing the player to discover things by themselves, which is far more satisfying than just doing what the designer wants.

PROBUILDER GEOMETRY

Geometry you create using ProBuilder will automatically have a collider attached, saving you the hassle of adding it manually. ProBuilder geometry is marked as non-convex, which enables you to make whatever shape you want without worrying about breaking the parts into convex chunks to get accurate collision. However, convex mesh colliders – and especially box, capsule, and sphere colliders – are much better for performance than non-convex mesh colliders. Not only that, but you will not be able to use non-convex mesh colliders with rigidbodies, so if you need to add collision to a moving object, such as a door, you may have to manually set up the collision shapes after building the mesh.

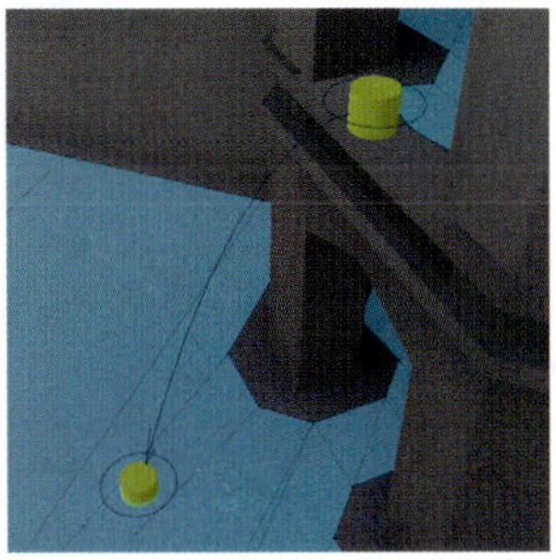

^ Obstacles and Off Mesh Links are used to make the zombies less predictable.

COMBAT DESIGN

Although combat design is also closely related to game design, it's also a vital part of level design for FPS games. It's especially important when there are multiple types of enemies with different abilities, as putting certain combinations of enemies can make situations more fun and engaging, or prove frustratingly difficult. Getting the right balance of enemies, along with power-ups (if relevant to your game), can be tricky.

In general, you should try to place each enemy where it will be most effective. If your game has flying enemies, make sure there's room for them to fly; if the game has charging enemies, make sure there isn't so much cover the player can avoid them too easily. If introducing an enemy for the first time, make sure to do it in a way that the player will notice it and see what makes that enemy different.

In *Zombie Panic*, the enemies use the navmesh to get to the player, so placement is less important for combat. What is important, however, is making sure zombies spawn relatively close to the player so that there are enough zombies to overwhelm the player at key moments. In our castle level, there are a few places where this can happen, one of which being the large courtyard.

"It's tricky to judge whether your own level is fun because you've spent so long making it"

Initially, the zombies pouring into the courtyard would chase the player in a relatively straight line that not only looked odd, but was also not at all threatening. In order to somewhat reduce this problem, I added some cover objects to split up the navmesh and hopefully force the zombies to take slightly different routes to get to the player. Doing this made the space feel a little more interesting, and also caused the odd zombie to split off from the pack and go a different way around the obstacles, increasing the chance the player could be surrounded.

Allowing zombies to jump down from above by placing Off Mesh Links to connect areas of the navmesh had a more positive effect on the combat, as it made the zombies feel a little less predictable and it became easier to surprise the player, such as the first time the locked door room is entered. In fact, the zombies in this room are some of the most fun to fight in the whole level.

TESTING AND REFINEMENT

Once you've built your level, it's really important you test it to make sure there aren't any major bugs and that it can be completed. Play through it a few times to make all the zombies spawn, doors open, and everything works as it should.

It's actually quite tricky to judge whether your own level is fun because you've spent so long making it, and will know every nook and cranny by the time it's finished. To really test your level, you should get a couple of friends who've never played it before. If you can, sit behind them and make notes as they play, but don't immediately tell them how to progress if they appear stuck. Be patient! Once your testers have finished their playthrough, ask them what they thought, whether they enjoyed it, and then ask specifically about issues you noticed while they were playing. Write notes of their answers and compile a list of changes you would like to make to the level. Don't just do everything your friends suggest, but try to think why problems occurred and how to fix or improve the level while staying true to the experience you were aiming to create.

Once the level has been tested by one player, make any changes you deem necessary and get someone else to test it. You can repeat the process until testers are not having any major problems and you're happy with the level.

JUST THE BEGINNING

This chapter barely scratches the surface of designing levels, which is an incredibly deep topic that would require an entire book to fully explain, but hopefully you now have enough basic knowledge to start creating interesting levels for your game.

Adding doors, triggers, and switches

Create elements that control the flow of your level

AUTHOR
ANDREW PALMER
Starting out as a hobbyist level designer in the nineties, Andrew has contributed to a long list of published titles in design, art, and technical art roles. He currently works for indie game developer 17-BIT, in Kyoto, Japan.

Having a big, open level full of zombies is a good start, but if there is nothing to control the flow, then all that players will experience is the basic mechanics of the game. Doors, triggers, and switches are some of the simplest methods of directing gameplay, but since they're easily understood by players and easily implemented, they are some of the most used and effective. Here, we'll implement a simple but expandable system for making doors that can be opened by switches, and add a new component that makes our spawners a whole lot more useful. Let's dive in.

TRIGGERABLE BASE CLASS

Before we start writing any code, it's important to take a moment to think about why it's needed and how it should work. In this case, we need doors that can be triggered by switches, and trigger volumes, but later on we may also want to trigger other things, such as spawners, animations, and sound effects in the same way.

To make this easier, I decided to create a base class, named Triggerable, that the door, spawner, or anything else that can be triggered can inherit from. This way, we don't need to write a separate trigger class for each type of thing we want to trigger, and our triggers can trigger a list of different Triggerable objects, and trigger them all at once and in the same way.

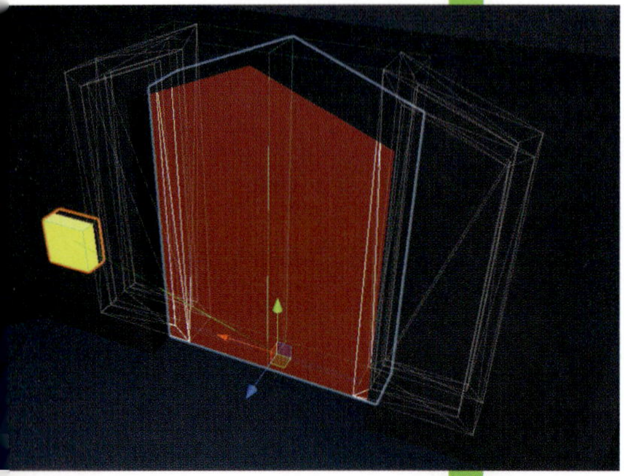

By adding the OnCollisionEnter function to the Switch class, we can make the Trigger activate its targets when the player touches the cube.

```
using UnityEngine;

public enum TriggerAction
{
    Activate,
    Deactivate,
    Toggle,
}

public abstract class Triggerable :
MonoBehaviour
{
    public abstract void Trigger (TriggerAction
action);
}
```

The code defines an abstract class, meaning an instance of **Triggerable** cannot be created, and any class deriving from it must override its members, which in this case is the single function named **Trigger**. The **enum TriggerAction** must be passed as a parameter to the **Trigger** function, and can be used to allow different functionality when **Trigger** is called, such as open or close in the case of the door.

```
public class Door : Triggerable
{
    public override void Trigger (TriggerAction
action)
    {
    }
}
```

This is the minimal **Door** class, with no functionality. As you can see, it derives from the **Triggerable** base class, and overrides the **Trigger** function. We could also modify the spawner code to derive from **Triggerable** in the same way, but it might be easier and more useful to make a script that activates or deactivates its parent GameObject, so let's just do that to see a simple example of a full **Triggerable** derived class.

```
using UnityEngine;

public class TargetActivator : Triggerable
{
  public bool deactivateOnAwake = true;

  void Awake ()
  {
    if (deactivateOnAwake)
    {
        gameObject.SetActive(false);
    }
  }

  public override void Trigger (TriggerAction
action)
  {
    if (action == TriggerAction.Activate)
    {
        gameObject.SetActive(true);
    }
    else if (action == TriggerAction.Deactivate)
    {
        gameObject.SetActive(false);
    }
    else
    {
        gameObject.SetActive(!gameObject.
activeSelf);
    }
  }
}
```

This **TargetActivator** class can be used to activate and deactivate any GameObject it's attached to. While we wouldn't want to do that for something that would visibly vanish when deactivated, it's perfect for our spawners. As you can see by looking at the code in the **Trigger** function, the **TriggerAction** parameter can be used to activate, deactivate, or toggle the GameObject on or off. However, we don't yet have a **Trigger** class, so let's make one.

THE TRIGGER

In order to call the **Trigger** function of our **Triggerable** derived classes, such as the TargetActivator just shown, or the door (which we'll get to in the next section), we'll need a **Trigger** class.

At its simplest, a Trigger is an invisible volume that calls the Trigger method on a targeted Triggerable component when something enters the volume. In order to detect when something enters the volume, we'll need to first create a new GameObject in the Scene view and attach a BoxCollider to it, with the 'Is Trigger' option enabled. Once that's done, we just need to attach a minimal Trigger script.

A plan view of the castle game environment; the red dots are zombies.

```
using UnityEngine;

public class Trigger : MonoBehaviour
{
    public TriggerAction action =
TriggerAction.Activate;
    public Triggerable[] targets;

    void OnTriggerEnter (Collider other)
    {
        if (other.CompareTag("Player"))
        {
            TriggerTargets();
        }
    }

    public void TriggerTargets ()
    {
        foreach (Triggerable t in targets)
        {
            if (t != null) // Check in case a
target is destroyed
            {
                t.Trigger(action);
            }
        }
    }
}
```

Our finished level with all its doors, switches, and triggers added.

Now place a spawner somewhere in the scene and add a TargetActivator component to it. The TargetActivator will set the spawner to inactive when the game begins, so nothing will spawn; we'll use the Trigger we just created to make things happen. In the Inspector, add the spawner to the 'Targets' list of the Trigger. Now when you play the game and walk into the Trigger, zombies should start spawning.

We may not even want to use a volume, and instead attach the Trigger to another GameObject, and directly trigger the targets when something happens in another script; for example, we could attach the script to an enemy and open a door only when the enemy is killed. In order to have this flexibility, the `TriggerTargets` function is public and can be called by other classes.

MAKING A DOOR

Now that we've seen how to create a `Triggerable` class, and have made a `Trigger` with which to trigger them, we can get to work on the door, which due to collision and animation is a little more involved than the `TargetActivator` class – but don't worry, it's not too difficult.

First of all, we need to create a solid object with a rigidbody, so create a cube and assign a Rigidbody to it, and make sure the 'Is Kinematic' option is on, as we'll control the movement of the door in code. Scale the cube to the shape you'd like your door to be. Next comes the fun part: writing the door code.

```
using UnityEngine;
using System.Collections;
using System.Collections.Generic;

[RequireComponent(typeof(Rigidbody))]
public class Door : Triggerable
{
  public float moveSpeed = 5f;
  public Vector3 moveOffset;

  private Vector3 _startPosition;
  private Vector3 _endPosition;
  private Vector3 _targetPosition;
  private Coroutine _update;
  private Rigidbody _rigidbody;

  void Awake ()
  {
    _rigidbody = GetComponent<Rigidbody>();
    _rigidbody.isKinematic = true;

    // Transform the offset so that it works
even when the door is rotated
    Vector3 offsetLocal = transform.
TransformVector(moveOffset);
    _startPosition = transform.position;
    _endPosition = _startPosition +
offsetLocal;
  }

  // Add the other functions here
}
```

The door's public variables define the speed at which it will move, and the offset of the movement from the door's initial position. Since we'll be moving the door with code, it's helpful to calculate the start and end positions of the door so we can avoid doing it every frame as the door moves. This can be done in the `Awake` function, and you should notice here that the offset is being transformed into the local space of the door before the start and end positions are calculated. Doing this means that once a door has been set up, it can be copied and moved around the level, and the offset will always be the same relative to the door's transform.

```
public override void Trigger (TriggerAction
action)
{
  // Support the door opening and closing
  if (action == TriggerAction.Toggle)
  {
    if (_targetPosition == _endPosition) {
_targetPosition = _startPosition; }
    else { _targetPosition = _endPosition; }
  }
  else
  {
    if (action == TriggerAction.Deactivate) {
_targetPosition = _startPosition; }
    else { _targetPosition = _endPosition; }
  }
```

```
  // Use a coroutine so we only update when
the door is moving
  if (_update != null)
  {
    StopCoroutine(_update);
    _update = null;
  }
  _update = StartCoroutine(MoveToTarget());
}
```

Since the **Door** is a **Triggerable** derived class, it must implement the **Trigger** function. In this code, the target position of the door is first determined by the **action** parameter, and then a coroutine is started in order to move the door. We could use an **Update** function on the door, but since doors are mostly stationary, it would waste a lot of CPU power if the game was constantly updating all the doors in the level, regardless of whether or not they were moving.

```
  IEnumerator MoveToTarget ()
  {
    while (true)
    {
      // Calculate distance to the target
position and also
      // the distance we can move this frame
      Vector3 offset = _targetPosition -
transform.position;
      float distance = offset.magnitude;
      float moveDistance = moveSpeed * Time.
deltaTime;

      // Keep moving towards target until we
are close enough
      if (moveDistance < distance)
      {
        Vector3 move = offset.normalized *
moveDistance;
        _rigidbody.MovePosition(transform.
position + move);
        yield return null;
      }
      else
      {
        break;
      }
    }

    // Ensure we move exactly to the target
    _rigidbody.MovePosition(_targetPosition);
    _update = null;
  }
```

The coroutine itself is quite simple, just moving the door a little each frame until the target position is reached.

Now that we've written the door code, try adding it to you cube door and hooking up a Trigger to activate it. The door should now open when you enter the trigger. Try adding another trigger to close the door, or better yet, modify the code to make the door open when the player enters the trigger and closes when they leave.

FUN WITH SWITCHES

The **Trigger** class we made works pretty well, but what if we want the player to be able to see it? Well, in that case, a switch might be a better tool for the job. A switch works in more or less the same way as a trigger, but has a visual representation that can change state to show that it has been activated, and collision can be handled differently so that it activates when the player pushes against it.

It's easy to create a switch by using the Trigger component we already made. First create a cube and add a Trigger component to it. The trigger won't work because the cube's default Box Collider isn't a trigger, but we want this for the switch, so leave it as it is. Create a new Switch script and add it to the cube. If we add an **OnCollisionEnter** function in the **Switch** class, we can make the Trigger activate its targets when the player touches the cube, but we also want a visual state change of the cube so that the player knows the switch has been pressed.

```
using UnityEngine;

[RequireComponent(typeof(Trigger))]
[RequireComponent(typeof(MeshRenderer))]
public class Switch : MonoBehaviour
{
    // The materials we will swap between when
the switch state changes
    // Active means the switch CAN be pressed,
inactive means it can't
    public Material activeMaterial;
    public Material inactiveMaterial;

    private Trigger _trigger;
    private MeshRenderer _renderer;
    private bool _pressed = false;
```

DOOR? I DIDN'T SEE NO DOOR!

Although the door will block player collisions, you might notice that zombies just pass straight through. While a zombie that can walk through closed doors is certainly terrifying, in the interest of fairness it's better if they're also blocked like the player. To make the zombies aware of the door, we must add a Navmesh Obstacle component. A Navmesh Obstacle is basically a collider that dynamically affects the navmesh. Assign a Navmesh Obstacle component to your door and enable the 'Carving' flag, which tells the Navmesh Obstacle script to update the navmesh when the parent object has stopped moving. Carving can be set to update while the object is moving, but this has a higher performance penalty, and is not really required for simple doors, although you might want to enable it for large and slow-moving doors.

```
    void Awake ()
    {
        _trigger = GetComponent<Trigger>();
        _renderer =
GetComponent<MeshRenderer>();
        _renderer.sharedMaterial =
activeMaterial;
    }

    void OnCollisionEnter (Collision collision)
    {
        if (!_pressed && collision.gameObject.
CompareTag("Player"))
        {
            _trigger.TriggerTargets();
            _renderer.sharedMaterial =
inactiveMaterial;
            _pressed = true;
        }
    }
}
```

As you can see, the basic code for the switch is very simple; it piggybacks on the functionality of the trigger and just adds a few additions, such as the material state change when it's triggered. This version of the switch is very simple and only works once, but you could modify it to turn things on, reset after a couple of seconds, and then turn them off the next time it's pressed.

DRAWING GIZMOS

We've placed our door and trigger setup in the level, but setting up the movement of the door was a bit annoying because we couldn't see where it would move to. Also, we can't see the trigger to select it, so we need to use the outliner, and once it's selected, we have to check the targets list to see which Triggerable objects it targets. If your game uses a lot of triggers, doors, and switches, then you might find yourself wasting a lot of time simply because setting them up takes longer than it should.

To make setting up switches, doors, and any other Triggerables we might make, we'll write some DrawGizmos functions that makes it obvious how they move and how they're connected. If you haven't used Unity's Gizmos class before, it's a handy tool that allows you to draw lines, primitives, and meshes in the Scene view, which can be helpful as a debugging aid, or to show extra information about the objects in your scene and the connections between them. For objects that are invisible in games, such as our trigger, we may also use gizmos to draw it in the Scene view to make selecting it easier.

First, it would be helpful to see which objects are targeted by a trigger without having to figure it out from the targets list. This can be accomplished by adding an `OnDrawGizmos` function to the Trigger script. In this example, in addition to the connection lines, a small cube is also drawn at the centre of the trigger to make it visible and easily selectable.

```
// Gizmos function for the Trigger
void OnDrawGizmos ()
{
    //Draw a cube to make it possible to
select the trigger in the scene view
    Gizmos.color = Color.green;
    Gizmos.DrawCube(transform.position,
Vector3.one * 0.25f);

    // This first null check avoids an editor
error on creation of the Trigger
    if (targets != null)
    {
        foreach (Triggerable t in targets)
        {
            if (t != null)
            {
                Gizmos.DrawLine(transform.
position, t.transform.position);
            }
        }
    }
}
```

Note that if you would like the gizmos to be drawn only when an object is selected, you can add an `OnDrawGizmosSelected` function instead. Both functions work together, so you can have the `OnDrawGizmos` function draw the small cube for selection, and then only draw the connection lines when the trigger is selected.

In order to make the setup of our `Door` class easier, we can add an `OnDrawGizmosSelected` function that draws a wireframe mesh preview in the position the door will move to when the door is selected in editor.

Figure 1: This TargetActivator class can be used to activate and deactivate any GameObject it is attached to.

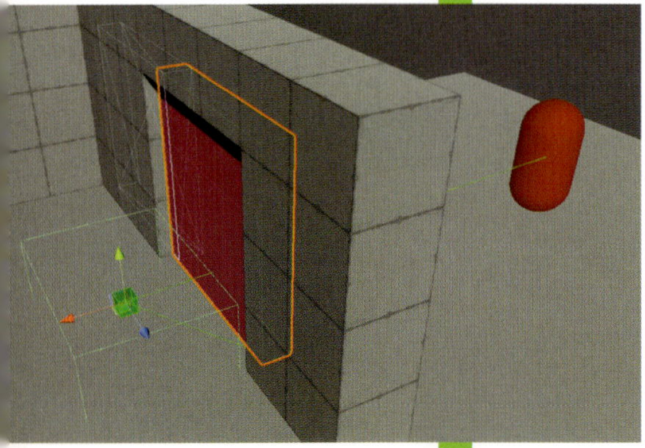

```
// Gizmos function for the Door
void OnDrawGizmosSelected ()
{
    // Gizmos will be drawn using the local
transform of the door
    // This means even if we rotate or scale the
door, the preview
    // will be correct!
    Gizmos.matrix = transform.localToWorldMatrix;

    MeshFilter mf = GetComponent<MeshFilter>();
    if (mf != null)
    {
        // Setting Gizmos.matrix means we only
need the offset here. Easy!
        Gizmos.DrawWireMesh(mf.sharedMesh,
moveOffset);
    }
}
```

Figure 1 shows an example of how our Gizmos look in the editor with a trigger targeting a door and a spawner. You can see that the switch is connected to the Triggerables by the green lines, and the door's open position is also visible.

ADDING FEATURES

It's now possible to add doors and operate them with triggers and switches, but we still need to add them to the level to block the player from running straight to the exit. One of the first ideas I had for *Zombie Panic* was to start the player in a dungeon, trapped in a cell they must escape from. You've probably seen this scenario in a hundred different games; the player's captured by the enemy and must stage a daring prison breakout. Zombies aren't particularly attentive prison guards, so breaking out isn't especially challenging, but the main gate is locked, and getting past the ravenous horde in order to open it may prove difficult. Let's take a look at the level with doors, triggers, and spawners in place.

From the handful of components we've made during this tutorial, quite a fun little level can be created. In *Zombie Panic*, doors are used both to suggest the route to the player, and also provide obstacles to progress. Triggers are used liberally to spawn zombies at the most inconvenient (but hopefully fun) time for the player, and I also took a few minutes to create a simple inventory and item system for the player, and modified the Trigger class to enable triggers that only activate when the player has a particular item.

LOCKED DOORS

Let's briefly look at how locked doors are made. In order to open a locked door, the player needs to have a key to open it. This means we need to store some kind of state about what items the player has picked up, and when the player enters the trigger to the door, the trigger must check this state and determine whether the player can open it.

To do this, I created a simple item and inventory system. The Inventory contains a list of the items the player is carrying, and items can be added or queried by other scripts. The Item is an object with a trigger collider and is visible in the scene. When the player collides with an item, the Item script gets the player's inventory, adds itself by name, and then removes itself from the scene, giving the effect of it being picked up.

When the player enters a trigger that requires an item to activate, their inventory is queried for the item, and if it's found then the trigger will activate its targets, and will do nothing if it's not. Additionally, I also added an option to remove the item from the player's inventory so that keys can be used up, making the system a little more flexible.

Without seeing any code, you can probably imagine the changes you need to make to the existing systems, so why not give it a shot? Try making your own locked doors and keys!

ADDING YOUR OWN TWIST

Now we've set up a system to control the player's movement through the level, try thinking about simple changes or additions that could be made to spice things up. With doors, triggers, and switches, it's possible to create more interesting gameplay without needing more enemies, weapons, or special abilities. In fact, a key principle of level design is working within the constraints of what's available to create variety and fun experiences for your players. In Unity, with components as our building blocks, making variety by combining them can provide endless fun for designers, too.

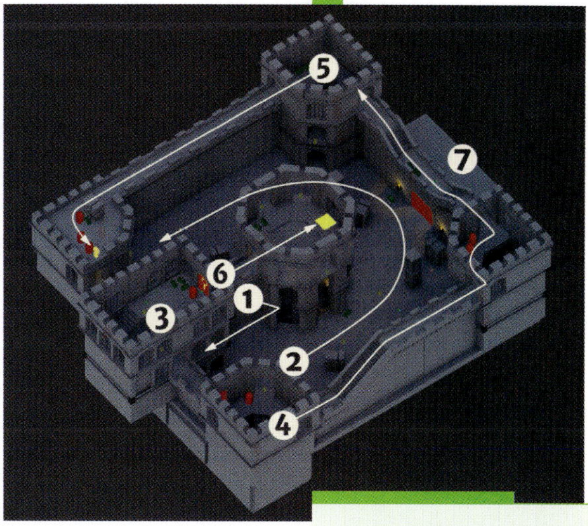

ESCAPE FROM THE CASTLE: LEVEL GUIDE

1. Escape from the jail cell and find a weapon.
2. Battle through the courtyard to access the second level.
3. A locked door! How was that implemented!? An exercise for the reader!
4. Blast through the hordes along the battlements.
5. Take down all the undead in your way to get that key.
6. Open the door to reveal the main gate switch.
7. Freedom!

Our level design and gameplay really starts to come together by adding some reasons for the player to explore our castle environment.

Expanding your level gameplay

Add risk-and-reward elements like medikits and limited ammunition

AUTHOR
STUART FRASER

Stuart is a former designer and developer of high-profile games such as *RollerCoaster Tycoon 3*, and has also worked as a lecturer of games development.

We've looked at various mechanics we can mix up to extend our base game, so we can now refocus on the level we've built and how to make it feel more cohesive by adding some risk and reward elements. At the moment, we have a weapon that has unlimited shots and the player has limited health that can't be replenished. We're going to look at how we can mix this up by limiting the ammo, but having ammo pick-ups around the arena. We'll also have a health pick-up that will allow the player to refill their health as the rounds get more intense. We're also going to provide the player with a basic melee attack when they have no ammo; as a trade-off, this could end with them taking damage. Finally, we'll add some more readability to the UI, and show an effect each time the zombies do damage. So let's get started.

The first thing we'll focus on is our two new pick-ups. We'll also revisit or replace some of our scripts to allow this to all work together. Let's start with creating the health pick-up; we'll just use the basic sphere by selecting Game Object>3D Object>Sphere from the toolbar. Select the Sphere in the Hierarchy and then in the Inspector, we'll rename this as HealthPickup for clarity.

BETTER MESHES

You can easily switch out the basic meshes on your pick-ups with something more suitable from the Unity Store or created yourself in Blender. All you need to do is change what object is listed by the Mesh Filter component for the object.

With that done, we can easily add a script that is similar to the one we created to send damage to the player. So while we're in the Inspector, we need to select Add Component > New Script and then set the name of the script to HealthPickup and create it. With that done, we can open the script and add our code as it is shown below:

```
using UnityEngine;

public class HealthPickup : MonoBehaviour
{
    public int healthAmount = 10;
    public bool respawn;
    public float delaySpawn = 30;


    void OnCollisionEnter(Collision other)
    {
        //We compare the tag in the other object
to the tag name we set earlier.
        if (other.transform.CompareTag("Player"))
        {
            //We disable the mesh renderer to
make it look like it's been picked up.
            gameObject.
GetComponent<MeshRenderer>().enabled = false;
            //We disable the collider once it's
picked up.
            gameObject.GetComponent<Collider>().
enabled = false;
            other.transform.
SendMessage("ApplyHeal", healthAmount);
            //If we choose to we can make it
respawn after X seconds.
            if (respawn)
            {
                Invoke("Respawn", delaySpawn);
            }
        }
    }

    void Respawn()
    {
        //We make the pickup visible again.
        gameObject.GetComponent<MeshRenderer>().
enabled = true;
        //The collider is enabled so we can pick
it up again.
        gameObject.GetComponent<Collider>().
enabled = true;
    }
}
```

The next step is to update the player so that the health pack is added to their health once it's picked up. Originally we created a script called PlayerDamage; while we could just edit this, the script name doesn't make sense. We will create a new script to replace it, and while we are there we improve the feedback for damage by adding an effect when the player is hit. We need to select our Player prefab in the Hierarchy and then either delete or disable the PlayerDamage script. Next, we can select Add Component > New Script and set the name of this script to PlayerHealth as this is more descriptive for handling both losing and gaining health. We can then open this new script and add the following code:

```
using System.Collections;
using UnityEngine;
using UnityEngine.UI;
[RequireComponent(typeof(AudioSource))]

public class PlayerHealth : MonoBehaviour
{
    //Use this to reference the text in the canvas
    public Text healthText;
    public Image damageFX;
    //Sets default health to 100
    public int health = 100;
    //Set the maximum value the alpha will reach.
    private float maxAlpha = 0.7f;
    //Check the effect is active;
    private bool isActive;
    //Add an audio effect;
    public AudioClip audioClip;
```

We can make our health pick-up look enticing to the player and easily readable. I've dropped in an emissive material and a point light to make the item pop in the environment.

ICONS

To add some more readability to how much health you have, or for that matter any other important UI information, think about adding some icons. You can easily add a new sprite and apply them to an image object on your canvas.

```
    private AudioSource audioSource;

    private void Start()
    {
        UpdateText();
        audioSource = GetComponent<AudioSource>();
    }

    void ApplyDamage(int damage)
    {
        health = health - damage;
        UpdateText();
        if (!isActive && damageFX != null)
            StartCoroutine(SetEffect());
    }

    void ApplyHeal(int heal)
    {
        //Stores the current health and subtracts the damage value
        health = health + heal;
        UpdateText();
    }

    void UpdateText()
    {
        //Make sure max health cannot go below 0 or over 100.
        health = Mathf.Clamp(health, 0, 100);
        //Check the health panel exists.
        if (healthText != null)
        {
            //Sets the text on our panel.
            healthText.text = health.ToString();
        }
    }

    private IEnumerator SetEffect()
    {
        isActive = true;
        //Grab the current alpha on the panel.
        float alpha = damageFX.color.a;
        //Grab the colour of the panel.
        Color color = damageFX.color;
        //Set the alpha to show the current colour of the panel.
        damageFX.color = new Color(color.r, color.g, color.b, maxAlpha);
        if (audioSource != null && audioClip != null)
        {
            audioSource.PlayOneShot(audioClip);
        }
        //Wait for 0.2 of a second.
        yield return new WaitForSeconds(0.2f);
        //Set the alpha back to fully transparent.
        damageFX.color = new Color(color.r, color.g, color.b, 0);
        //Wait for 0.4 of a second, so we are not constantly flashing.
        yield return new WaitForSeconds(0.4f);
        //Make sure we know we can run the coroutine again.
        isActive = false;
        //Exit.
        yield return null;
    }
}
```

Once saved and back in Unity, we need to do some setup with the Canvas: we need to expand the canvas and rename the Text object we previously added to Health for clarity.

While we're here, we'll create a panel to act as our screen effect when the player gets hurt. All we need to do is right-click on the Canvas and select UI > Panel. We then select the Panel and in the Inspector, rename this to DamageFX. We also need to set the Color parameters on the Image script by setting the pallet to a red colour and set the alpha to be fully transparent.

"You should be able to heal up to a maximum health of 100"

Now to set some references for your script so it can control the UI elements. We select our Player in the Hierarchy and, in the Inspector, drag the Health object onto the Health Text slot of our script; then the DamageFX object to the DamageFX slot on our script. With that done, we've created our pick-up; to test this, you can place a pick-up in the level and then preview the game by selecting the Play button. You should be able to get hurt by the zombies and heal up to a maximum health of 100 by picking up the medikit. Once you've finished testing, remember to exit out of the preview.

We can make the ammo pick-up in almost the same way, but instead of SendMessage, we use BroadcastMessage. We're doing this as the script that we're communicating with is a child of the Player prefab, but instead of us directly stating the child object, we're using this command to

Now you've created the panel, you need to make sure you've set the colour for your damage overlay to something suitable. Remember to set the alpha to be fully transparent or you won't be able to see the viewport in the editor.

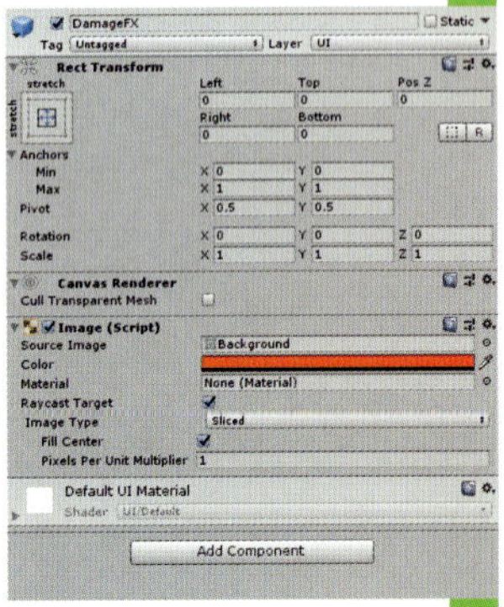

talk to all the child objects. This isn't the most efficient way to do this, but as our player only has a small amount of attached objects, it makes sense to do it in this way.

Let's start on making the pick-up and the script we need. Firstly, select Game Object > 3D Object > Cube from the toolbar. Next, scale down the cube to make it look more like an ammo box. We should rename this in the Inspector to be called AmmoPickup, and then we can select Add Component > New Script. As usual, we want to name this script; in this case, we'll call it AmmoPickup. With that created, we can add our script.

```
using System.Collections;
using System.Collections.Generic;
using UnityEngine;

public class AmmoPickup : MonoBehaviour
{
    public int ammoAmount = 10;
    public bool respawn;
    public float delaySpawn = 30;

    void OnCollisionEnter(Collision other)
    {
        //We compare the tag in the other object
to the tag name we set earlier.
        if (other.transform.CompareTag("Player"))
        {
            //We disable the mesh renderer to
make it look like it's been picked up.
            gameObject.
GetComponent<MeshRenderer>().enabled = false;
            //We disable the collider once it's
picked up.
            gameObject.GetComponent<Collider>().
enabled = false;
            //We broadcast to the player and all
children.
            other.transform.
BroadcastMessage("ApplyAmmo", ammoAmount);
            //If we choose to we can make it
respawn after X seconds.
            if (respawn)
            {
                Invoke("Respawn", delaySpawn);
            }
        }
    }

    void Respawn()
    {
        //We make the pickup visible again.
        gameObject.GetComponent<MeshRenderer>().
enabled = true;
        //The collider is enabled so we can pick
it up again.
        gameObject.GetComponent<Collider>().
enabled = true;
    }
}
```

We can now save this and turn our attention to implementing a limitation on the amount of shots we can fire. We'll also wrap this up with adding our melee attack. This is reminiscent of the original *Doom* games, where the player could punch enemies if they had run out of ammo. The first thing we need to do is make a few small changes to make sure we query what collider we're touching rather than what object we've collided with. This is a one-line change, but the code below is provided in full. We need to first open the EnemyDamage script and update it as below:

```
using UnityEngine;

public class EnemyDamage : MonoBehaviour
{
    private int hitNumber;

    private void OnEnable()
    {
        hitNumber = 0;
    }

    void OnCollisionEnter(Collision other)
    {
        if (other.collider.transform.
CompareTag("bullet"))
        {
```

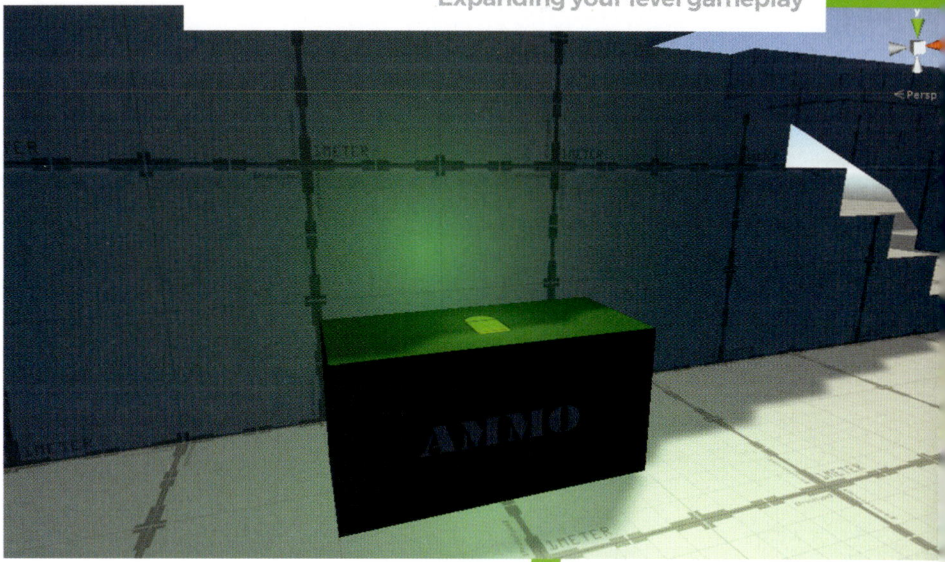

The last thing you want to do is skip over an ammo box when in the middle of a rush of zombies.

ART OF NOISE

As an optional extra, the script allows us to add audio for when your player gets hurt, you can record your own audio or find a suitable effect and add it to the project. To use this you will need to also make sure you include an AudioSource component on the Player prefab. For more on adding sound to your game, turn to page 70.

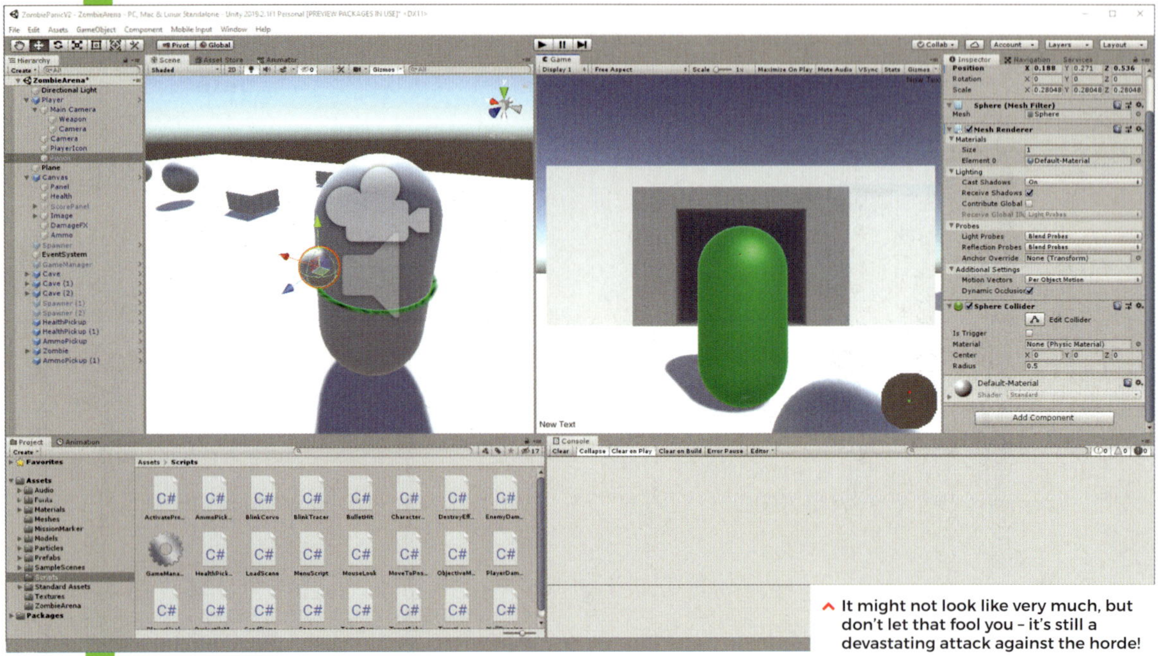

It might not look like very much, but don't let that fool you – it's still a devastating attack against the horde!

```
                //If the comparison is true, we
increase the hit number.
                hitNumber++;
            }
            if (hitNumber == 3)
            {
                gameObject.SetActive(false);
            }
        }
}
```

Save this and then we need to edit the SendDamage script in the same way:

```
using UnityEngine;

public class SendDamage : MonoBehaviour
{

    void OnCollisionStay(Collision other)
    {
        //We compare the tag in the other object
to the tag name we set earlier.
        if (other.collider.transform.
CompareTag("Player"))
        {
            //If the above matches, then send a
message to the other object.
            //This will also pass a value of 1
for our damage.
            other.transform.
SendMessage("ApplyDamage", 1);
        }
    }
}
```

With all this done, we're ready to work on our Player prefab back in Unity. We want to add something to represent our player's fist. So for this, we're going to right-click in the Hierarchy and select 3D Object > Sphere and rename this Punch in the Inspector.

We then want to make this more representative of being the player's hand. We should rescale the sphere to be about fist size, and place it just in front of the player capsule and slightly lower than our head height. You may want to play around with this so that you can see the sphere in the first-person view. We should also change the tag for this object to be tagged as bullet; while this is a bit strange, we're using the same logic. Ideally, we may want to change the name of the tag, but you would need to update all script references as well as your tag.

The next thing to do is to select the Weapon object in the Hierarchy. We're going to need to disable or remove the ActivateProjectile script and replace it with a similar script that will handle some additional aspects. To create this new script we'll select Add Component > New Script and call this script UseAttacks and complete the process of creating the script. We can then open the new script and add the modifications we need as below:

```
using UnityEngine;
using System.Collections;
using UnityEngine.UI;

public class UseAttacks : MonoBehaviour
{
```

```
    public int ammoAmount = 10;
    public float meleeRepeatDelay = 0.25f;
    public GameObject projectile;
    public GameObject punchMesh;
    public Text ammoPanel;
    private bool punchActive;

    private void Start()
    {
        //Update text to display the player ammo.
        UpdateText();
        //Hide the hand when we start the game
and have ammo.
        punchMesh.SetActive(false);
    }

    // Update is called once per frame
    void Update()
    {
        if (Input.GetButtonDown("Fire1"))
        {
            if (ammoAmount > 0)
            {
                ammoAmount--;
                UpdateText();
                var clone =
Instantiate(projectile, gameObject.transform.
position, gameObject.transform.rotation);
                //Destroy after 2 seconds to stop
clutter.
                Destroy(clone, 5.0f);
            }
            else
            {
                if (!punchActive)
                {
                    punchActive = true;
                    StartCoroutine(MeleeAttack());
                }
            }
        }
    }

    void ApplyAmmo(int ammo)
    {
        ammoAmount += ammo;
        UpdateText();
    }

    void UpdateText()
    {
        //Check the ammo panel exists.
        if (ammoPanel != null)
        {
            //Sets the text on our panel.
            ammoPanel.text = ammoAmount.
ToString();
        }
    }

    IEnumerator MeleeAttack()
    {
        punchMesh.SetActive(true);
        yield return new WaitForSeconds(0.1f);
        punchMesh.SetActive(false);
        yield return new
WaitForSeconds(meleeRepeatDelay);
        punchActive = false;
        yield return null;
    }
}
```

Now we have that done, we need to make sure we've added a new text object to our canvas to display the ammo count, and that we've linked up the references to our new script. First, we can right-click on the Canvas object and select UI>Text and rename the new object to Ammo in the Inspector.

While we're here, we can use the Anchor Presets and the Pos X and Pos Y values to make sure we're happy with the position this information is displayed on the canvas. Now we select the Weapon object in our Player prefab again, and we can then drag over the Ammo text we just created into the Ammo Panel. The next task is to drag the Punch mesh we parented to the Player onto the Punch Mesh slot of this script. Finally, drag the Projectile prefab from the Project panel onto the matching slot of the script.

With all that done, it's a good time to make sure that all your prefabs are updated, and we should create a prefab for the ammo pick-up by dragging the game object into the Project panel. With all this done, you should see that when playing the game you have a limited ammo supply that can be replenished with the pick-up. You should also have a short-range punch ability when all ammo has been depleted. This has shown us another way to expand our gameplay from being just about avoiding and shooting the zombies: it forces the player to explore more of the carefully crafted level, and use the environment to try to outlast the hordes of enemies as they endlessly approach.

RESPAWNING PICK-UPS

As an optional extra for each pick-up, there are parameters built into the script to change the amount that you get of health or ammo from each pick-up. You can also set them to respawn, and how long that takes in seconds.

With our additional text object added to the canvas in our Hierarchy, we can display how much ammo the player has picked up.

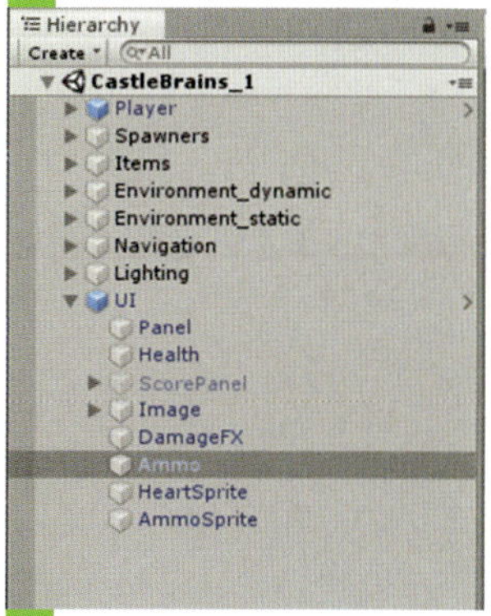

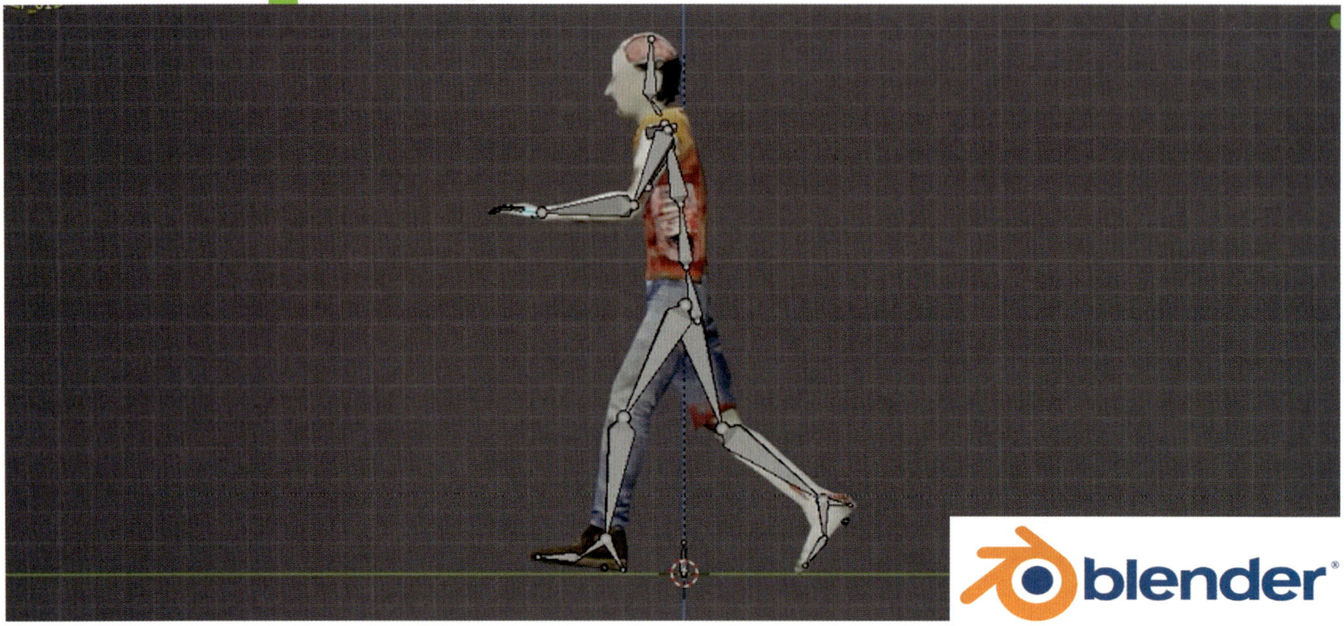

Creating and rigging a character in Blender

Here's how to construct, texture, and animate a walking zombie and import it into Unity

AUTHOR
MARK VANSTONE

Mark is Technical Director of TechnoVisual, and the author of the educational game series, ArcVenture.
education.technovisual.co.uk

Although the realm of 3D modelling might sound daunting at first, it's become increasingly easy – not to mention affordable – to get into with the advent of software like Blender. In this tutorial, we'll build a low-polygon humanoid mesh, and then transform it into the twisted form of a zombie. Then we'll add textures, a walking animation, and finally import the model into Unity and connect it up to the rest of our game.

To get started, make sure that you have Blender 2.8 – the newest version at the time of writing – installed. To download it, head to **blender.org**. Once we have the program installed, we can start work on our model.

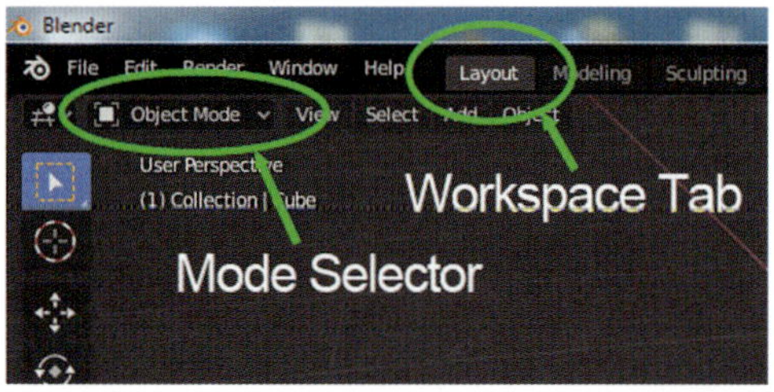

› **Figure 1:** You can switch from Object Mode to Edit Mode by clicking the arrow circled on the left.

MODELLING THE BASIC BODY

With Blender loaded, you should see the default grey cube in the middle of the display. Look at the top right and you'll see that you're in Layout View, while the default mode is set to Object Mode. This means you can select whole objects and move them around. We need to be in Edit Mode; so, with the cube selected, switch from Object Mode to Edit Mode from the drop-down

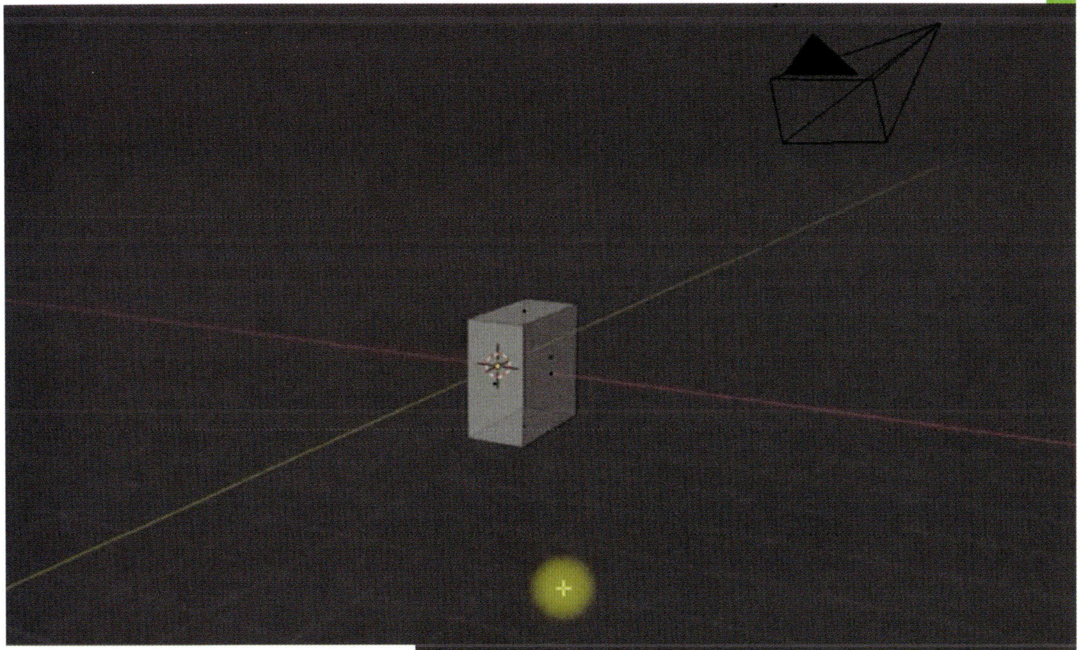

Figure 2: We've erased all the faces of the cube lying to the right of the z axis. We're almost ready to start modelling our zombie head.

menu at the top left of the view (**Figure 1**). Our cube will go from grey to orange, with orange dots on each corner. We're in Vertex Selection mode, as shown by the icons to the right of the Mode selector drop-down. The three icons are (from left to right): Vertex Select, Edge Select, and Face Select. Remember these tools – you'll be using them a lot.

As a base for our character, we want to create a humanoid shape which is symmetrical – and if we use the mirror modifier, we only have to model one half of our mesh. Thanks to the modifier, anything we do on one side will be reflected on the other side, too. To add our mirror modifier, first change to Front Orthographic view (**1** on numpad). We're going to mirror our object across the z axis (denoted by the blue line), but we have half of our cube on each side of it.

We need to chop the cube in half, so make a loop cut by pressing **CTRL+R** while hovering over the cube, and an orange line will appear down the centre of the cube. Left-click twice to select and cut. Change to Face Select Mode (from the icons on the top left) and select all the faces on the left of the cube. To make sure you get the back faces and the front faces, you'll need to set the 'Show X-Ray' mode, which you'll find in the top right of the view; it looks like two squares. Hit the **DELETE** key and, from the pop-up menu, select Faces. Now you should have just half a cube on the right of the z axis (see **Figure 2**).

We can now add our modifier. Select the Spanner on the Properties panel to the right of the view. Drop down the Add Modifier selector and choose Mirror from the Generate column. When the modifier has been added, you'll see the other side of the cube reappear. Now everything we do to the right-hand side will also happen in reverse on the left. Don't apply the modifier yet; we will do that when we've finished modelling the mesh.

We used a loop cut to chop our cube in half, but loop cuts are also a good way add extra faces to our model. We want to make a head shape, so we'll need some extra faces. You can make two loop cuts by hovering over the cube and pressing **CTRL+R** – make sure you see an orange horizontal line, then rotate your mouse wheel, and another orange line should appear. Left-click twice to select and slice, and you now have three faces instead of one (**Figure 3**). Now do the same in Top Orthographic view (**7** on the numpad).

Figure 3: By making loop cuts, we've made extra faces on our mesh.

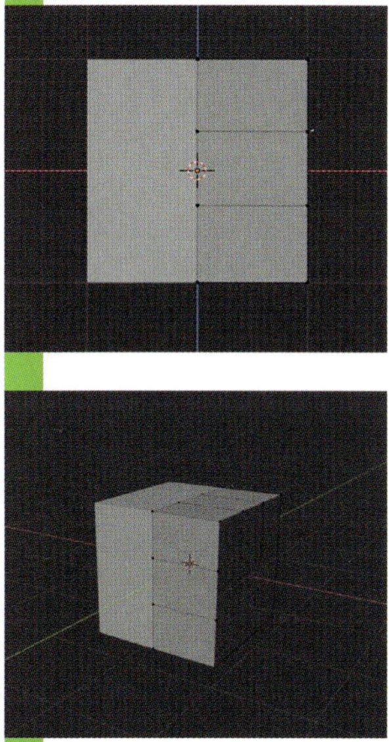

ON WITH HIS HEAD

Now our cube should be split into nine segments on the right side and mirrored on the left. We can now go back to Vertex Select mode (from the icons top-left) and start forming our cube into a head shape. It will be very rough at →

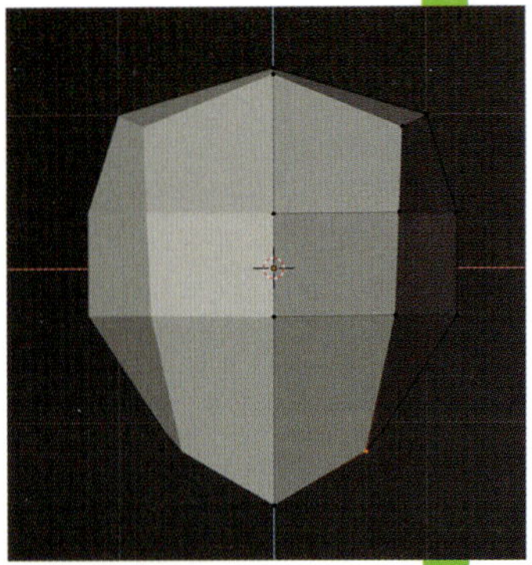

Figure 4: Our mesh viewed from the front. We're gradually moving the vertices to form the rough shape of a human head.

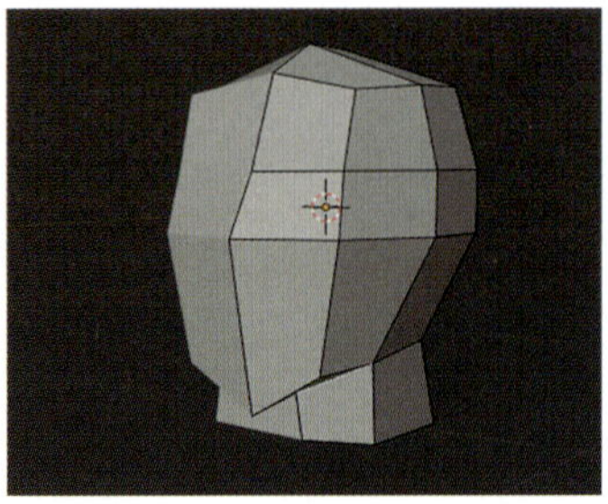

Figure 5: With the head roughly modelled, we can select the polygons beneath the jaw and extrude them to form the neck, as seen here.

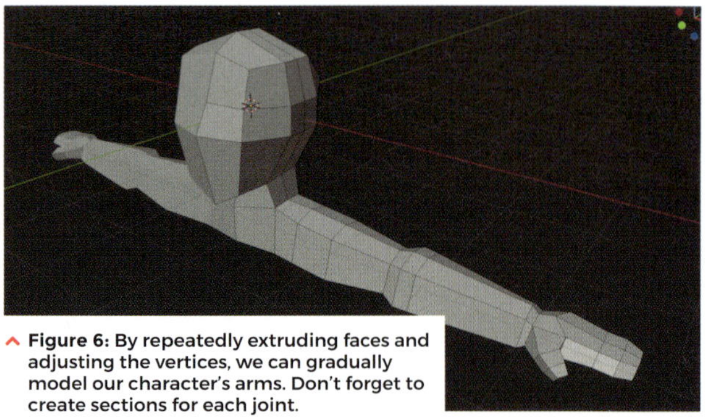

Figure 6: By repeatedly extruding faces and adjusting the vertices, we can gradually model our character's arms. Don't forget to create sections for each joint.

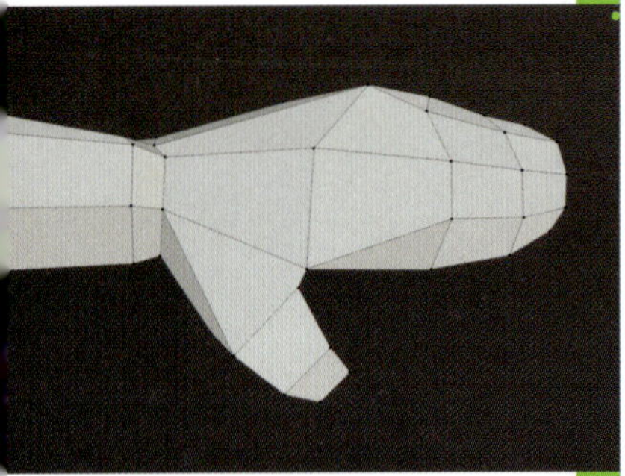

Figure 7: Because we're creating a low-poly character, we're keeping the hand shape simple here – something along the lines of a mitten or oven glove.

the moment, but we'll improve on that as we go on. Go back to Front View (numpad **1**) and select the top-right vertices by dragging a selection box around them (left-click and drag). This will select all the vertices that are hidden behind the front one, as we're still in Show X-ray mode. Then move these vertices by pressing **G** and moving the mouse towards the z axis. You should see the mirror modifier working as you move. Then left-click to fix the vertices in place. Do the same with the bottom-right vertices. We want to make a sort of oval shape from the front view (**Figure 4**), perhaps a bit thinner at the bottom to form the chin, and a bit wider at the top. Now do the same with the top view and make a rough circle shape, then switch to the side view and move the vertices to make the shape of a head from the side.

MAKING THE BODY

When you're satisfied with the shape of the head, you can select the lowest face of the shape (where the neck would start), switch to front view, and press **E** to start extruding the neck (**Figure 5**). You will notice that the extrusion doesn't go straight down, so press **Z** to extrude along the z axis. Left-click to fix the extrusion. At this point, you can either scale the new faces by pressing **S** and dragging out the shape, or continue to extrude another section which will form the collar bone part of the body. From there, you can use the same process to select the right side face of the new section and extrude it out to start forming the shoulder and then the rest of the arm.

BENDY BITS

As you work your way along the arm, you will need to extrude the arm in sections, because the arm will need to bend in places. You'll need to have a couple of sections for the shoulder, three for the elbow, and another couple for the wrist (we'll get on to the hand in a moment). Think of these sections as hinges which will allow us to bend our character's limbs when we come to animate it later on (**Figure 6**).

When you get to the hand, we can make a mitten shape hand by more scaling and extruding (**Figure 7**). Make sure you have a section for each joint in the hand. Make a thumb by selecting a face from the side of the hand and extrude out three sections. Once you've done all this, you'll probably want to refine the shape a bit. You could add a loop cut on the top and side of the arm shape so that you can make it a bit rounder. Move any vertices around to give a better shape by going into vertex select mode, select the vertices, press **G** to move, and left-click to fix in place.

"We can also have a bit of the skull missing, exposing some brains"

THE REST OF THE BODY

Once you have an arm shape, you can continue with the rest of the body by selecting the underside faces of the collar bone and shoulder (in face select mode) and extruding then down. You will probably need at least five sections from the collar bone down to the hips (**Figure 8**). Then select just the outside face and extrude down and slightly right for the thigh bit of the leg. You will need an extra section or two for the knee joint and the ankle. The foot can be extruded from the front face of the ankle section. By the time you get to the end of the foot, you should have a roughly human shape. You may well at this stage want to add a bit more detail to the model, making the legs more rounded with additional faces or getting the proportions better. Once you're happy with the shape, you can apply the mirror modifier. Making sure the model's selected, go back

USEFUL TOOLS

Blender provides a huge array of built-in tools, but you'll need a couple of other things to create your zombie character. The first is a camera or mobile phone. Rather than try to find copyright-free images that fit exactly what you need for your model textures, you can use photographed items from real life. Try to start with the largest, best-quality images you can get. The other tool you'll need is an image manipulation program, such as Photoshop or the free-to-download GIMP.

Once the basic shape's finished, we can start to add more detail.

Figure 8: Again, we've extruded existing faces and manipulated the vertices to create a rough humanoid shape.

into Object Mode. Go to the spanner on the properties view and select Apply. You'll see the modifier disappear from the properties view, and if you go back into Edit Mode you will see that the mesh is editable on both sides of the z axis now.

FACIAL FEATURES

Now we'll take our humanoid model and turn it into a zombie. Starting with the head and face, we can make the zombie have a crooked mouth and an eye hanging out of the socket. For the mouth, we can add a couple of loop cuts to the bottom of the head and make one side go down a bit. You'll probably want to add two more loop cuts to the eye area, and cut each side of the middle of the face to model the nose. The hanging eyeball can be done by adding an Ico Sphere whilst in Edit Mode and placing it on the cheek. Then stretch out the vertices nearest the face to look like it's joined to the eye socket. We can also have a bit of the zombie's skull missing, exposing some brains – so one side of the head needs to be remodelled to look like a bit is missing (**Figure 9**).

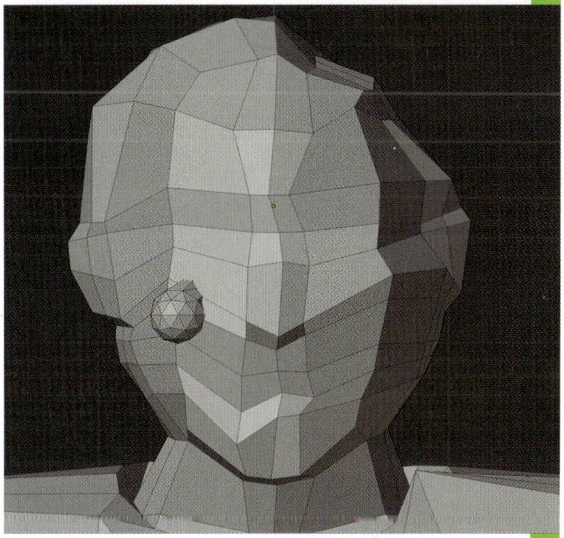

Figure 9: We're moving vertices around to make the model look less symmetrical, while the addition of a sphere will serve as a detached eyeball. Nice.

ADDING CLOTHES

There are several ways of adding clothes. For high-polygon models, the clothes are often separate meshes, but with low-poly characters it's best to make the clothes part of the same mesh. The reason being that if you only have a few polygons with some on top of others (like a shirt sleeve over an arm), when those faces are deformed to bend, often the inside faces can show through the outside faces. We're going to have our zombie wearing a sleeveless jacket with a bite taken out of it, and jeans with one leg torn off so you see a withered leg which the zombie will drag along as it walks (**Figure 10**). →

Figure 10: We're starting to add gnarly details to the body now: note the missing chunk from the torso on the bottom right.

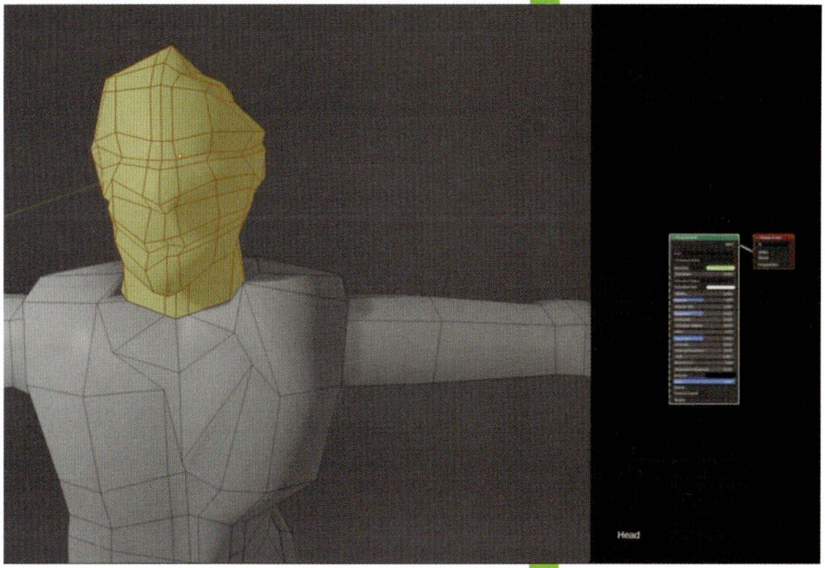

The jacket can be made by extruding the back and then the front of the torso area, then adding some extra faces down the front to make a collar opening. You'll probably want to move a few of the vertices around to make the shape a bit less symmetrical, and add a few creases. The same can be done with the shirt and jeans, adding some extra faces to provide some creases in the material. For the chunk of body warmer that is missing (and showing exposed ribs), select the whole side section of the torso and extrude inwards, and then scale to create a recessed area. Don't get too hung up on the fine-tuning of the mesh here, as we can add the detail with textures later.

ADAPTING LIMBS

Our zombie's going to have one arm half missing and one leg dragging along the floor behind it. For the damaged arm, we can just select the hand and forearm and delete the faces (delete and select faces from the pop-up menu). Then extrude and scale faces to form a bone sticking out of the missing arm. With the leg, you can move existing vertices and scale faces to make the leg thin and bony (**Figure 11**). When you've remodelled to your satisfaction, you may want to switch back to Object Mode, make sure you have your zombie selected, and then from the Object menu select 'Shade Smooth'. This irons out all the sharp edges of your mesh and makes everything look smooth. It doesn't actually change the geometry – just renders it differently. You can switch between this setting and 'Shade Flat' to see the difference.

ASSIGNING MATERIALS

Now it's time to start putting some colour on the mesh. We're going to be putting textures onto the faces, but first it's a good idea to separate the different parts of the mesh and allocate them to separate materials. This way, we can easily select and deselect these parts as we're working with different textures. To see the materials that you set up on your mesh, you will need to be in shading mode. The controls for Viewport Shading are in the top right of the 3D view and look like four spheres; the one you want to select is the second from the right and is called 'Look Dev'.

In Edit Mode, select all the faces that make up the head and neck. You can use Show

Figure 11: A better view of our zombified human model. You can copy our design or come up with a grotesque character of your own.

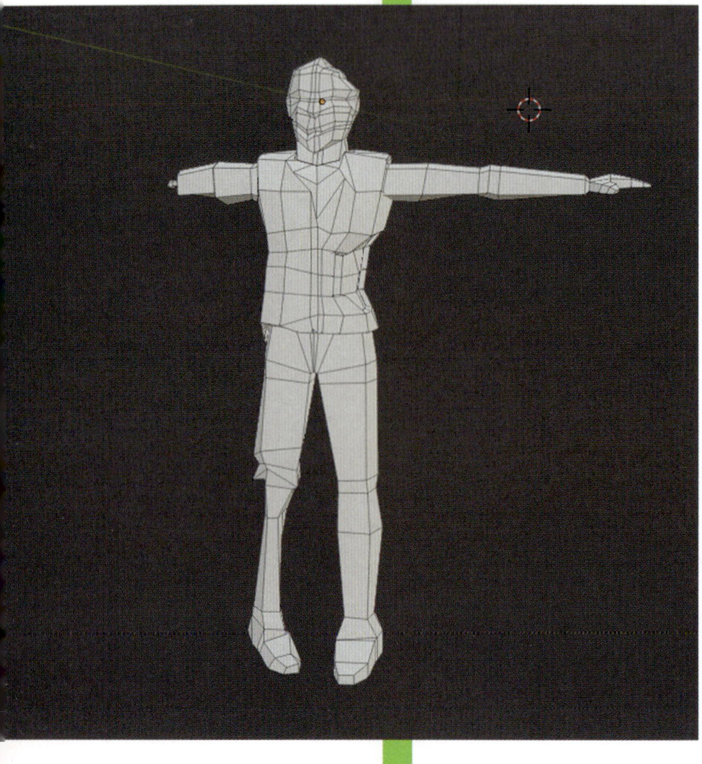

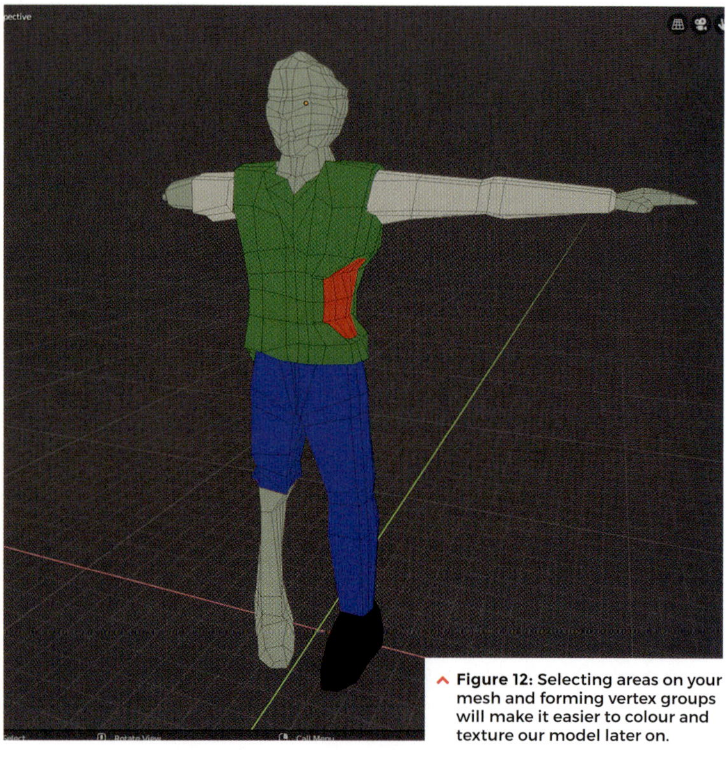

Figure 12: Selecting areas on your mesh and forming vertex groups will make it easier to colour and texture our model later on.

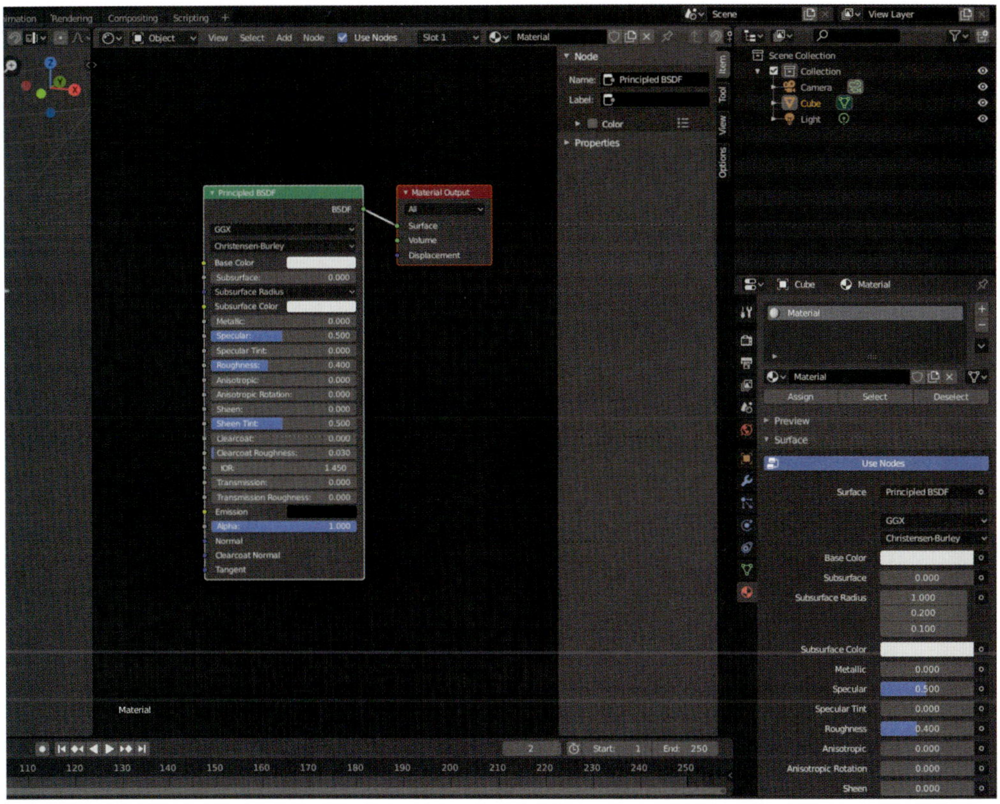

Figure 13: You can select, add, and adjust textures by opening up the Shader Node Editor.

X-Ray mode to make sure you get all the faces selected. You can either select faces with a box select, individually selecting each face with shift and left-click, or you can press **C**, which goes into paint select mode (press **ESC** to exit again). When you've selected the faces of the head and neck, go to the object data tab on the Properties view, and you'll see a section called Vertex Groups. Select the + button and then the Assign button to add this part of the mesh to the new group. Rename this 'Head'. Vertex groups allow you select and deselect parts of the mesh.

With the faces still selected, switch to the Material tab in the Properties view and create a new material (+ button), then select Assign. If you now change the Base Color setting of this material you will see the head changing colour. Rename this material to 'Head' as well. Now do the same with each part of the body that will have a different texture (**Figure 12**). We've made groups for the Head, Body Warmer, Side Guts, Trousers, Sleeves, Hand, Stump, Leg, and Boot.

ADDING TEXTURES

Now that we have our material groups sorted out, there are various ways we can add texturing to the faces of the mesh. We'll start by making a texture for each of the materials. Ideally, we'll want to have a single texture for our character when we import it into the game, but we'll deal with that later. Separate textures are much easier to work with in Blender. We don't need to worry too much about texture sizes at this stage, but we tend to stick to images measuring 1024×1024 or 2048×2048, as these sizes have been supported by 3D engines for some time.

There are various tools you can use to map textures onto a mesh. The first and easiest way is to get an image and add it to your material. If we select one of the materials in the materials tab, we can look at the nodes that make up that material (or shader). We can open up a Shader Node Editor view by splitting our 3D view into two (right-click while hovering over the bottom edge of the 3D view and select Split Area), then select Shader Editor from the drop-down selector in the top left of this new view (you can also press **SHIFT+F3**). In this editor, we can edit all the properties of the material (**Figure 13**).

To add a texture to the material, select Add from the menu and choose Texture then Image Texture. This will create a new node that we can connect to our Material Output Surface. When you connect your Image Texture Color output to the Material Output Surface channel, the →

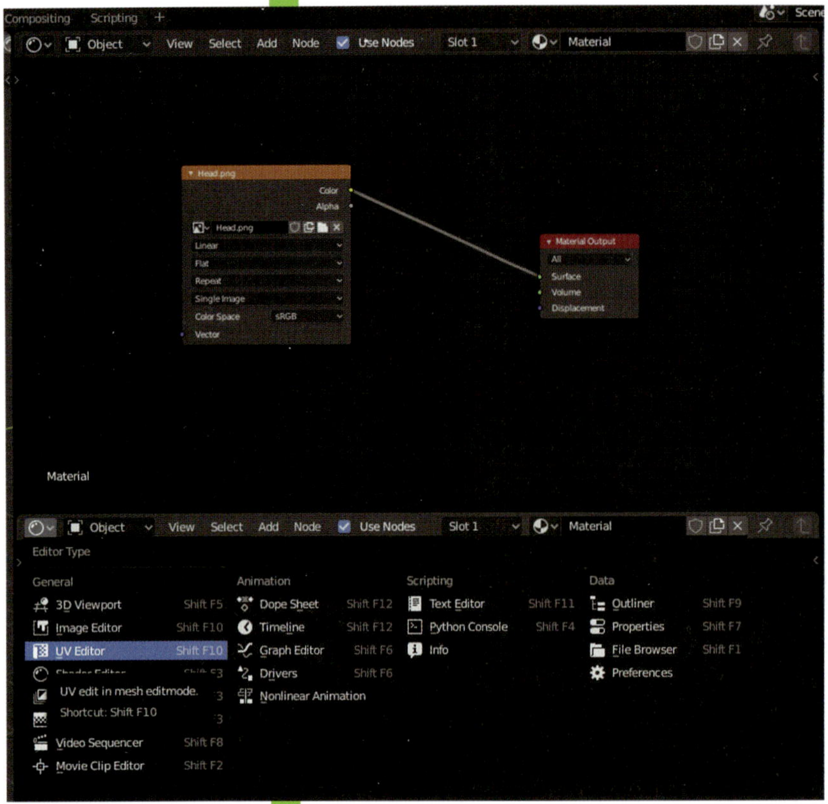

Figure 14: Once applied to our model, we can adjust our textures' positioning with the UV Editor.

faces that are assigned to that Material should go black. That's because there is no texture loaded yet. Select the Open button on the Image Texture node and load in your texture. You should now see the image wrapped around the part of your model to which it's assigned in the 3D viewport.

EDITING TEXTURE COORDINATES (UVS)

With a texture now on your mesh, you can now adjust its position – this is where the UV editor comes in. First, split your Shader Editor view horizontally and change this new view to the UV Editor. From here, we can select our image from the image selector drop-down (top middle of the view) and then in Edit Mode, if we select faces of our mesh in the 3D view, we'll see what part of the image is being mapped to the face (**Figure 14**). You can move the points around on the image in the same way you move vertices. As you move the points, you'll see how the texture is remapped in the 3D view. This means we can align details on our textures precisely with specific points on our mesh. All we need to do now is make some images to use as textures, which is where your camera and image editor will come in useful.

UV UNWRAPPING

When we attached our texture to the material, it gave us a set of default mapping points for each face. If we want to start from a more suitable mapping point, we can use the UV menu in the 3D view. You'll probably want to experiment with all these options, but a useful way to get things done quickly is to line up your mesh in the 3D view by looking at the faces you want the texture on (make sure just the faces you want to map are selected) and choose 'Project From View' from the UV menu. This will create a set of UV points which you can lay over the area of your image that has the details you want on those faces (**Figure 15**).

It will take some time, and probably a lot of trial and error, to get good texture mapping on your character model, so start off with flat colours and small details that can be easily positioned. Most of the zombie character has been textured using the Project From View unwrapping and then filled in with our next texturing tool: Texture Painting.

TEXTURE PAINTING

You may want to fill in a few details or iron out a few seams on your textures once you have them mapped onto your mesh. If you change your workspace to the Texture Paint Tab at the top of the Blender window, you'll see a toolbox of items to help you do this. All you need to do is select a tool from the tool palette on the right-hand view and start painting on your model (**Figure 16**). You'll see the changes appear both in the 3D

Figure 15: Project From View allows you to see how a texture will line up with your model's faces.

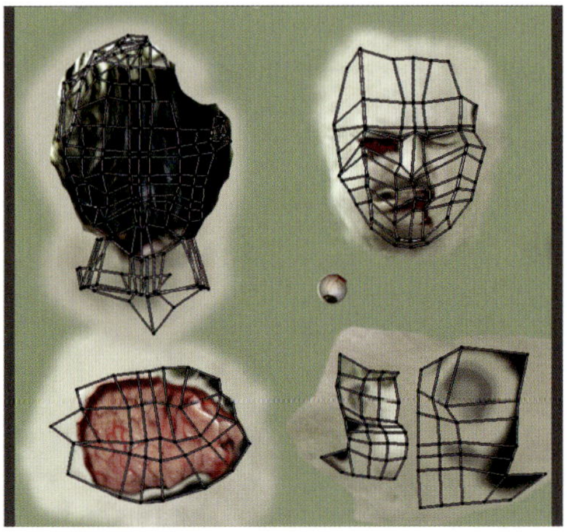

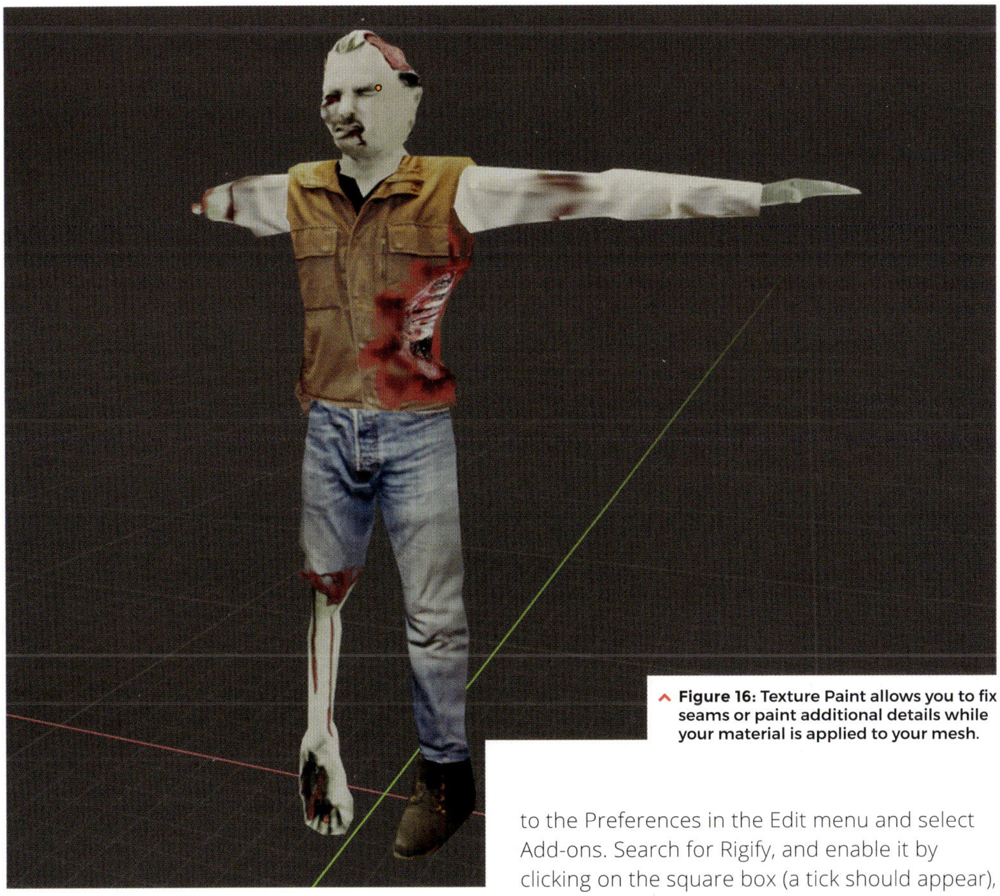

Figure 16: Texture Paint allows you to fix seams or paint additional details while your material is applied to your mesh.

version and in the Image view on the left. Make sure you save any images that are changed (the Image item in the menu will have a star after it if it needs saving) by selecting Save from the Image menu in the left-hand view.

RIGGING THE CHARACTER

We now need to start thinking about how to make our zombie move around – and for that we need bones, which will allow us to move and animate our model's joints, not unlike a real skeleton. (Note: a set of bones is often known as a rig, but it's called an Armature in Blender.)

In Object Mode, go to the Add menu and select Armature. You'll see a triangular shape object with a sphere on top appear at the cursor position. If you go into Edit Mode and press **E** to extrude, you'll see that another connected bone appears. You can make a string of bones like this and position them to match your mesh.

There's a far less time-consuming way to rig a humanoid model, however: we can use Rigify. Rigify is a plug-in that provides a ready-made skeleton of bones for humanoid characters (and some other forms, too). To enable it, go to the Preferences in the Edit menu and select Add-ons. Search for Rigify, and enable it by clicking on the square box (a tick should appear), then close the Preferences window. Now, in Object Mode, if you go to add an Armature, you'll see some new options. Select the Basic Human(Meta-Rig) option and you'll see a skeleton appear at the cursor position.

Now you need to match the bones on the skeleton to your mesh. You may need to scale it up or down, and you'll probably need to move and rotate some or all of the bones. A useful setting so that you can see where the bones are without them being hidden by your mesh is to go to the little stick figure icon on the properties view and, under Viewport Display, you'll find a setting called 'In Front'. Select that and you'll be able to see your bones through the mesh. Make sure that your bones line up in all directions with your mesh. You can delete bones that you don't need – in this case, the lower arm bones of one arm (**Figure 17**).

SKINNING

When we have all our bones lined up with our mesh, we need to attach the two together so that when we move a bone, the mesh moves too – this is known as Skinning. In Object Mode, select your mesh, then **SHIFT**-select your skeleton so that both are selected at the same →

Figure 17: Rigify will automatically generate a humanoid skeleton, which you can resize and adjust to fit the limbs on your mesh.

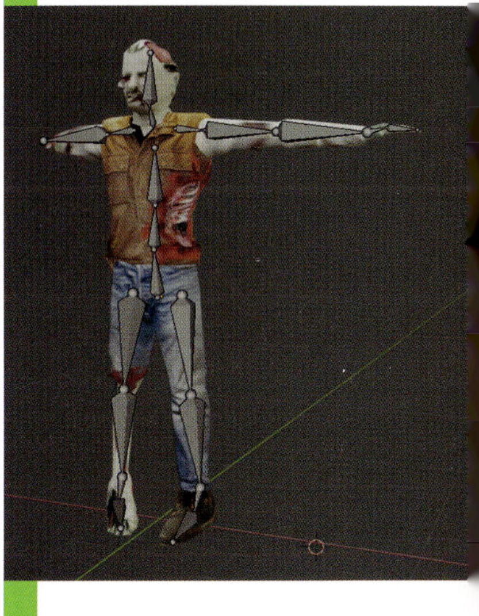

time. Your mesh will have an orange line around it, while the rig will have a yellow line around it. From the Object menu, go to Parent, and then, under Armature Deform, select 'With Automatic Weights'. This will join the rig and the mesh together, and associate the bones with the faces of the mesh that are closest to it.

TESTING THE RIG

Select the rig in Object Mode, then go to the Mode selector and select Pose Mode. Next, select one of the arm bones. If you press **R** to rotate then move the mouse, you should see not only the bone rotating, but also the mesh deforming to follow the bone's movement. Test a few bones and if it all seems to have married up properly, we can start thinking about animating our zombie.

ANIMATING THE ZOMBIE

The Blender animation system is much the same as other timeline-based animation packages, in that you can move backwards and forwards through your frames and set keyframes for various properties. Blender 2.8 has a workspace designed for animation, so you can select that from the workspaces tabs at the top of the window.

To create our zombie's walk cycle, we want to view our character from the side (numpad **3**) and we will need to be in Pose Mode, as we were when we tested the rig. At the bottom of the window you'll find two views. The first is the Dope Sheet, which shows keyframes as we set them. Beneath is the timeline where you' ll see controls for play, forward, and rewind.

MAKING A WALK CYCLE

Our walk cycle will last for 24 frames, so change the End value on the bottom right of the timeline to 24. We'll divide those 24 frames into four – the four stages of our walk – and once played back at 24 frames per second, our zombie will move at a natural-looking pace.

Our first keyframe will be on frame 1, and we want to have our zombie with its left foot forward with its heel touching the floor, and its right foot back with its toes touching the floor – you can see what this first pose should look like in **Figure 18**. To set this pose as a keyframe, make sure you have all the bones selected, and then from the Pose menu item, go to Animation and then Insert Keyframe. You'll be presented with a list of types of keyframe. Select LocRot, which will set keyframes for location and rotation.

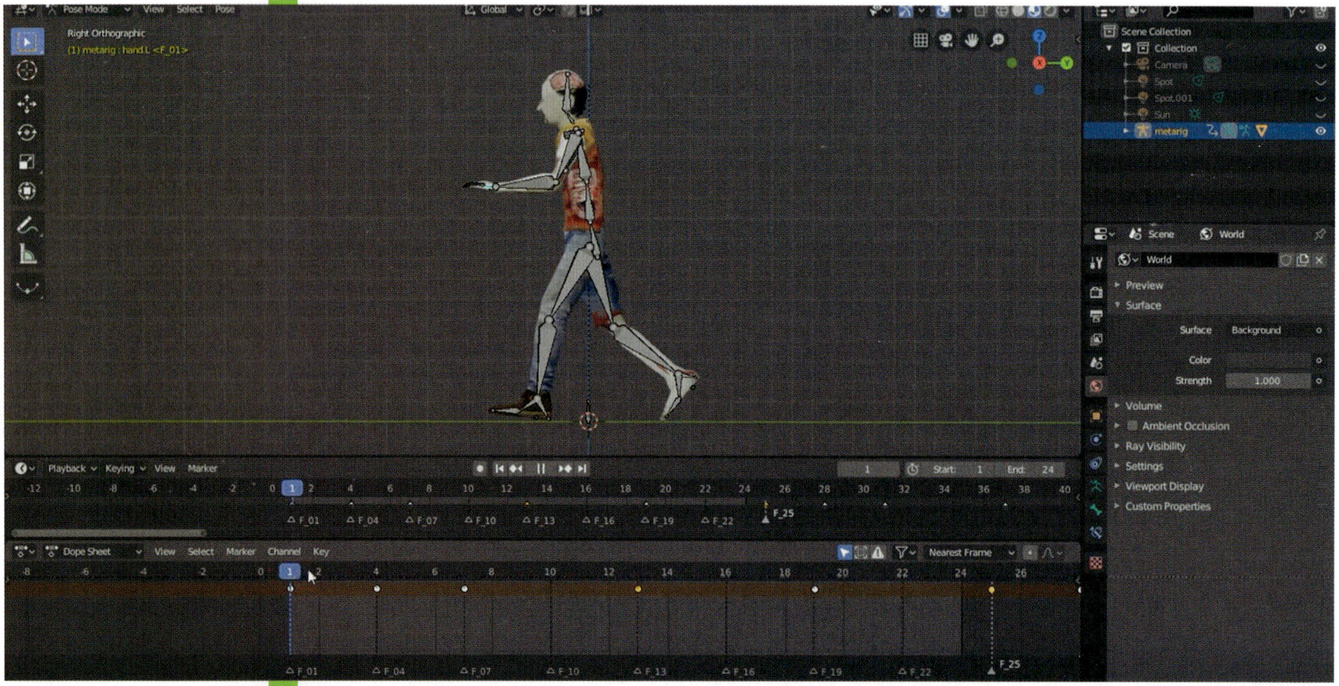

Figure 18: It's much easier to set your walk animation poses by viewing the model from the side as you adjust the bones.

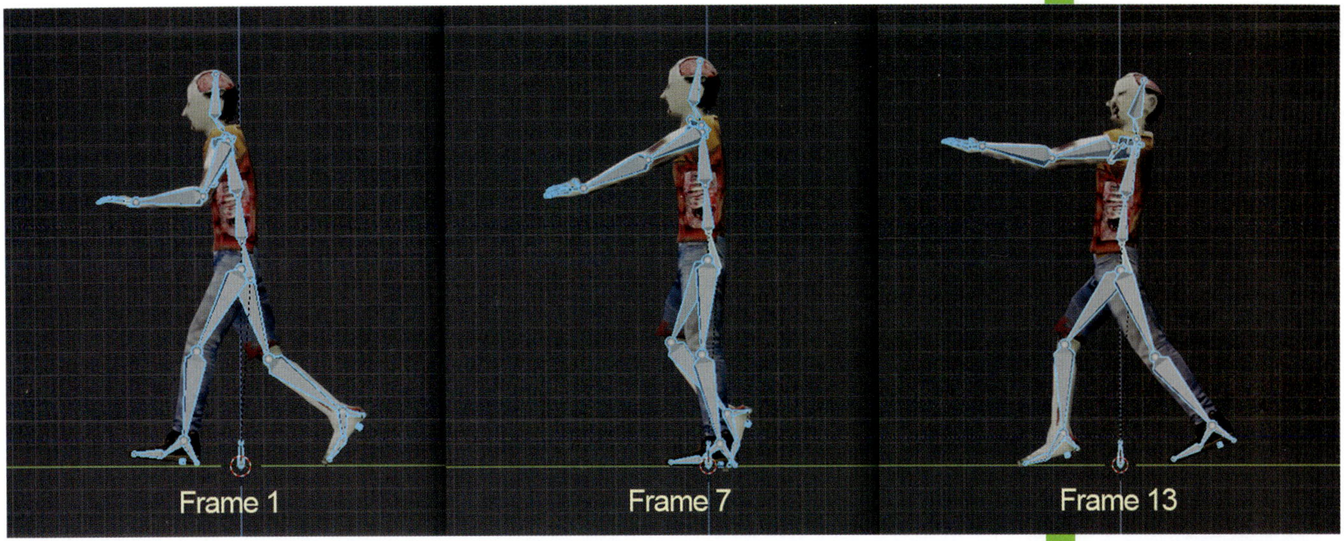

Figure 19: The basic poses for our zombie walk cycle. It may take a bit of refinement to get a nice, shambling trudge.

Now we need to do the same with the other key parts of the animation (**Figure 19**). The next keyframe to go to will be frame 13. The pose needs to be the opposite to the first frame: right foot forward and left foot back. When that frame's done, we can set the loop part of the animation by copying the keyframes from frame 1 to frame 25 (yes, just outside our animation range). We can then go to frame 7, where both feet are in the middle but the left foot is flat on the floor and the right knee is slightly bent. Then on frame 19 we have the opposite to frame 7. Use the Play button on the timeline to preview the animation.

The walk cycle's a bit stiff right now, so you'll probably want to add a few extra keyframes and wave the arms around a bit too. Make sure you always have a copy of frame 1 at frame 25 so that it loops smoothly. You might want to add other animations to the character, like an idle cycle or a lunging action. These can be added to the same timeline in a different position.

"If it all seems to have married up properly, we can start thinking about animating our zombie"

COMBINING TEXTURES

While adding textures to a mesh, it's much easier to work with multiple images for each section. Once it's time to import our character to Unity, however, we need to start thinking about being more efficient with our use of texture maps. By merging our separate textures into one – to make something called a texture atlas – we can save memory and ensure we don't end up with lots of files associated with a single character.

The first stage of the process is to create a new image (perhaps 2048×2048 or maybe larger) which our textures are going to get rendered to. Go into the UV Editor (or split the screen and switch to UV Editor) and create a new image from the menu. Rename it to something like 'AllTextures'. With your zombie selected, go to the Object Data tab in the Properties view and find UV Maps. Add a new one and call it 'AllMaps'. Now open up a Shader Editor view and select the Head material. Add a texture node and an Input UV Map node, and connect the UV to the Vector input of the Texture node. Load your AllTextures image into your new Texture node and for the UV Map node, select your AllMaps UV set. Now add an Input UV Map node with the UV set to your original UVMap and attach it to your existing Head Texture, UV to Vector input.

Now to populate the AllMaps UV Set. Select your zombie, go into Edit Mode, and select all faces (press **A**). Then, with the AllMaps UV set selected in the Object Data section in Properties, from the UV menu in the 3D view, select Smart UV Project. Change Island Margin to 0.03 and select OK. Your whole model will be unwrapped and shown as a wireframe on your new image in the UV Editor. Now, in the Shader Editor, copy the new nodes that you made in the Head material to all the other materials and connect them in the same way.

In your 3D view, make sure you have all faces selected, go to your UV Editor, and make sure you have all the UVs selected, then go through →

USING REFERENCES

If you're having difficulty making a head shape – or modelling anything in Blender, really – you can use reference images to guide you. In Object Mode go into Front View, then go to the Add menu, go down to Image, and select Reference. You can then browse for your reference image and it will be added as a plane into your scene. You can then do the same for the side view, and when you go into Edit Mode you will have a reference image to match your vertices to.

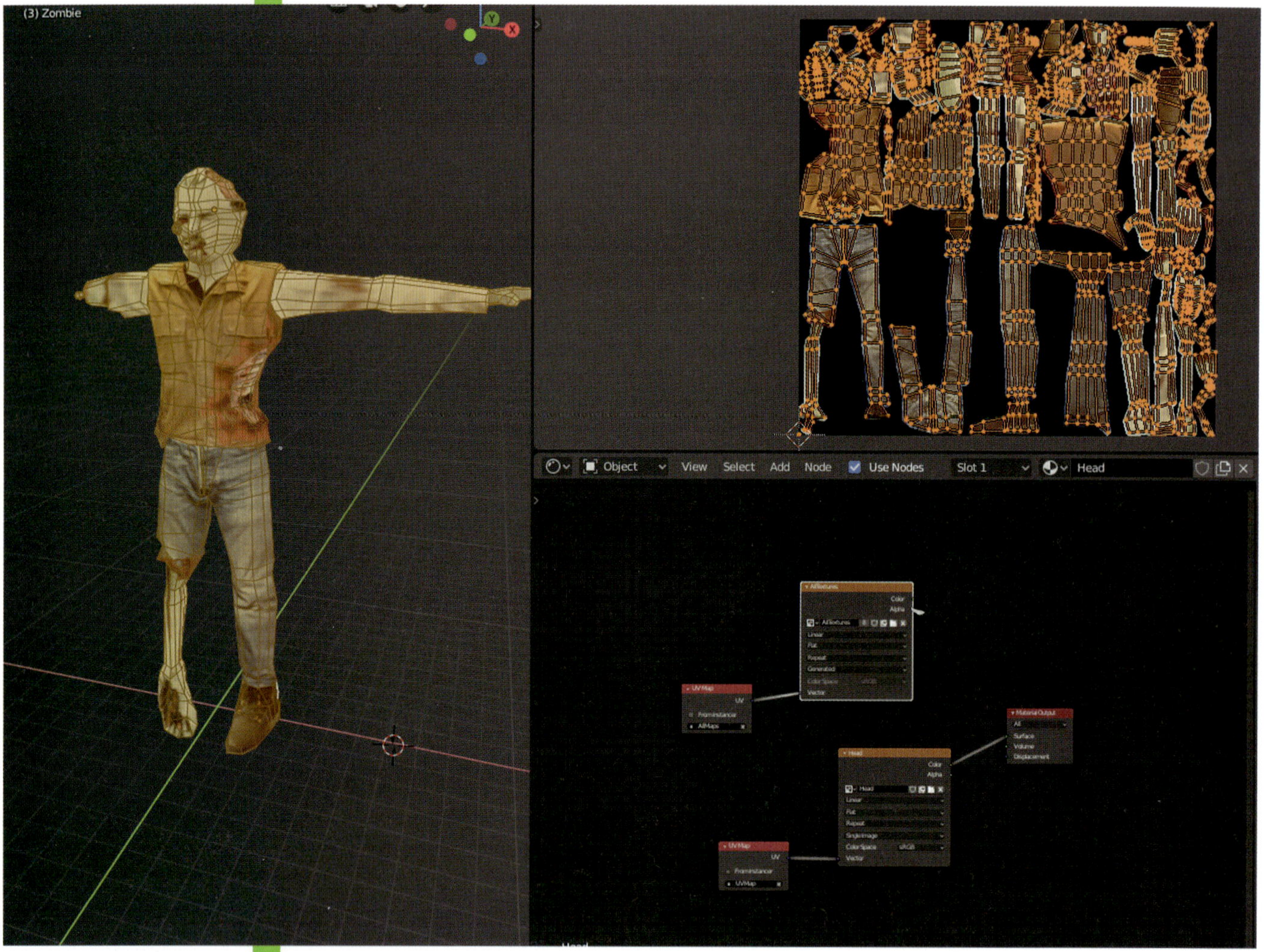

Figure 20: Once you've hit Bake, all your separate textures will merge together.

each material, selecting the new AllTextures node. When all that is selected at the same time, go to the Render tab in the Properties view, and select Cycles as the Render Engine. Go to the Bake options and select Combined as the Bake Type, and deselect Direct and Indirect (we just want the texture with no lighting). Now hit Bake. After a few moments, your combined atlas of textures will appear in the UV Editor (**Figure 20**). Now make sure you save the new image.

This new texture can now be attached with the AllMaps UV set to all your material surfaces. If you want to be even more efficient, the best thing to do is make a new material, attach the new texture atlas and UV set to it, and apply it to the whole mesh. Then you'll just have one material and one texture to worry about.

"You can drop your zombie into a scene by dragging it into the Hierarchy window"

IMPORTING INTO UNITY

To get our zombie into a game in Unity, we will need to import it and hook it up to other game elements. Unity will allow you to import your .blend files directly, but it won't import the textures with it (this is why it's a good idea to have one texture to reconnect). To import your zombie into an open Unity project, just drag and drop your .blend file into the Assets view. This will create a new asset which you can expand to see the rig, animation, and AllTex material (this won't contain its texture).

Next, drag and drop your texture file into the Assets view, select your zombie asset, and from the Inspector, select Materials. Select Extract Materials and confirm the folder to save them in. This will enable us to edit the zombie's

Figure 21: Our fully textured zombie model safely imported into Unity.

materials; you should see that the AllTex material has moved out of the Zombie asset and into the main Assets directory. Now click on the AllTex material and drag the Zombie Texture onto the 'Albedo' property in the Inspector. If you go back to your zombie asset, it'll now be correctly textured.

You can drop your zombie character into a scene just by dragging it into the Hierarchy window, but you may want to attach it to other game objects. In our *Zombie Panic* game, you can swap the capsule mesh for your zombie just by creating an empty game object in your placeholder asset in the Hierarchy, and then dragging your zombie asset onto that object. You may need to change the scale of your zombie. Then, in the Inspector of your placeholder object, uncheck the Mesh Renderer component. Your zombie should have replaced the placeholder capsule (**Figure 21**).

MAKING THE ANIMATION WORK

The last piece of the puzzle is to get the animations you set up working in the game. Mesh animations are controlled through an Animation Controller. First, select your zombie asset and go to the animation section in the Inspector. Create a new clip with the + button under Clips and rename the clip to 'WalkCycle'. Set the End frame to 24, check the Loop Time box, and scroll down to hit Apply. Now create an Animation Controller (from the Asset window right-click menu), call it ZombieAnim, select it, and click Open in the Inspector. You will see a flow-chart-type view open. Drag your WalkCycle icon (inside your zombie asset) onto the flow chart; you will see it connects up to the 'Entry' block.

Selecting the zombie that you have put inside the placeholder object, you'll see that there's an Animator component. Set the controller to be your ZombieAnim Animation Controller. You can set Culling Mode to Always Animate and now when you play your game, you should see an animated zombie where your placeholder was.

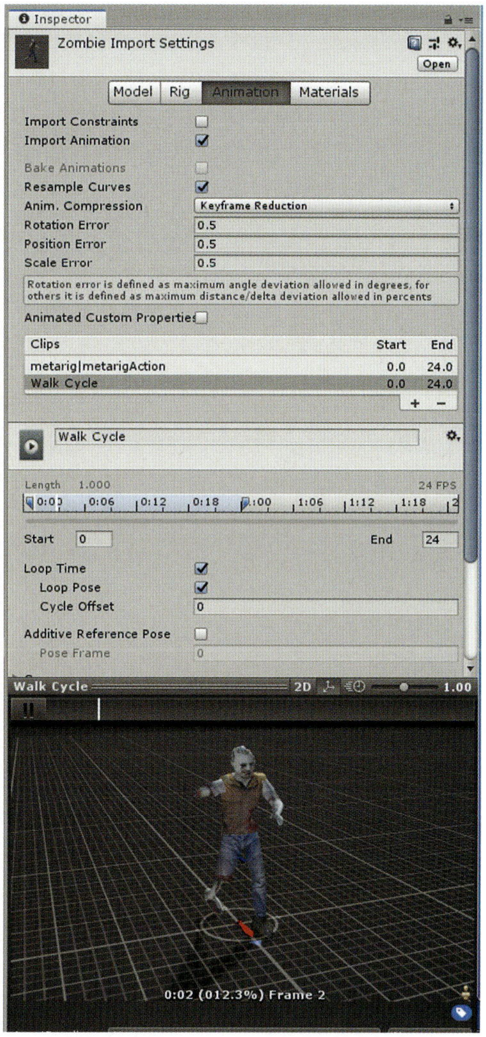

The animation we created in Blender can be assigned to our zombie model in Unity's Inspector.

Our flesh-eating zombie is complete, and ready to start hectoring our player.

Add lighting and atmospheric visual effects

Lighting and effects generate atmosphere and highlight points of interest to the player. Here's how to get started

AUTHOR
RYAN SHAH

An avid developer at The Multiplayer Guys with a strong passion for education, Ryan Shah moonlights as KITATUS – an education content creator for all things game development.

Lighting is one of the most powerful tools in a creator's toolkit. From illuminating important goals to adding spooky atmosphere – the importance of light and understanding light cannot be overstated.

To use the lighting tools within Unity, we must first know our limitations. There are two main types of lighting to consider: baked and dynamic. Baked lights are ones that are pre-calculated by Unity, whereas dynamic lights are calculated at runtime. The benefits here are that baked lights are essentially 'free' in terms of performance within your game, and also offer high-quality shadows for static objects. With dynamic lights, you gain the advantage of having shadows for moving objects, as well as total control of adding, removing, or altering lights at runtime.

The drawbacks of one type of lighting are complemented by the other. For example, a big drawback for baked lighting is that your game requires more memory to read the lighting data. As dynamic lighting doesn't pre-compute this data and creates it on the fly, this is more lightweight in terms of memory requirements; the trade-off is that dynamic lights are more performance-intensive.

Figuring out what lighting to use in your project may seem like a daunting task at first, but the process becomes much easier when you start to break things down. A good example of this is sunlight. Does your scene have any outdoor elements, such as open spaces or windows to the outside world? If so, you're going to need a sun. Does the sun move (is there a change to time of day during playtime)? If so, we'll need to dynamically change the light properties at runtime, and thus rely on dynamic lighting. Even if the sun doesn't move, if you have a lot of moving objects in your scene that need to cast shadows, dynamic lights are still required.

You don't have to use just one type of light in your scene, however. It's possible to mix static and dynamic lights together to get the best of both worlds in terms of their functionality. Here, we'll use a number of different lights and lighting profiles to add atmosphere to our scene.

LIGHT IT UP

To get started, let's look at Environment Lighting. First, head into the lighting menu by going to Window > Rendering > Lighting Settings (see **Figure 1**). Inside this lighting menu, there are a number of features we can use to fully exploit Unity's lighting features to our advantage. The first one we're going to look at is the Environmental Lighting feature. This is useful for lighting that has no origin within the scene but still needs to exist. You may be thinking that this doesn't make sense – after all, if you're creating

▾ The Lighting tab has a plethora of options to choose from.

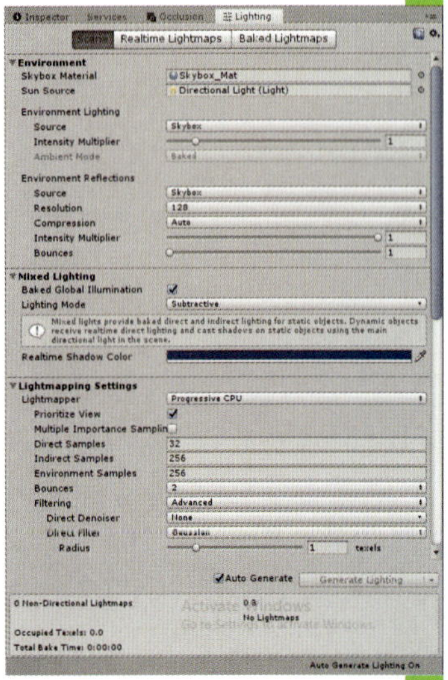

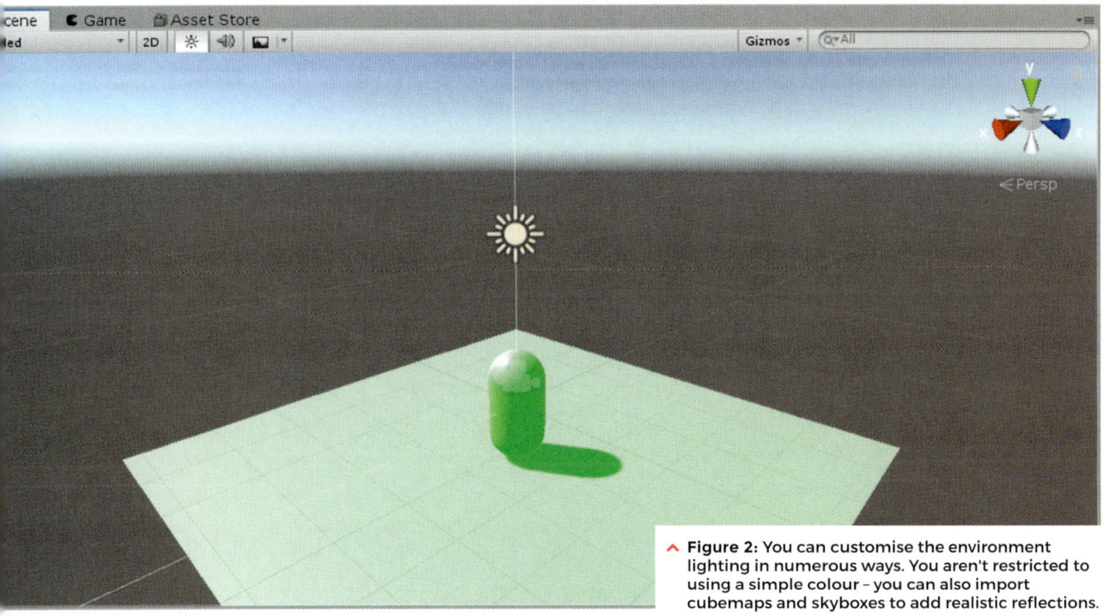

^ **Figure 2:** You can customise the environment lighting in numerous ways. You aren't restricted to using a simple colour – you can also import cubemaps and skyboxes to add realistic reflections.

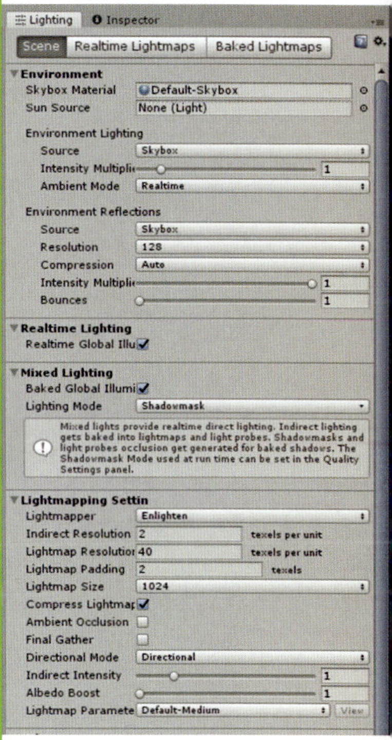

^ **Figure 1:** The Lighting Settings window allows us to make a number of changes to the lighting in our scene to help us achieve the effect we're looking for.

a realistic game, you want your lights to come from natural locations. But there are important benefits to using environmental lighting, even in realistic scenes.

In most movies, lighting emanates from sources outside the scene captured by the camera. In many behind-the-scenes videos, you may notice additional lights and fixtures behind or around the camera. Environmental lighting is usually to either diffuse the existing lighting within the scene – to brighten up dark corners, or to highlight an object or character in the foreground.

"In most movies, lighting emanates from sources outside the scene captured by the camera"

We can do this in Unity with Environment Lighting. We have three main options in this section: source (which defines where the light's coming from), intensity (how strong the light is), and ambient mode (if you have global illumination turned on for your scene, this would control how this light should be treated). As you may have guessed, in the source section, Skybox means the light will come from the sky. Gradient deals with our scene in three chunks: the sky, the distant horizon, and the ground. With the gradient, you can set specific colours for each of these three areas and Unity will blend these colours together based on location, to coat your scene in a naturally blended light. The colour option blankets the whole scene with a colour of your choosing, which is great for diffusing your scene.

As a cool example, let's coat our scene in a luminous green (see **Figure 2**). This will not only give us an effect akin to *The Matrix*, but will also brighten our shadows a little to make sure our scene isn't too dark. To do this, head back to Environment Lighting and change the source to Color; for Ambient Color, click the colour (to open up the property window) and add these values: R: 0, G: 185, B: 22 (alternatively, you can set the hexadecimal value to 00B916). If you take a look at your scene now, you'll notice everything is coated in a bright shade of green – even our dark shadows have a green tint to them.

There are still plenty of steps we can take to improve the atmosphere of our level. As our scene takes place outdoors, we're going to need some sunlight. In most cases, especially in modern games, sunlight is displayed using a Directional Light. In Unity, there are four key lighting types: Point, Spot, Directional, and Area. Point lights are placed in the scene and emit light in a spherical fashion. Spot lights act like real life spot lights – they radiate a cone of light from the point of origin. Directional lights have no clear point of origin, but act as if the light is omnipresent (like a sun) and blanket the whole scene with lighting based on the rotation of the directional light. Finally, area lights are a baked-only light that emits rays uniformly within a rectangle. →

< Here are the three options for Environment Lighting, where you can change the source of the lighting, the intensity multiplier, and the ambient mode.

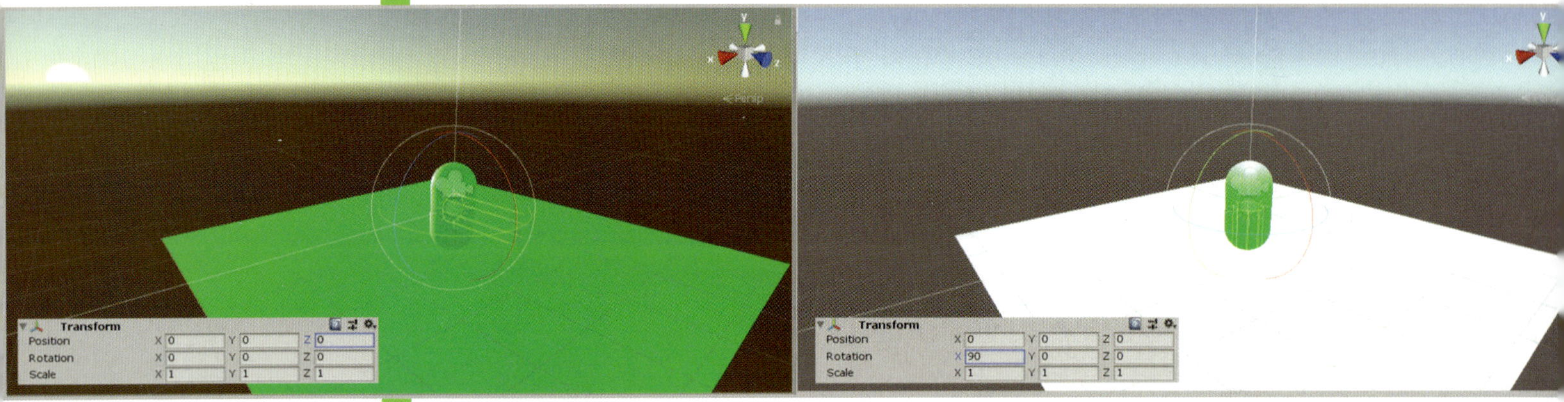

^ **Figure 3:** The rotation of a directional light will change the time of day of the default skybox in your scene.

The best way to understand these different lighting types is to use them in practice, so let's get started by creating a sun. Take a look in your scene Hierarchy (usually on the left-hand side of the main editor view). If you see a Directional Light in there, delete it by selecting it and pressing the **DELETE** key on your keyboard. Now our scene is lit solely by the ambient lighting we set up earlier. To make a new directional light, right-click inside your Hierarchy; within the menu that pops up, select Lights > Directional Light.

"The best way to understand these different lighting types is to use them in practice"

Wherever directional lights are placed, they'll blanket the whole scene in light. What does matter with directional lights, however, is rotation. If you select the Directional Light and press **E** to edit rotation mode, grabbing the X axis (the red spherical line) will let you spin the light. You should immediately notice that the time of day for the skybox changes when you do this. This is because this light is simulating your in-game sun. An X rotation of 0 is dawn, where the light bleeds over the horizon, an X rotation of 90 is mid-day and an X rotation of 180 is dusk (see **Figure 3**). Unity does this because using a directional light as sun or moon light is about as helpful as this type of light can be. Let's create a warm, dawn sunlight by setting our rotation (via the Inspector) to X: 0, Y: 0, Z: 0.

We now have a spring morning breaking out across our scene. As we've already covered, this light is a dynamic light (that doesn't use pre-baked lightmaps) because it has to calculate shadows for objects that move. You can see what lighting mode the light is set to by clicking the light and, within the Inspector, going to the Mode area, where you will see Realtime for our directional light.

Before we dive deeper into the lighting system, let's look at a couple of effects we can add to our scene to further flesh out the atmosphere.

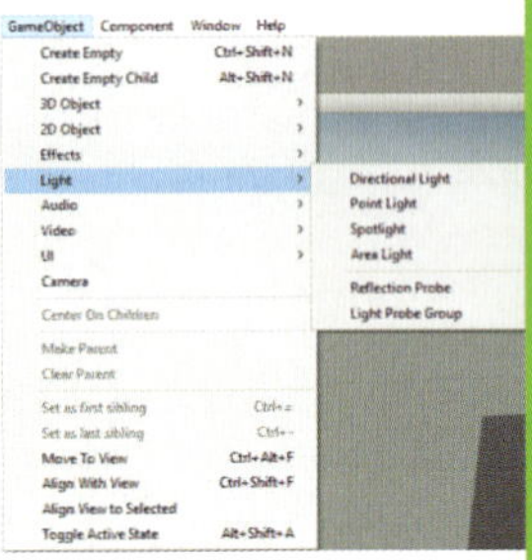

^ The four lighting options can be accessed via right-clicking in the Project tab, or by using the drop-downs at the top of the Unity Editor.

POST-PROCESS

To really add atmosphere to our scene, let's use the post-process feature. A post-process adds effects to the rendered image just before it's displayed to the end user. It's useful adding atmosphere and style to your scenes. If you haven't brought in the Post Process tool yet, you need to add it via the package manager. To do this, you can go to Window > Package Manager. Once it's loaded, on the left-hand side select Post Processing, and press the Install button on the top right of the window to install it into the project.

To start using the post-process, we need to do two things. First, we need to add a Post-Process layer to our camera. This tells the engine, "Hey, this camera gets affected by the post-process settings we're going to make." In order to do this, select the camera within your scene, head over to the Inspector, and select Add Component.

Now select Rendering > Post-Process Layer. There are a few options in the Rendering submenu, so ensure you select the correct

> You can select the colour of your directional light and the kinds of shadows it creates in the settings menu.

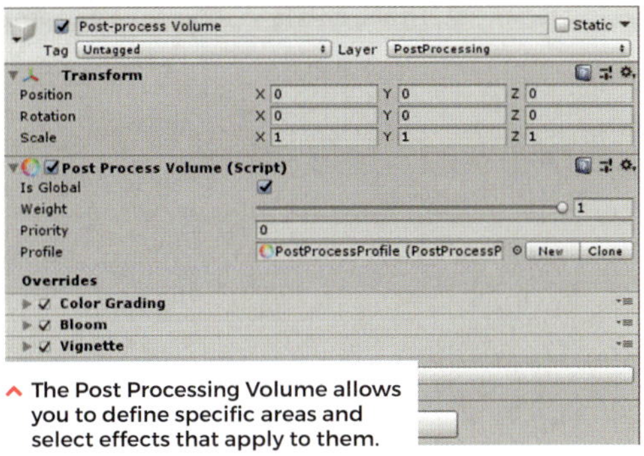

The Post Processing Volume allows you to define specific areas and select effects that apply to them.

option. To ensure this camera captures our post-process work, within the newly created Post Process Layer section in our Camera, go to Layer and select Everything. This means that the camera will react to every post-process volume in the scene – as opposed to the default value of none, which means none of the post-process volumes can affect the camera.

The second step to deal with is the post-process volume. These are trigger boxes placed within your scene that can either affect the area covered inside them or the whole scene. We will look at how to set this up in just a moment. Before we do, we must first spawn a Post-Process volume in our scene. To do this, head over to the Hierarchy and create a new component. Select 3D Object > Post-Process Volume to spawn the system we need.

We now have a working post-process system in our scene, but there are still a couple of things we need to do before we can tune the settings. Click the post-process volume and, over in the Inspector, tick the Is Global checkbox so it's true. This tells Unity that instead of turning the post-process on if the camera is inside this trigger volume, it should apply it to the whole scene. If you're wondering when would be the right time to have Is Global set to false, if you had multiple post-process effects in your scene, if Is Global was set to true then they would conflict and cause unintended results. Basically, if you have more than one post-process, turn Is Global off and scale the trigger volumes accordingly to cover the area you want said post-process to appear in. If you only have a single post-process that you want to cover the whole scene, set Is Global to true.

There are a few other settings both within the Post-Process Volume and the Post-Process Layer we've created. Many of them are designed to be tweaked by hand to get the exact specific aesthetic you're trying to achieve. For the purposes of what we're doing here, we're simply going to focus on the last piece of the puzzle: the Post-Process Profile. This is where the magic happens – this is the asset we can use to adjust the post-process settings we want to implement in our scene. To create a Post Process Profile, either head to the content browser and create it there, or you can press the handy New button next to the Profile heading in the Post Process Volume. Go ahead and create one now.

From here, open the newly created profile by either double-clicking the asset or double-clicking the now filled-in variable within the Post Process profile. Within the Inspector, we can now add and alter effects for our post-process profile. Getting a post-process to look exactly how you want will be a subjective experiment, turning on and tweaking effects as you see fit to get the exact atmosphere that you're looking for.

Below is a list of the effects you can implement with this post-process profile system:

Ambient Occlusion: Darkens calculated ambient shadows between objects and surfaces.

Auto-Exposure: Mimics the human eye's reaction to light. It simulates those few seconds where, if you're in a dark room and then head outside on a sunny day, your eyes take a few seconds to adjust.

Bloom: Makes the light around a bright object leak out a little, creating the illusion of a really bright light source – a common artefact with real life cameras. You can also add dirt masks to emulate a dusty lens. →

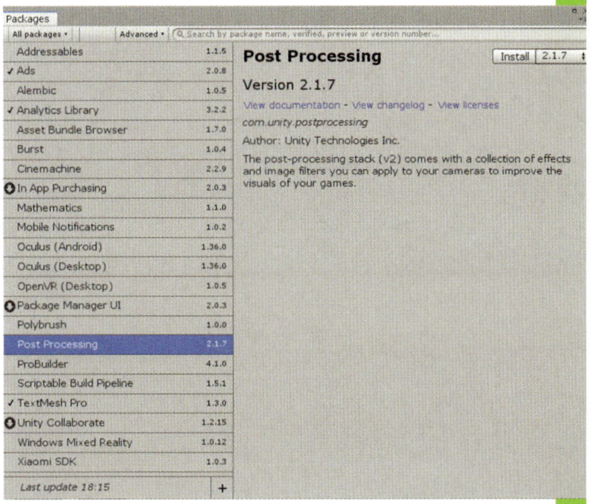

The package manager is filled with utilities and packages you can use to improve the look and feel of your project.

DOUBLE INSTALL?

If you're having trouble activating post-processing features – if you find there are options missing, for example – you might have a 'double install'. This is where you have two instances of PostProcessing in your project. The package manager is the intended way of using the system, so take a look in your content browser and delete any folders marked PostProcessing (that isn't a Packages subfolder).

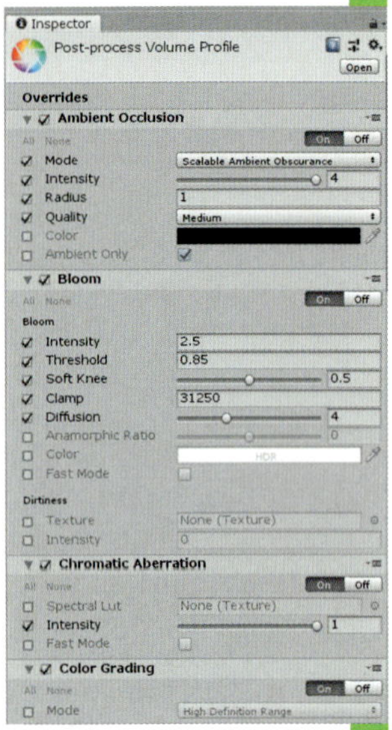

With Post-Process Volume Profiles, keep performance in mind, as some of the effects can bring a large performance cost.

Spot light settings give you plenty of control over things like angle, range, colour, and intensity.

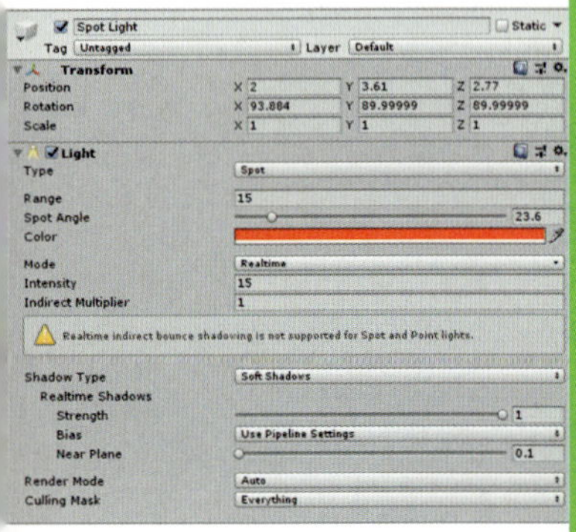

Chromatic Aberration: Emulates the multicoloured halo effect sometimes seen on real camera lenses.

Colour Grading: Uses a look-up table to adjust the palette and tone of colours in a scene.

Depth of Field: Replicates the focal point of a camera lens. You can change what objects are blurred out and what's in focus, just like a real camera lens.

Grain: A film grain effect which can be used to mask jagged lines or to provide a classic cinematic feel.

Lens Distortion: Changes the shape of the virtual camera lens to provide a distorted effect made commonly seen in skateboarding videos of the nineties.

Motion Blur: Enhances the look of a fast-moving object. A popular technique in modern video games.

Screen-Space Reflections: Alters the appearance of objects that appear in reflective materials, such as a puddle or a mirror. This effect saves having to render geometry twice by using the depth buffer to calculate how the reflection should look.

Vignette: Darkens the edges of the image to emulate a real camera. This effect is used a lot in horror games because it adds to the spooky atmosphere.

I have included an example below of a post-process file you can use, but feel free to tweak with the settings within this profile until you come up with a visual style and aesthetic that suits your project:

- **Ambient Occlusion:**
  - **Mode:** Scalable Ambient Obscurance
  - **Intensity:** 4
  - **Radius:** 1
  - **Quality:** Medium
- **Bloom:**
  - **Intensity:** 2.5
  - **Threshold:** 0.85
  - **Soft Knee:** 0.5
  - **Clamp:** 31250
  - **Diffusion:** 4
- **Chromatic Aberration:**
  - **Intensity:** 1
- **Color Grading:**
  - **Mode:** ACES
  - **Temperature:** 9
  - **Saturation:** 1.2
  - **Contrast:** 1
  - **Channel Mixer:**
    - **Red:** 40
    - **Green:** 110
- **Depth Of Field:**
  - **Focus Distance:** 15
  - **Aperture:** 3
  - **Focal Length:** 70
- **Grain:**
  - **Colored:** False
  - **Intensity:** 0.15
- **Motion Blur:**
  - **Shutter Angle:** 310
  - **Sample Count:** 20
- **Vignette:**
  - **Intensity:** 0.425
  - **Smoothness:** 0.2

One important thing to note with post-process effects is that they're not all created equal in terms of performance. Some effects come with a large performance cost, and it's down to you to decide if the effects are worth the performance trade-off, or if you want to disable (or in some cases enable) specific effects on specific devices.

Before we go back to talking about lights, let's look at one last effect we can use to add atmosphere and further stylise our project. Head back into the Lighting window. If you've closed it, you can find it again in Window > Rendering > Lighting Settings. If you scroll through the list, you'll find Fog. Fog has been a staple of video games for many years as an easy way to build atmosphere, as well as hide any imperfections in your game's world. Select the checkbox next to Fog to turn the feature on and play with the settings until you find a look that suits you. For my project, my settings are:

- **Fog:**
  - **Fog:** True
  - **Color:** (Hexadecimal) D2C1C1
  - **Mode:** Linear
    - **Start:** 0
    - **End:** 150

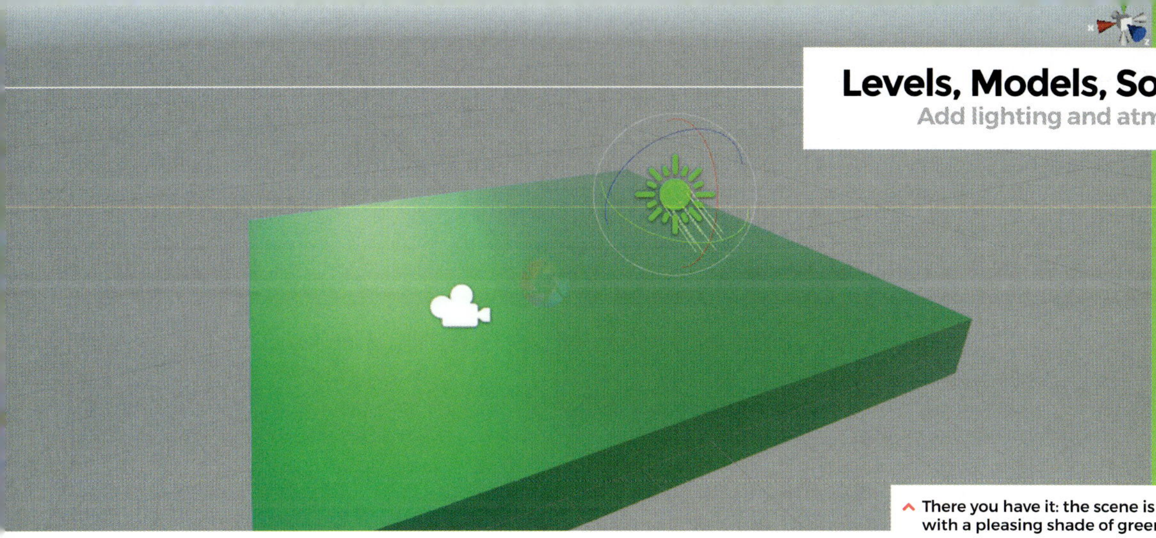

There you have it: the scene is lit with a pleasing shade of green.

There are many different tweaks and changes you make in both the Post-Process settings and the Lighting settings, so I highly recommend going through and making tweaks to values until you find a style you are happy with.

Now that we've covered post-processing, let's add a few more lights to gain a deeper understanding of the options available to us.

IN THE SPOT LIGHT

There are two important light types we touched on earlier, but are worth exploring in more detail: point lights and spot lights.

Let's start by making a spot light. You can do this by right-clicking in the Hierarchy and selecting Light > Spotlight. Earlier, we looked at how we can emulate a real-world spot light; here, we'll use a spot light to create a torch.

Find the camera in your Hierarchy and drag the spot light on top of the camera. You'll notice that your spot light now becomes a child of this camera. We changed the parent of our spot light, but it has stayed in the same location it was in before the merge. To fix this, select the camera and head into the Inspector. Set the location and rotation to: X: 0, Y: 0, and Z: 0. This will move the spot light to the camera, creating the illusion that the torch is being held by the player character.

Below, I've provided settings to create a realistic-looking flashlight. Again, feel free to tweak these values as you see fit.

- **Light:**
  - **Range:** 10 – How far into the distance does the light affect.
  - **Spot Angle:** 45 – This is how big the cone of the light should be.
  - **Mode:** Realtime – As this is supposed to act as a flashlight, we will need real-time shadows due to the many moving objects within our scene.
  - **Intensity:** 10 – Intensity deals with how bright the light source is.
  - **Indirect Multiplier:** 5 – Deals with how much light bleed you get from this light.

The last light I wanted to touch on is the point light. These are ideal for areas in your scene that require a realistic-looking light bulb, or an area of your scene that requires a particular light or hue that you're not getting from your direction light, such as an exaggerated glow from a neon sign.

You can create a point light in almost the same way as we've created the other lights within the scene. Within your Hierarchy, right-click and select Lighting > Point Light. For our example, we'll pretend there's a street light at the corner of our scene that has an evil, red tint. I've placed my point light at the position: X: 0.5, Y: 2.5, Z: -5.

Earlier, we saw how point lights emit light evenly with from the centre of a sphere, so rotation isn't necessary in most cases. Here are the settings I'm using for my red light (if you'd like to emulate them, or create your own style; make sure the point light is selected and head into the Light section of the Inspector):

- **Light:**
  - **Range:** 15
  - **Color:** (Hexadecimal) FF0000
  - **Mode:** Baked – This light isn't used to shadow dynamic items within this scene; it is simply used to further colorize our in-game world so we can go for the more performant Baked option.
  - **Intensity:** 15

As we have a number of lights in our scene – and process effects that also affect the visuals – it might be hard to see this light while playing your game. To combat this, you'll have to tweak your various lights and post-process settings until you get the style you're looking for – it's a case of balancing your project's systems until they look right.

We've just taken our first steps into the lighting and effect systems within Unity, but this is just the tip of the iceberg. If you are interested in taking these systems a step further, I strongly suggest looking into global illumination and how to alter lights via code – for example, you could create a spooky, flickering light in a lonely hallway.

PREVIEWING

You can instantly see the results of your post-processing effects by heading over to the Game viewport. The Scene viewport doesn't include post-process effects due to performance and usability risks.

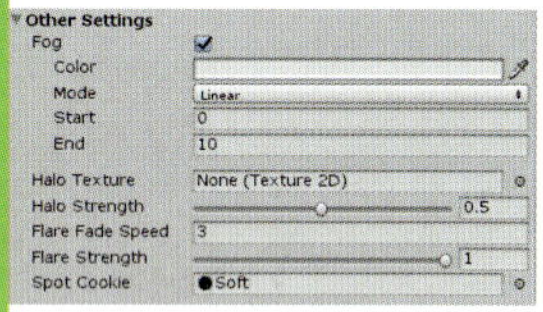

The Lighting Settings window contains many helpful settings to further tweak the visual style of your scene, from fog settings to global illumination.

When viewed in the game, our point lights give off a sickly orange glow, and generate the kinds of shadows you'd expect from a sinister castle.

Adding sound and audio

Heighten tension and excitement with music and sound effects. Ryan shows you how

AUTHOR
RYAN SHAH

An avid developer at The Multiplayer Guys, with a strong passion for education, Ryan Shah moonlights as KITATUS – an education content creator for all things game development.

Sound in your projects is extremely important. Watch a film with the volume turned down and you'll immediately notice the impact sound and audio has on the experience. Adding audio to your project is a great way to provide an immersive atmosphere, and can even provide new gameplay experiences.

When it comes to audio, there are a number of different tools you can use in Unity, and there are many different ways to use said tools, too. Let's go over the core features of Unity's audio systems and learn all about AudioClips, AudioSources, and the powerful Audio Mixer toolset.

In games, you can categorise sounds into five core areas – Music, Dialogue, Effects, UI, and Master. Master is the overall volume of your project, which is a helpful way for your players to turn down the overall volume of sounds without having to adjust music, dialogue, effects, and user interface sounds separately.

Before we can start working with audio within Unity, we need sounds to use. For the purposes of what we're doing here, you can either record some audio in your favourite recording program (such as Audacity or Adobe Audition), or you can browse the asset store to find sounds that you'd like to use. Most (if not all) of the Unity example content also features sound files, so go ahead and either make or find some sounds to use.

It's worth touching on how to import sounds into Unity – it's handy to know how, even if you're not using your own sounds for this guide. Unity supports many audio formats, such as MP3, OGG, WAV, and more. When Unity builds your project, it will convert the file into OGG for desktop and consoles, or MP3 for mobile platforms. In general, most people use WAV files due to their lossy format, but if you use OGG files on import, you're not going to get any degradation in quality compared to your built files (if you're building your project for desktop and console) because no conversion will take place.

Once you've got your audio files ready to import, there are three main ways you can bring them into your project. The first method is to manually drag and drop the audio file from your file explorer into Unity's content browser. The second method is to go to Assets > Import New Asset... and import the files that way. The third way is quite similar to the second method, but instead of using the menu system, you can right-click in an empty space inside the content browser to bring up the requisite menu.

With your audio files inside the project, we can now bring them into our scene. We'll quickly test to ensure our audio is coming through and

You can choose from multiple templates depending on your project's requirements.

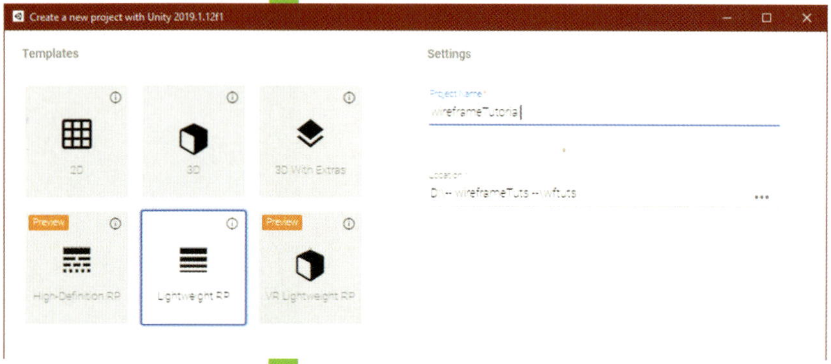

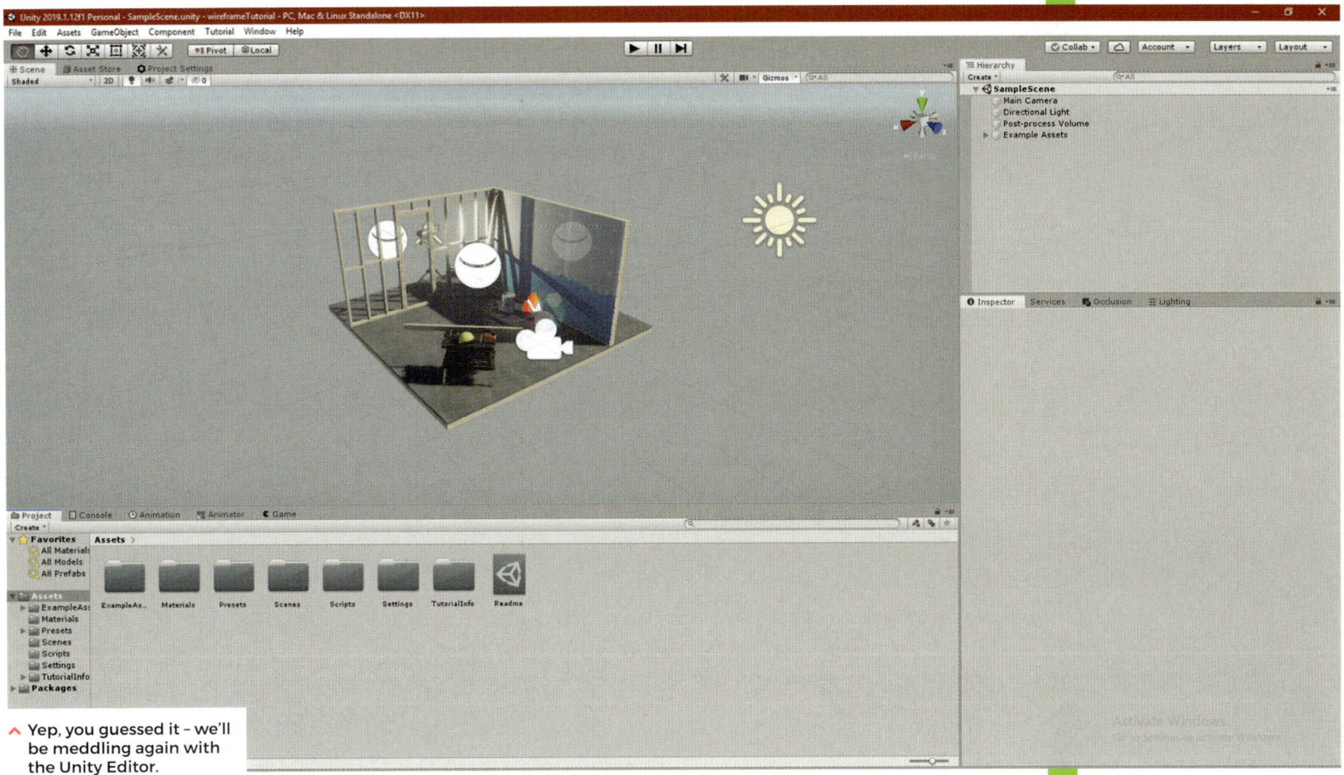

Yep, you guessed it – we'll be meddling again with the Unity Editor.

playing correctly. There are two key ways to do this. The first way is to select the audio within the content browser. With the audio selected, you'll be able to see some properties on the right-hand side of your screen. If you look at the very bottom of this properties area, you'll see a section with a waveform inside. Just above the waveform on the far right, you'll see some play controls: volume, looping, and play/pause. You can use these controls to test out the audio within Unity.

Another way of testing the audio is to put it in the scene. To do so, simply select an object within the scene (or create an empty GameObject) and drag your audio file into the properties panel. You'll see that it creates an audio component for you, and sets up the audio to automatically play on game start. If you were to test the project out now, you should immediately hear the sound playing.

By now, we can confirm the sound is imported and works in the scene. The next stage is to fire this sound off with a piece of code, so that we can understand how to activate a sound when a gun is fired, a door is opened, or a footstep is made.

"We're now going to create a sound that fires every three seconds"

NOISES OFF

We're now going to create a sound that fires every three seconds – this will give us a basic understanding of how audio works in code within Unity. To get started, we're going to need a new C# file. If you haven't done this yet, you can do so by right-clicking the content browser and selecting the Create option. From here, select New C# Script and this will generate the files needed. Give it any name you want, but for the purposes of synchronicity, I'll be calling mine 'AudioTester'.

When the C# file is generated, we're given `Start()` and `Update()` functions – `Start` obviously fires when this script is run, and `Update` runs during every update loop of the game. We don't need the update loop for testing our audio, so go ahead and remove this function. We're going to add a requirement to our script, because we don't want our code to fire if there's no audio present. This is to prevent any errors or bugs within our project at runtime. To add a requirement, head above the class (the line that says `public class XX : MonoBehaviour`) and add the following:

```
[RequireComponent(typeof(AudioSource))]
```

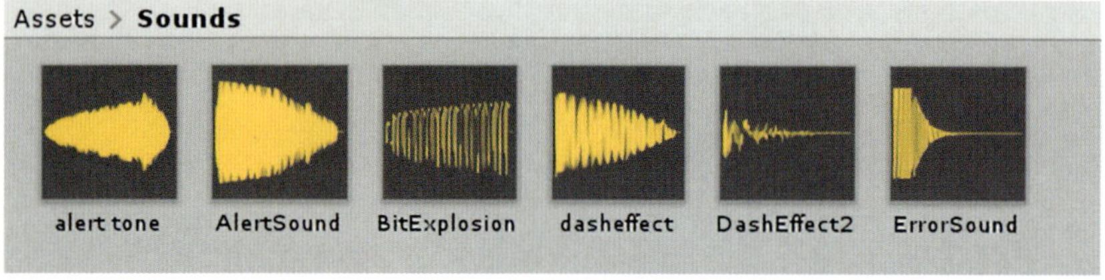

Here's all of our imported sounds in the editor – the wavelengths give a visual clue as to what they'll sound like.

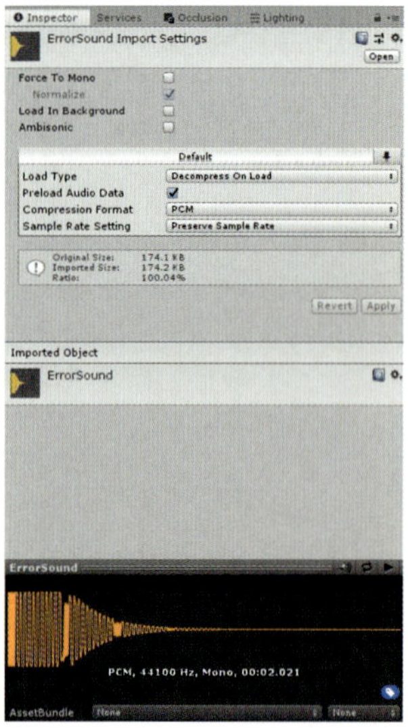

What your sound will look like in the Inspector.

FLOATS

The dynamic floats we can use to alter values on our Audio Mixer are between -80 and 20, with -80 being 0% and 20 being 120%. This means a value of 0 is actually 100% audio, and any further is artificially increasing the audio output of the channel.

This line of code ensures that when this script is placed on an object, an audio source is present. If one isn't present, it will create one for us.

It's almost time to add the code that will fire our sound every three seconds. Before we do so, we need to set up the audio source to accept the sound we want to use. To do this, we're going to store the sound we want into a variable (exposed to the Unity Editor) and tell the AudioSource component to use that variable.

Just above the `void Start()` function, go ahead and add the line `public AudioClip soundToPlay;`. This will create a variable we can set within the Unity editor for use with our script. We also want to store the AudioSource as a variable so we can talk to it a little easier (instead of having to find it every time our code fires, which will be once every three seconds). After the line you've written, add a new line and copy `AudioSource audioSourceToUse;` into your script. You should now have the following:

```
using UnityEngine;
using System.Collections;

[RequireComponent(typeof(AudioSource))]
public class AudioTester: MonoBehaviour
{
    public AudioClip soundToPlay;
    AudioSource audioSourceToUse;
   void Start()
    {
    }
```

Once you've added that line, head into the `void Start()` function and add the line: `audioSourceToUse = GetComponent<AudioSource>();`. This line looks at the object this script is attached to and finds the audio source. We then save the found audio source to the variable we made, so we can talk to it without forgetting who we need to talk to.

All that's left now is to fire the sound every three seconds. To do this, we're going to create another function. For those who haven't understood what a function is yet, just take a look at `void Start()` – the default function that was created when our script file was generated. Create a function called `FireSound` and place it after your `void Start()` function. Your script should now look like this:

```
using System.Collections;
using UnityEngine;

[RequireComponent(typeof(AudioSource))]
public class AudioTester : MonoBehaviour
{
    public AudioClip soundToPlay;
    AudioSource audioSourceToUse;
    void Start()
    {
        audioSourceToUse =
GetComponent<AudioSource>();
    }
    void FireSound()
    {
    }
}
```

Inside your `FireSound` function, adding `audioSourceToUse.PlayOneShot(soundToPlay);` will be enough for our example. This line of code gets the created AudioSource and tells it to play whatever sound file is stored in the `SoundToPlay` variable. All we need to do now is fire the function we've created every three seconds. To do this, head back into the `void Start()` function and add this line of code: `InvokeRepeating("FireSound", 1.0f, 3.0f);`. This is telling Unity that it should fire the function `FireSound` one second after this script is run. After that, it should repeat firing the function every three seconds. Here's how it should look:

```
using System.Collections;
using UnityEngine;
[RequireComponent(typeof(AudioSource))]
public class AudioTester : MonoBehaviour
{
    public AudioClip soundToPlay;
    AudioSource audioSourceToUse;
    void Start()
    {
        audioSourceToUse =
```

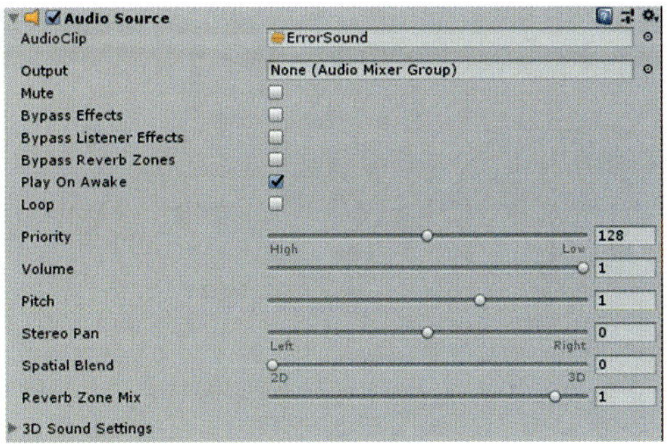

Sounds can be manipulated further once applied to a GameObject.

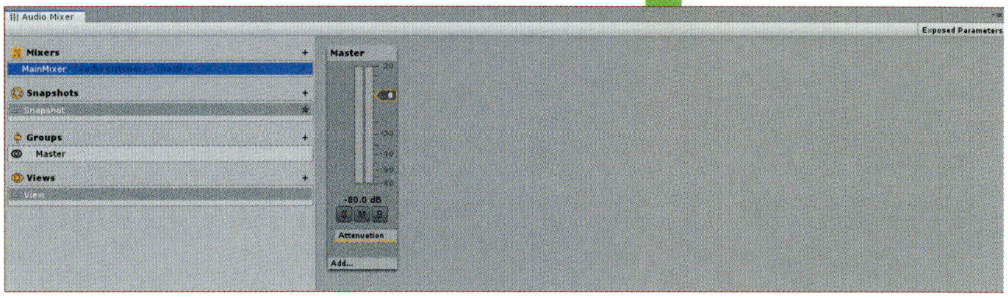

The Audio Mixer tab may look intimidating at first, but it's simple once the basic functions are broken down.

```
GetComponent<AudioSource>();
        InvokeRepeating("FireSound", 1.0f,
3.0f);
    }
    void FireSound()
    {
        audioSourceToUse.
PlayOneShot(soundToPlay);
    }
}
```

We now have a working audio system that we can use to test our sound in-game. Again, this will fire every three seconds. To activate this script, make sure you save the script, and then head back into Unity. Find an object within the scene of your Unity project and drag and drop the script from the content browser. If the object didn't have an AudioSource, you'll see one is generated. All that's left now is to add a sound file into the `audioSourceToUse` variable of your script by pressing the button and selecting your sound and you're ready to test and hear your audio.

Now that we've learned about audio files and how to use them via scripts in Unity, it's time to learn about the audio mixer. Remember we talked about how sounds can be filtered into five categories (Music, Dialog, Effects, UI, and Master)? We can use Unity's audio tools to filter our sounds via said categories, which gives us the power to alter the volume of each element. An audio mixer can also store multiple sounds in one place, so instead of storing and playing audio on objects, you can have one master audio object that drives the audio within your scene.

IN THE MIX

To get started with the audio mixing system, we need to create an Audio Mixer. You can do this by going to Window > Audio Mixer. This will create the Audio Mixer window within your editor. We now want to make a mixer, so move over to the Mixers heading within the Audio Mixer and press the plus sign to do so.

As the Master is the owner of the other mixers – its values directly affect all the others – we need to make some child mixers. Although independent in nature, these will always inherit data and values from their parent, which in our case is the Master mixer. To create these children, head over to the Groups heading and press the + button four times. Name these mixers 'Music', 'Dialogue', 'Effects', and 'UI' respectively. Make sure that these created mixers are only children to the Master mixer and not each other. If you have a child of a child, you can click and drag it in the Groups view to ensure its only parent is Master.

"We can use Unity's audio tools to filter our sounds via categories"

The audio mixer tool is a powerful one, and if we were to go into every facet, we'd be here all day. Instead, I want to focus on getting you started and give you enough breathing room to experiment with the system to gain a deeper understanding of the many features the system contains.

At this point, none of the sounds in our scene will be using the new mixer system we've made, and any changes we make to values here won't be replicated to the audio within our scene. Let's fix that now.

Head into a sound that's in the scene and find the Audio Source properties. There's a section ➜

Scripts can be easily applied to GameObjects in the editor.

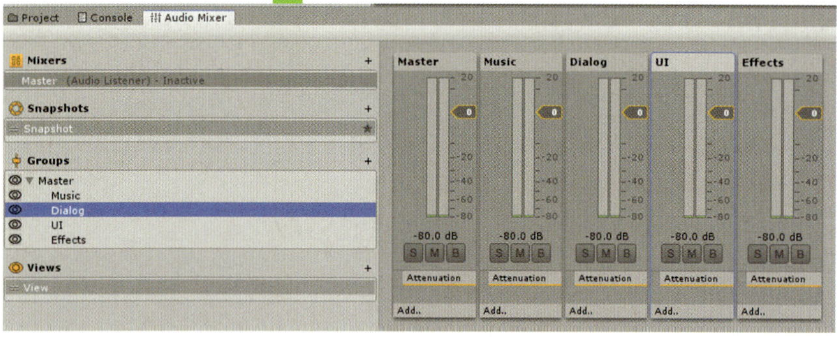

The Audio Mixer can accept multiple different channels, mixers, and dynamic properties. It's a powerful tool for all things audio manipulation.

The Audio Mixer allows you to add all kinds of different effects. Using what we've learned here, you can extend the possibilities of the system through code.

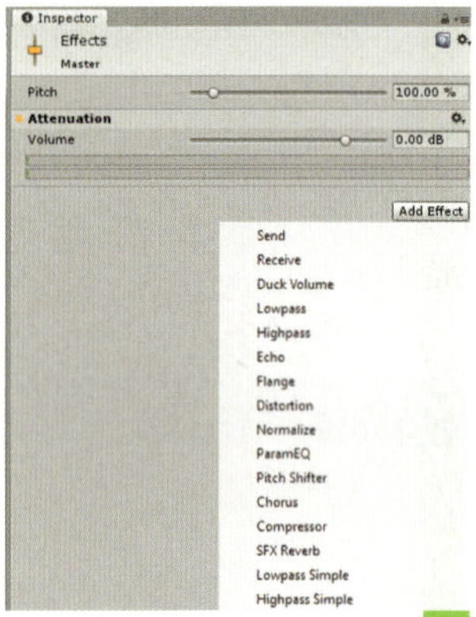

marked 'Output'. Select the circle button next to the 'None (Audio Mixer Group)' box, and select the audio mixer you'd like this sound to play through. Now, if you test your game with the audio mixer open, you'll see that when the audio plays, the audio mixer tied to the audio should react accordingly.

Excellent! Now our audio is being pushed through the audio system, which allows us to monitor each channel separately and make changes to each channel accordingly. For now, we're going to focus on altering the values of our channels through the power of code to gain a deeper understanding of this system.

STICK TO THE SCRIPT

We need a new script file for our Audio Mixer script; create one and call it **MixerTest.cs**. Now open it up in your IDE. We need a variable to store the Audio Mixer, which can be created by adding the line `public AudioMixer mixerToUse` just inside the class. This touches on the same ground we covered earlier; putting this after the class header tells the class we want this variable to be a part of it, while putting 'public' before the variable tells Unity we want this exposed to the editor.

You may notice that your IDE is complaining about not being able to find any class called AudioMixer. This is because we haven't included the code to tell our IDE where to learn about this class. To fix this, head to the top of the code file, where you'll see `using UnityEngine;` on a new line, add `Using UnityEngine.Audio;` to include access to the audio code within this script. Here's how it should look:

```
using System.Collections;
using UnityEngine;
using UnityEngine.Audio;

public class MixerTest : MonoBehaviour
{
    public AudioMixer mixerToUse;

    void Start()
    {
    }
}
```

We now have a variable storing our AudioMixer – but we're not currently doing anything with the variable. Let's add some functionality into the `void Start()` function so our code fires when this script is executed. Inside the function, the line `mixerToUse.SetFloat("currentVolumeForFX", -10.0f);` will find a parameter called `currentVolumeForFX` and set it to -10.0; notice the use of quotation marks and the `f` within the line of code. The quotation marks around `"currentVolumeForFX"` tell the code that this is the text to look for, and to treat what's inside the quotations as literal text. The `f` tells unity that what we're giving it here is a float and not an integer.

```
using System.Collections;
using UnityEngine;
using UnityEngine.Audio;

public class MixerTest : MonoBehaviour
{
```

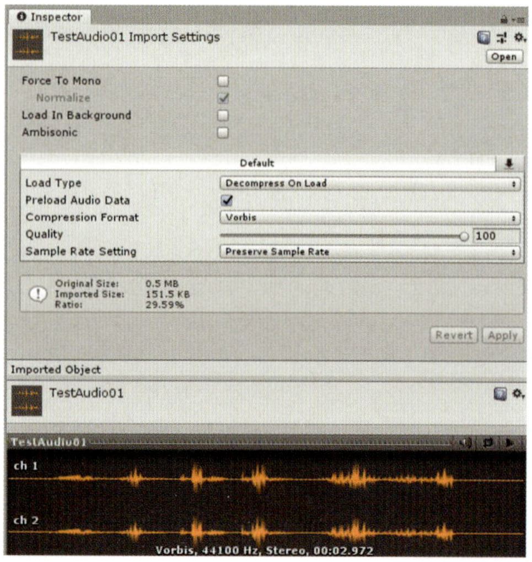

The Properties panel for your imported audio has a number of settings that you can use to change various properties, such as looping, blend time, and timing.

In scripts within Unity, marking variables as Public exposes them to the editor window – allowing you to dynamically set variables inside the editor instead of through code.

```
    public AudioMixer mixerToUse;

    void Start()
    {
        mixerToUse.
SetFloat("currentVolumeForFX", -10.0f);
    }
}
```

With the skills we've learned here, we can now start adding sound effects to our shooter.

The code's now complete, but it won't currently fire. We still have a few steps to take before this code will successfully execute; first, we need to add this script to an object within a scene. We then need to set the correct audio mixer. But, most importantly, we need to add the `currentVolumeForFX` variable to our mixer.

Make sure your code is saved and, once you're happy, close the IDE and head back into Unity. You can put the script on anything in your scene, so I'll put mine on the MainCamera, just as a test and in the same place I put the test script for our audio earlier. Remember, to do this, you can select the object in the scene hierarchy, scroll down in the properties to an empty space, and drag the script in from the content browser. Our script now shows up on the object you've placed it on, and it has an empty variable. Go ahead and feed in the Audio Mixer we set up earlier (which should be titled 'Master'). Finally, we need to set up the 'currentVolumeForFX' link within our AudioMixer.

Head back into the AudioMixer and select the group that you want to adjust the volume for. In my case, it's the 'Effects' group. Go ahead and select the one you need by left-clicking it either in the 'Groups' drop-down or in the rack. You'll notice the properties page opens up on the far right of your screen. There should be a single effect currently applied to your audio group: Attenuation. The simplest (albeit not scientific) way to think of attenuation in this case is volume – which is exactly what we're looking for. There's some empty space with the Attenuation area of the properties window in the section marked 'Volume', between the title and the scrollbar. Right-click in this area and select 'Expose Volume (of XX) to script'. Now head back to the AudioMixer window. If you look carefully in the top-right of this window, you'll see a section marked, 'Exposed Parameters (1)'. If you're not seeing the '(1)' at the end of the text, it means you've not set up the parameter correctly.

"You should now feel comfortable adding audio to your scenes"

When you have the correct text, left-click this button and find the parameter we created. All we have to do now is right-click the parameter within this menu and select 'Rename'. This needs to be the same name as in our code, which in my case is 'currentVolumeForFX'.

If you've followed everything correctly, when you test your scene, any audio that is a child of the AudioMixer group with an exposed parameter will have its volume changed accordingly. You can even see the changes live if you have the Audio Mixer open when testing the scene.

Audio is such a massive subject within Unity, and we've only just scratched the surface. From what you've learned, you should now feel comfortable adding audio to your scenes, and be able to adjust their properties and effects accordingly. Using your new knowledge, you should be able to create such atmospheric effects as an echo in large, empty spaces, or distorted sounds when the player swims underwater, and lots more besides.

Additional mechanics

Customise your shooter experience with these optional mechanics

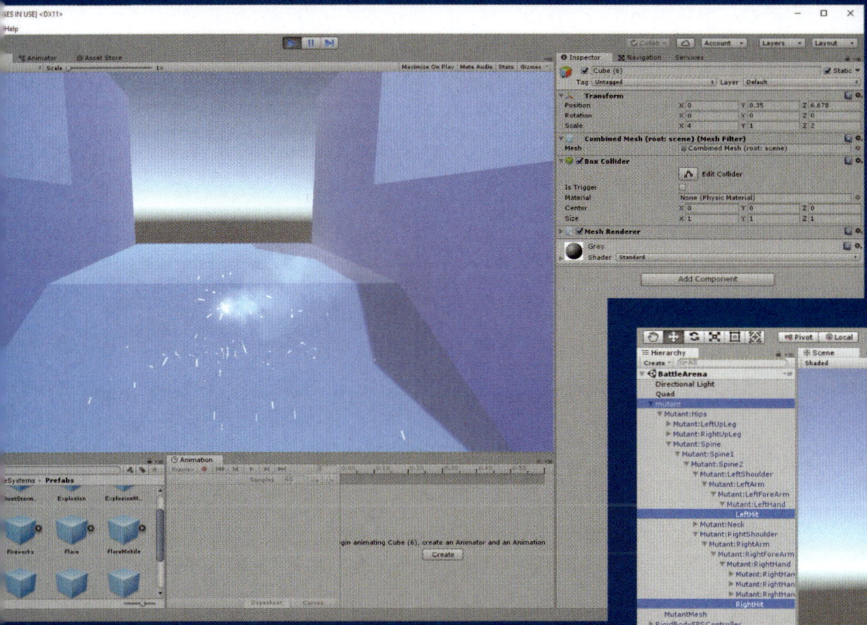

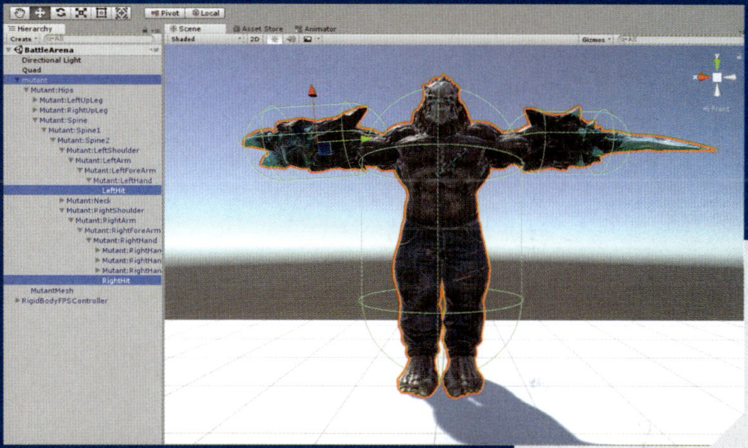

Add mission markers, extra player abilities, and even a boss battle with our additional mechanics.

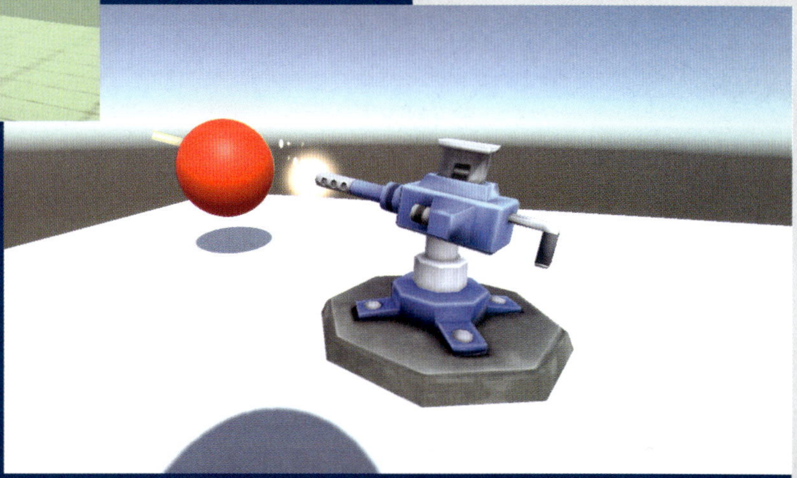

Creating a mission marker in Unity

Guide players through your game with a simple mission marker. Stuart shows you how to set one up

AUTHOR
STUART FRASER

Stuart is a former designer and developer of high-profile games such as *RollerCoaster Tycoon 3*, and also worked as a lecturer of games development.

In this tutorial, we're going to look at adding a mission or objective marker: this will point towards a specific goal and let the player know the direction they must go in. This is used in all sorts of game genres, and there are various ways that it can be presented. In our case, we'll make a simple arrow that rotates to point towards the next goal, and it will also display an approximate distance to that location. Also, we'll make the marker fade when you're very close and can see the objective, so we stop cluttering the player's view.

We can go ahead and open our first-person character project. Once complete, we will make a new scene for us to test-prototype this mechanic by selecting File > New Scene from the toolbar. Firstly, we should delete the Main Camera object as we are going to replace this with our player camera. We will then add our Player prefab from the Project panel into our Hierarchy view. Then we can make a simple floor by selecting GameObject > 3D Object > Plane from the toolbar. You may need to use the transform tools in the Scene viewport to adjust your FPS Character to be above the landscape.

Next, we need to add our UI elements, and we also need to create or download an arrow texture. At this stage, we can use a simple

^ You don't have to guide the player with arrows: *Shadow of the Colossus* ingeniously let players find their next objective with the glint of their sword.

arrow that points upwards and ideally has a transparent background; I suggest saving using the PNG format. Once done with creating the arrow, you will need to simply drag the image into your Project window and then select it so we can set some parameters. We need to make sure that in the Inspector for this new arrow texture, we set the Texture Type to sprite and select Apply. You should see a preview of the arrow on a chequered background to indicate it is transparent.

The next thing to do is go to an empty area of our Hierarchy panel and right-click, then select UI > Canvas. Next, we need to select the Canvas object in the Hierarchy and then right-click and select UI > Image. If we now select the Image object that we added and move to the Inspector, we can see the image script. Select the circle icon to the right of where it says Source Image; this will open a new window in which we can select our arrow image. If we are successful, the arrow will appear in the centre of the screen.

"We'll make a simple arrow that rotates to point towards the next goal"

WAY TO GO

We also need to add a text object so we can display how far away from the goal or target the player is. Select the Canvas in our Hierarchy and then right-click and choose UI > Text to add it to our Canvas. The first thing you may notice is that the text appears offset and is also covering our arrow; we can simply double-click the Text object in the Hierarchy and use the Unity transform tools to move it down in the Y direction in the Scene viewport. We can also fix the alignment by going to the Inspector and using the Alignment options to centre the text – these are under the Paragraph heading for our Text component.

The next thing we want to do is add the script – we will do this now, as this script will attach to our Image object and not the player, ➔

^ We've used a plain arrow for this tutorial, but you could create a more stylish one for your own game.

v You should be at the point where the arrow will be correctly rendering to the screen. Don't worry that the canvas is much larger than your player – this is expected.

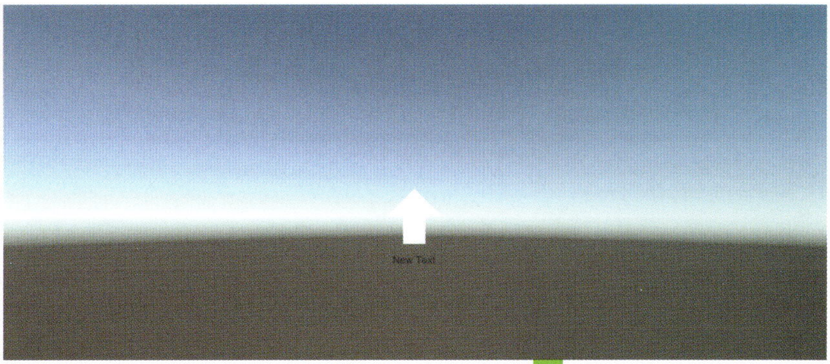

Mission markers are handy for showing objectives, but also consider giving players the option to turn them off, as Arkane did with its shooter, *Prey*.

The alignment tools work like a text alignment tool in any word-processing software. All you need to do is select the option below to centre your text, so it no longer appears offset.

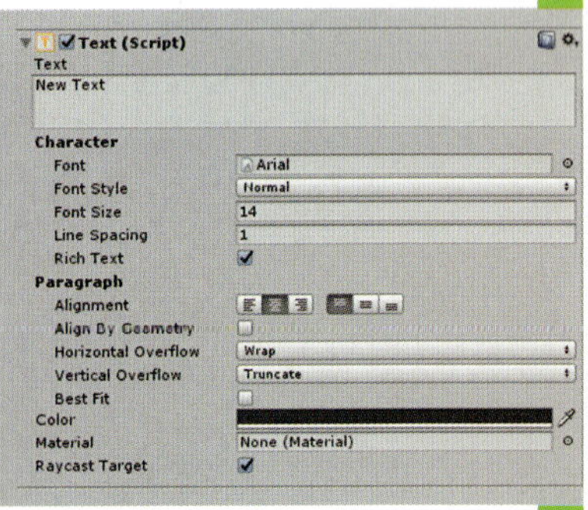

so make sure we are still selecting the Image object. We want to select Add Component from our Inspector and then select New Script and type ObjectiveMarker as the Name and then select Create and Add. We are ready to double-click this new script and open it in a script editor, then we can add the following code.

```
using UnityEngine;
using UnityEngine.UI;

public class ObjectiveMarker : MonoBehaviour
{
    public Transform target;
    public Text display;
    public float distance = 3f;
    public float fadeTime = 0.3f;
    private float angle;
    private RectTransform rectTransform;
    private GameObject player;
    private Image img;

    // Start is called before the first frame
update
    void Start()
    {
        rectTransform =
GetComponent<RectTransform>();
        player = GameObject.FindGameObjectWit
hTag("MainCamera");
        img = GetComponent<Image>();
    }

    // Update is called once per frame
    void Update()
    {
        float currentDist;
        transform.LookAt(target);
        //When we have a target, rotate our
arrow to its approx direction.
        if (target != null)
        {
            Vector3 relative = player.
transform.InverseTransformPoint(target.
position);
            angle = Mathf.Atan2(relative.x,
relative.z) * Mathf.Rad2Deg;
            //Fixes the fact that we want
to rotate the arrow clockwise and not anti-
clockwise.
            angle *= -1;
        }
        //Sets the rotation for our visual
arrow.
        rectTransform.transform.eulerAngles =
new Vector3(0, 0, angle);
```

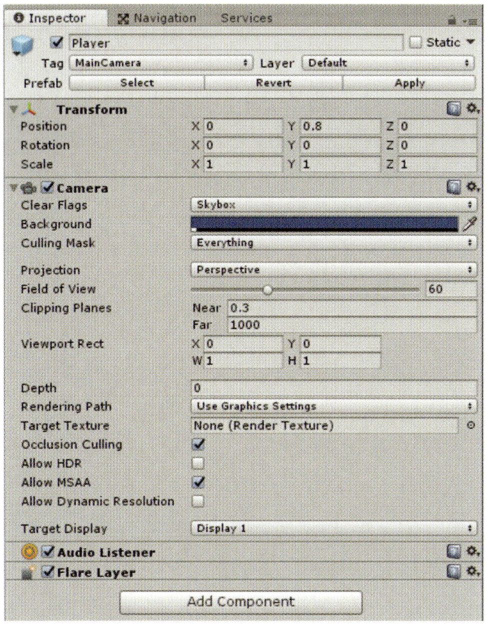

It's vital to set the premade tag of MainCamera on our game object that has the Camera component. The above script uses this to reference our player position against the position of the objective.

```
        //Find the distance from the player.
        currentDist = Vector3.
Distance(player.transform.position, target.
transform.position);
        //Display the distance in meters.
        if (display != null)
            display.text = (Mathf.
Round(currentDist * 10f) / 10f).ToString() +
" Meters";
        //If we are looking at the target and
in X meters of the target.
        //We will fade off the arrow so it
doesn't clutter the screen.
        if (angle <= 30 && angle >= -30 &&
currentDist < distance)
        {
            img.CrossFadeAlpha(0, fadeTime,
false);
            if(display!=null)display.
CrossFadeAlpha(0, fadeTime, false);
        }
        else
        {
            img.CrossFadeAlpha(1, fadeTime,
false);
            if (display != null)display.
CrossFadeAlpha(1, fadeTime, false);
        }
    }
}
```

FLYING ARROWS

There are various tools out there for creating your arrow; some are paid, and some are free. Take some time to research your options and see what other developers recommend. If you enjoy the more artistic side of development, you can always spend time theming your arrow and being more creative with it than the ones presented here.

"We want to select Add Component from our Inspector and then select New Script"

We can save this and then return to Unity; the actual base script is now usable, apart from we need to give it three frames of reference so it knows about the player, the objective, and can display the distance correctly.

First, we will look at the FPS Character, more specifically the camera it uses. You will need to find your FPS character and expand it so you can see the sub-objects. You should see an object that has a camera component attached; in this case, make sure that the Tag in its ➔

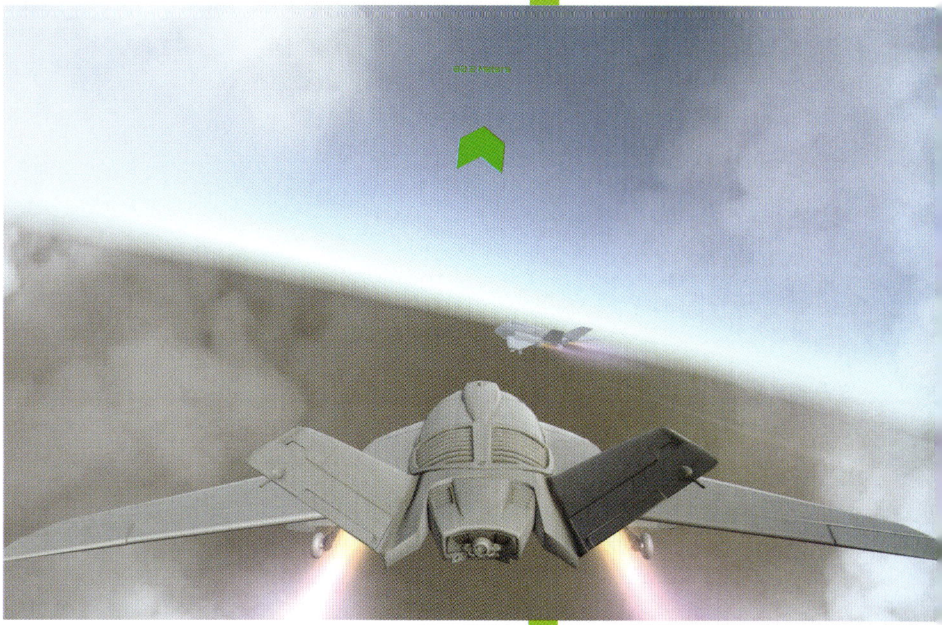

You can always reuse this in another project; imagine you need to highlight targets for a flight combat game.

^ The marker shows the player which direction the exit is – though they'll have to get past the zombies before they can reach it.

Inspector is set to the Main Camera. In the case that it hasn't been set, simply use the drop-down to set it correctly.

We will then need to link our objective; at the moment we don't even have an object to represent it. So, from the Unity toolbar, select GameObject > 3D Object, choose the Cube, and place it somewhere in your test level. With that done, we can select the Image object we made earlier and then look for our script in the Inspector. The next stage requires you to drag the game object we just added in the Hierarchy on the slot of the Target variable in our attached script. While we are here, we should also drag the Text object we made earlier into the Display parameter on the script. This effectively tells the script that this is the element we want to draw our text to, so it's important to remember to do it.

"There are other ways you can present the marker and make it your own"

SNEAK PREVIEW

With that all complete, we can preview the game in Unity by selecting the Play button from the toolbar. We should see the arrow rotate to the position of our target object. As we get closer to the object and it remains in view, we should see that the arrow will fade off as we don't need it any more. We should also see the distance to the target displayed in metres – this should update correctly as we move around.

Let's say we wanted to have the player navigate to this point as an exit to your level. We have previously looked at loading up our scenes based on if we click the Start button on our main menu. We can do the same when we touch the Cube object. Firstly, we should save this as a new scene before we make any further changes. Next, select the Cube in the Hierarchy and then, in the Inspector, expand the Box Collider component; check the Is Trigger option. While still in the Inspector, select Add Component, then select New Script and name this LoadScene, and Create and Add. Once we have that set up, we need to open our script and add the code below.

```
using UnityEngine;
using UnityEngine.SceneManagement;

public class LoadScene : MonoBehaviour
{
    public int sceneId;

    public void OnTriggerEnter(Collider
```

PLACEMENT

You can move the arrow to a more suitable location rather than having it remaining central to the screen. Do your research and find out what works for other games and what feels best for your situation.

v Once we have reordered the build list, we can set the index of the scene from our scene list. This will then be the level that we load up next.

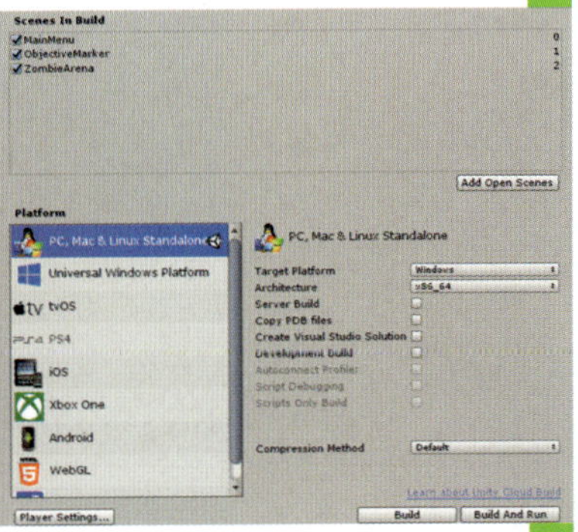

^ *Payday 2* shows enemy alerts and has similar directional arrows to show information about where threats are coming from.

```
other)
    {
        if (other.CompareTag("Player"))
        {
            SceneManager.LoadScene(sceneId);
        }
    }
}
```

Save it and return to the editor; we are going to make some changes to our build settings. We need to select File > Build Settings... in the Toolbar and then select Add Open Scenes to add this scene to the list. Let's suppose we want to load to our main menu – we would just load this scene and then our zombie area. We need to move our current scene to be above the zombie arena. Note the numbers to the right-hand side of the list: you should see the zombie area will have the id value of 2; this will be useful shortly.

Once we have that done, close these settings and select the Cube in the Hierarchy; in the Inspector, we can see the script we added. At the moment, the Scene Id is wrong – it's set to 0, which is our main menu. We need to change this number to be 2 as this is the value of the id for our zombie arena scene. We need to make sure we save this scene again, so that the new id is remembered. We can preview our loading script by pressing the Play button on the Toolbar – you should now be able to trigger the level transition. It's pretty easy to see how we could build out our level and use the objective marker to guide the player to a destination.

There are certainly other ways you can present the marker, and there's room to make it your own; for instance, you might want the arrow to be more dynamic to your screen rather than moving around an axis. But for now, this is a great way of displaying information to the player and guiding what they need to do next.

ON TARGET

In our example, the target isn't very exciting or dynamic, but this is purely for testing that our marker works. Imagine the wide variety of goals you might have in your game; there could be many ways to use this marker to help highlight key quests and awesome rewards to your player.

^ *Dishonored 2* kept its mission markers and on-screen info tastefully minimal.

Adding a minimap to your Unity game

Players can spot the location of enemies and more with a minimap. Here's how to make one

AUTHOR
STUART FRASER
Stuart is a former designer and developer of high-profile games such as *RollerCoaster Tycoon 3*, and also worked as a lecturer of games development.

We're now going to look at how we can add a minimap to our first-person shooter. Minimaps have appeared in all kinds of video games, from *Halo* to *World of Warcraft*, and have stood the test of time in terms of notable (and useful) UI features. They can highlight specific information to the player, from important mission goals to the location of any enemies in the player's proximity. There are several ways to add a functional minimap to your game, but we're going to look at a relatively cheap and efficient way to add this to any game. We can also achieve this without needing to use any C# scripts.

The *Halo* minimap is useful for finding enemies, but has a clever and rewarding mechanic, in that it only highlights them if they are making excessive noise or already visible to the player.

The first thing we need to do is open our first-person character project. We can use the main first-person level where we added the zombie enemies, as we can easily add our minimap into the scene without any major changes or additional coding. You should also have the player and the enemy prefabs we already created as part of implementing our initial project. This is great, as we can just adjust these and save the changes and we should be good to go.

SETTING UP THE MINIMAP

Our initial step towards setting up our minimap is to draw icons for the positions of our player and any other objects we wish to highlight on the map. To achieve this, we're going to use another camera that is placed above our player. We select the Player object in the Hierarchy and right-click, and then select the Camera object. You should see an additional camera preview in the Scene viewport, but for what we need next, it's the completely wrong orientation and position.

First, in the Inspector, we need to set the rotation for X to 90, then set our Y position to 10. We also need to set the drop-down option for Projection to Orthographic.

With that done, we also want to add our player icon that will appear on the minimap. So, what we need to do is select the main Player object in the Hierarchy view, then right-click

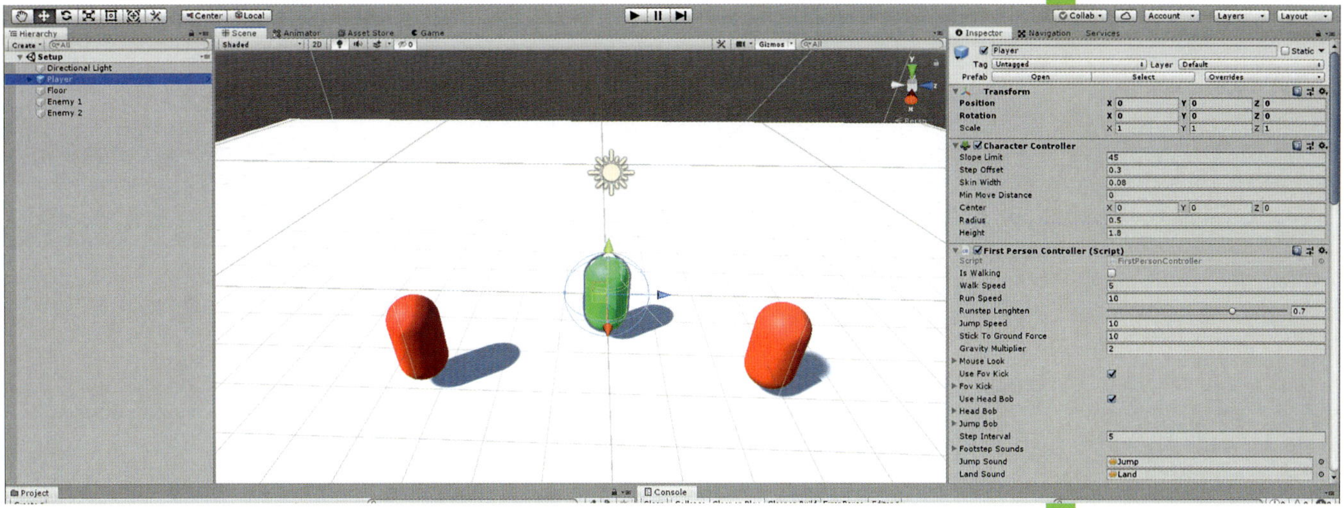

We already have a basic level where we spawn enemies for displaying on the minimap. Now we're ready for implementation.

and select Create Empty. Select this new empty object and move to the Inspector panel.

In the Inspector, we can name this as 'Player Icon' and then we need to select Add Component > Rendering > Sprite Renderer. Once added, select the Sprite entry to open the Select Sprite window and select the Knob sprite image. I would also set the Color value to a green hue. Finally, we should set the value for the X rotation to 90 and the X, Y Scale values to 4. In the preview for the camera added, you may be able to see the icon, but it will be clipping with the player capsule – this will be fixed later. We need to apply our current changes, so we must select the Player object in the Hierarchy, and in the Inspector select Overrides and Apply All.

Next up, we'll find our Zombie prefab in the Project panel, and in the Inspector, select Open Prefab. We can then simply right-click and select Create Empty to create an empty object. As before, we select this and in our Inspector we're going to name this 'Enemy Icon'. We're then going to repeat the process of adding our Sprite Renderer and then our Knob sprite image. In terms of the colour of the sprite, this time I would go with a red, and we need to set our rotation and scale as with the ones above for our Player Icon. We can then select the back icon next to the Zombie text in the Hierarchy to return the objects in our main scene.

RENDERING OUR MINIMAP

The next thing to focus on is rendering our minimap to our screen somehow. We're going to use a render texture; in effect, this can be used to render what is usually rendered to our camera viewport to a texture which can be placed anywhere in the game world. This method can also be used to create a mirror or portal to another location. To create this render texture, we need to right-click in our Project window and select Create > Custom Render Texture and this should then appear. I would take time to rename this as 'Minimap' so we know what it will be used for.

"We're going to look at a relatively efficient way to add this to any game"

We now need to find the camera we created which points top-down onto our player character. Simply drag the render texture to the Target Texture slot on the Camera component. Next, we want to use our Render Texture in the game and show it somewhere on the UI, so we need to create this. We already have a canvas ➜

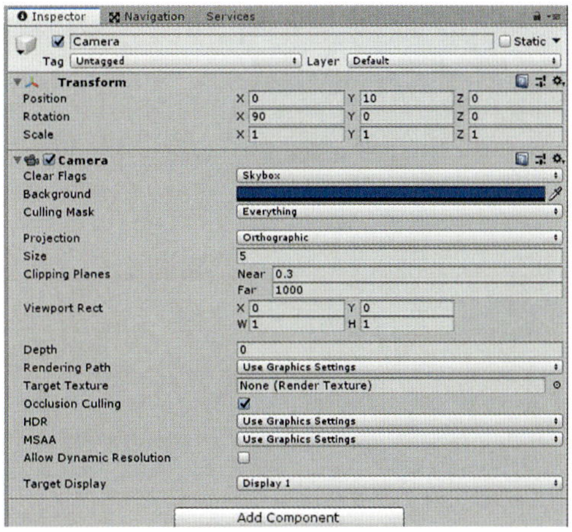

With our additional camera added, and a few quick tweaks, you can already see how this can be used to draw our minimap viewpoint.

MASKS

By setting what we can and cannot see in the Culling Mask, we can choose what appears to the player in either their view or what is shown on the minimap.

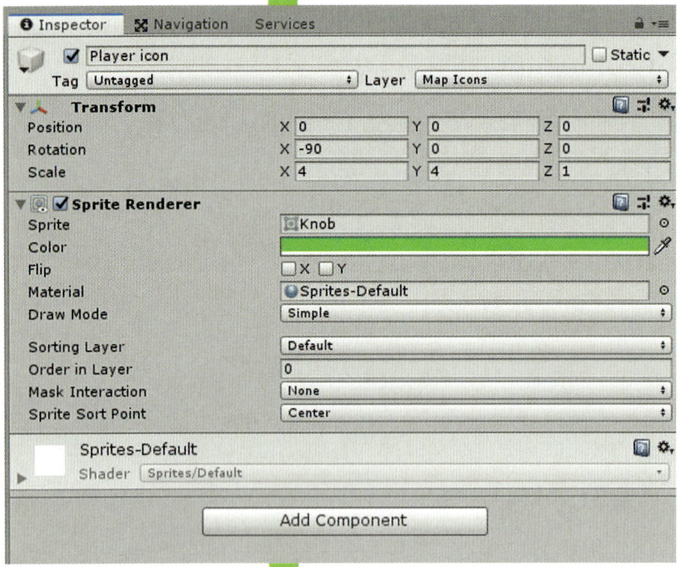

^ We should make sure to correctly orientate the rotation of our minimap sprites so that they're seen by our overhead camera.

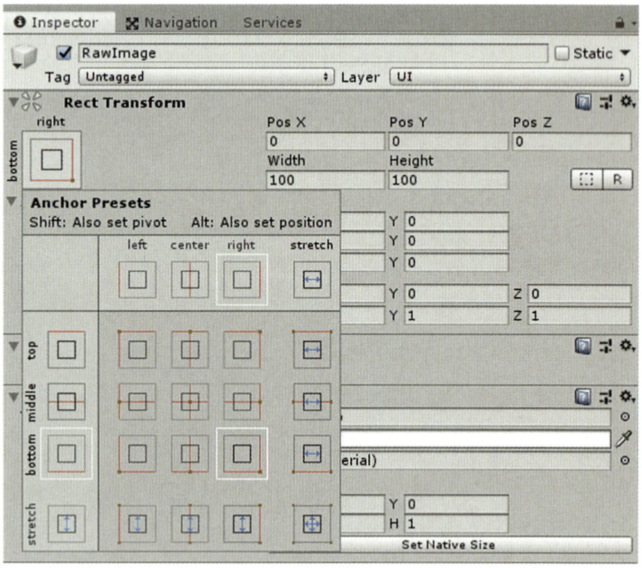

^ The anchor presets allow us to quickly align our Canvas elements to various positions on the screen. Perfect for trying our various UI configurations.

object to render our player health, so we can select this in the Hierarchy. We need something to render the texture on; so, with the Canvas still selected, right-click and select UI > RawImage.

You may have noticed that a white box appears in your camera view on the Game preview. We don't want a minimap in the centre of the screen, so we can simply fix this by keeping the Image object selected and heading to our Inspector. We can now look at adjusting the position of the image by changing values in the Rect Transform.

> **"The red circles that represent the enemies appear on the minimap"**

The easiest way to do this is to use the Anchor Presets; we used this before, and it looks like a target with a red circle in it. If we select it, we can then click the icon that corresponds to the bottom-right of the matrix you're presented with. You should repeat that action, but with the **SHIFT** key held down to make the pivot also adhere to the bottom-right of the screen. Next, we want to set our Pos X to -5 and Pos Y to 5 to add a buffer between the map and the edge of our screen. At this point, you should see that the white texture appears in the bottom-right corner with some padding.

We can now drag the Minimap that is our Render Texture to the Texture slot on our Raw Image component. You should see what looks like the view from the secondary camera we set up appear. While this is great, it doesn't show our icons and doesn't come across as a traditional minimap. To fix that, we'll use Layers. To set these up, we'll create a new layer for our camera to use. We can do this by selecting the Layer drop-down on the Inspector and then selecting Add Layer... from the options.

You should now be shown the layers that are already in use for this project. If we select an empty entry, we can then type in a new layer name of 'Map Icons'. We're going to have to adjust both cameras as part of our setup. First, we need to find the camera that has the tag 'Main Camera' in the Hierarchy panel. In most cases, this is going to be the camera that our player uses to look around the game world. We'll then look in the Inspector for this camera and select the Culling Mask. In there, you should see the Map Icons layer. Deselect it.

Next, select the top-down camera we added for the minimap. In the Inspector, we first want to select Nothing as our Culling Mask, then reselect the Culling Mask and choose our Map Icons layer. The final task is to select our Player Icon and the Enemy Icon we created

PREFABS

An important element we should have set up during the initial development was to create our Player object as a Prefab. You should see your Player object in the Project panel. If this isn't the case, you can easily open the original scene and drag the Player object from the Hierarchy to the Project panel to achieve this.

v The render texture will allow us to draw what our top-down camera sees. We can then apply this to any mesh or surface in the game.

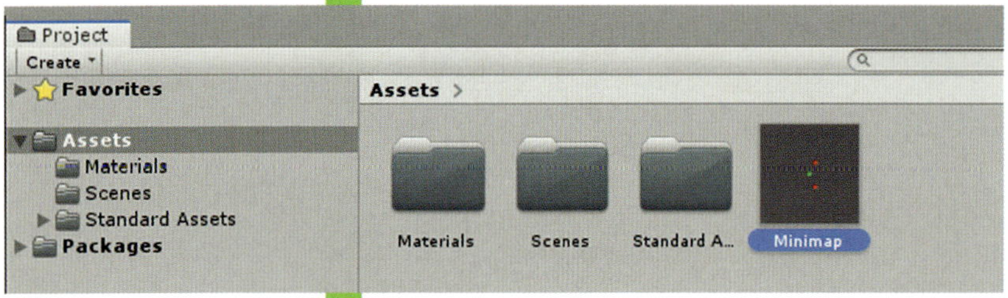

The minimap is now being rendered to our UI and we can start seeing the enemy position markers correctly displayed on it.

ANCHORS

We can use the anchors to adjust where the minimap or any canvas UI element will appear. Feel free to try an alternative position to have your minimap display in.

and set their Layer drop-down to Map Icons in the Inspector. You may have to go through the process from earlier to modify the Zombie prefab. With that, we should be able to select the Play button and preview our game. Notice as you walk around that the red circles that represent the enemies appear on the minimap. Once you are happy, we can select the Play button again to end the preview.

You may notice the minimap has a very narrow field of view of where the enemies are; this could do with widening. To fix this, we're going to increase the size of the viewport. This is very simple: all we need to do is select the top-down camera we made in our Hierarchy. We can then look at the Camera component in the Inspector and change the Size parameter from 5 to 12. You may notice the displayed icons are too small; to fix this, increase the X & Y scale values from 4 to 6. Once you're happy, it's a good idea to select the Player and make sure to apply all the prefab changes.

While we're here, we will make the minimap render look more like a compass. This is going to be extremely crude, but we can always improve it by making a bespoke texture. For now, we're going to select the Canvas in the Hierarchy, right-click, and select UI > Image. With this selected, in the Inspector we need to select the Knob sprite again as our Source Image. We also need to select Add Component and then select UI > Mask. We need to set our Anchor position to the bottom-right; remember to do this once to set the position, and again with the **SHIFT** key held to move the pivot. We also need to repeat the values for the Pos X and Pos Y, setting them to -5 and 5 respectively. Finally, we want to drag our RawImage object onto this new Image object so that it's a child of it. We should see this update, so we have a basic circular look to the map to emulate a typical minimap design.

We can then preview our changes by selecting the Play button; this feels a bit better and allows us to see more of the playing area. It all depends on the game you're creating, though. Now we've developed this basic minimap, we can think about improvements like additional theming, adding more visualisation for the architecture of the level, or even adding a fog of war effect to limit how much we can see on the map. It's time for your imagination to run wild and come up with some creative solutions to achieve these.

WARNINGS

If you're seeing warnings about multiple audio listeners, then look at your cameras; you can remove all other listeners that aren't attached to your Main Camera.

We now have more visibility on the minimap and can see enemies at a greater distance, as well as something that looks more like a recognisable map shape.

RPG games like *Divinity: Original Sin 2* have minimaps that hide the path ahead with a 'fog of war' effect. Have a look at shader programming to efficiently achieve this effect.

Creating a deployable gun turret in Unity

Help the player fend off relentless waves of enemies with a special auto-firing weapon

AUTHOR
STUART FRASER

Stuart is a former designer and developer of high-profile games such as *RollerCoaster Tycoon 3*, and also worked as a lecturer of games development.

You can download a package and import it into the project you're developing at any time. This gives you access to assets and tools that help speed up the development process.

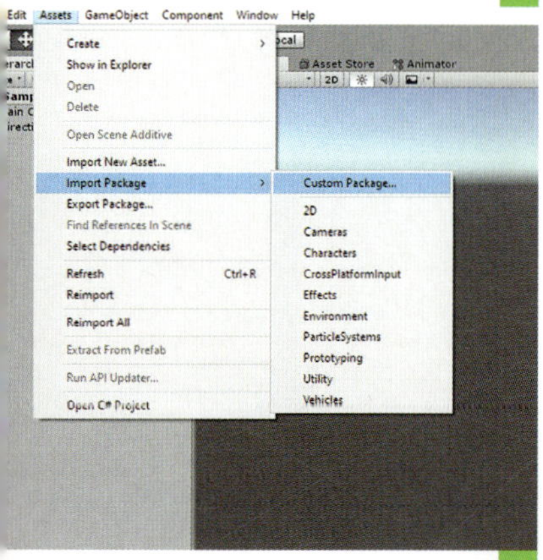

We're going to make our own deployable turret that will fire for us when it's set down, similar to the ones used by Roland in *Borderlands* and Torbjörn in *Overwatch*. We'll use a hitscan method to determine if an enemy takes damage; hitscan has been used in shooters since the original *Doom*, and means that a shot from our turret will instantly hit its target (you can find out more about this subject on page 128).

BUILD THE TURRET

We can open the first-person shooter project we've already created and modify this to include our deployable turret. While we're prototyping this new mechanic, I would develop this in a new scene. We can simply select File > New Scene from the toolbar and then delete the Main Camera. Next, we can simply drag in the Player from the Project panel and we should have our playable character ready to go.

We then need to find a suitable mesh to represent the turret; luckily, Unity has provided an ideal asset in one of its packs on the Unity Store. We are going to use assets from the 'Tower Defense Template' which Unity provides for free. I've created a new package that only includes the assets we need, to make it a bit easier to organise.

Download this asset package from **wfmag.cc/fps-turret**. In the Unity editor, select Assets > Import Package > Custom Package... and locate the MachineGunTower1.unitypackage from your Downloads folder. You can import everything, but you don't really need to include

In *Overwatch*, one of Torbjörn's abilities is his deployable turret, which can track the enemy team.

the scene file provided. We also need to add a simple floor by selecting GameObject > 3D Object > Plane. Feel free to adjust the position of your Player prefab so it's not clipping into the ground. You could also scale up the floor to give yourself some more room for testing the mechanic.

We want the turret to fire at a target when we deploy it, so we're going to add an object for testing this feature. In the Unity toolbar, select GameObject > 3D Object > Sphere and place it somewhere in the level. We need to make sure this is tagged suitably, so select the Sphere in the Hierarchy; then, in the Inspector select the Tag drop-down and pick Add Tag... to create a new tag. We'll then select the + icon and set the New Tag Name as Target for testing purposes, and then save it. We also need to make sure the Target tag is applied from the Tag drop-down, as it's not applied by default. This is achieved by reselecting the Sphere in the Hierarchy and then changing the drop-down in the Inspector.

Next, we're going to add a script to our turret so that it tracks various targets; we'll also have it spawn a particle effect and play a sound to indicate when it's active and shooting. This will also contain an event that we can use to track damage on the target. To get started, we need to expand Prefabs > Towers > MachineGun from the Project panel, and select the MachineGunTower_1 prefab, then drag it into the Hierarchy panel. Next, from the Hierarchy, we expand the MachineGunTower_1 prefab and select the Turret_MachineGun_L02 sub-object. With this selected, click on Add Component in the Inspector and select New Script, add the name TurretBehaviour, and then select Create and Add.

We then double-click the new script and open it in our script editor to begin writing our code, as displayed below:

```
using UnityEngine;
using System.Collections;
using System.Collections.Generic;

public class TurretBehaviour : MonoBehaviour
{
    public ParticleSystem particleFX;
    public AudioClip soundFX;
    public float damageAmount = 10;
    private AudioSource audioSource;
    private GameObject target;
    private bool lookingAt;


    void Start()
    {
        StartCoroutine(Fire());
        audioSource =
GetComponent<AudioSource>();
        if (soundFX && audioSource)
        {
            audioSource.clip = soundFX;
        }
        else
        {
```

PARTICLE COLLISIONS

You might notice that the turret particle effect will travel through the wall. A way to fix this is to select the Tracer child object in the MachineGunTower prefab and enable Collision for that Particle System. We will also need to set the following parameter values: Type should be set to World, and Lifetime Loss to 1.

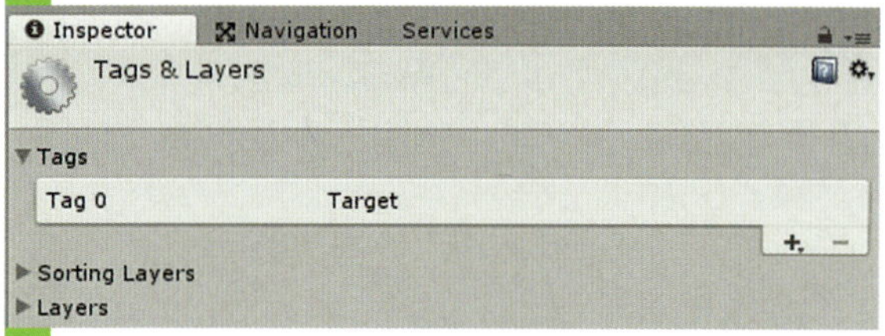

> Make sure that you've created your tag and also assigned it to the objects you want to be targeted by the turret.

```
            Debug.LogWarning("No audio source
and/or effect assigned.");
            return;
        }
    }


    public GameObject FindClosestEnemy()
    {
        GameObject[] gos;
        gos = GameObject.FindGameObjectsWithTa
g("Target");
        GameObject closest = null;
        float distance = Mathf.Infinity;
        Vector3 position = transform.position;
        foreach (GameObject go in gos)
        {
            Vector3 diff = go.transform.
position - position;
            float curDistance = diff.
sqrMagnitude;
            if (curDistance < distance)
            {
                closest = go;
                distance = curDistance;
            }
        }
        return closest;
    }


    void Update()
    {
        target = FindClosestEnemy();
        Vector3 fwd = transform.
TransformDirection(Vector3.forward);
        RaycastHit hit;
        Vector3 targetDir;
        // Rotate the camera every frame so it
keeps looking at the target
        if (target != null)
        {
            targetDir = target.transform.
position - transform.position;
            float step = 2 * Time.deltaTime;
            Vector3 newDir = Vector3.
RotateTowards(fwd, targetDir, step, 0.0f);
            transform.rotation = Quaternion.
LookRotation(newDir);
            if (Physics.Raycast(transform.
position, fwd, out hit))
            {
                Debug.DrawRay(transform.
position, fwd * 20, Color.green);
                if (hit.collider.tag ==
"Target")
                {
                    lookingAt = true;
                }
                else
                {
                    lookingAt = false;
                }
            }
        }
        else
        {
            lookingAt = false;
        }
    }


    IEnumerator Fire()
    {
        while (true)
        {
            yield return new
WaitForSeconds(0.5f);
            //Firing effect and damage will
only occur if the target can be seen.
            if (lookingAt)
            {
                //Play the particle effect.
                if (particleFX != null)
                {
                    particleFX.Play();
                }
                //Play our firing audio
effect.
                if (audioSource && soundFX)
                {
                    audioSource.Play();
                }
```

SOUND EFFECTS

Unity provides a weapon placement sound with the turret asset, which we could easily use as an audio cue when we deploy the gun in our game. For this, we can use the same audio source and audio clip code in our turret script, but remember to make sure to attach an audio source component.

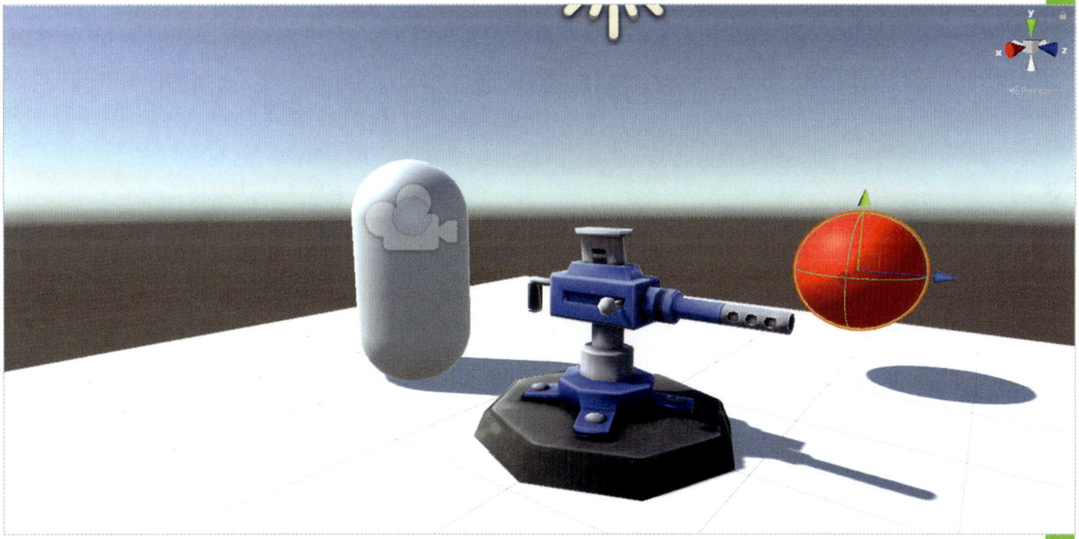

We can start throwing together a test area for the turret, bringing in our shooter character and some other assets to represent our enemies.

```
            //Apply damage to the target
via send message function.
            target.transform.
SendMessage("ApplyDamage", damageAmount);
         }
         yield return null;
      }
   }
}
```

Save your script and return to the editor. We're almost ready to preview the turret behaviour, but first we have a few options that we can set on the above script. In the Inspector, you will see two new entries for Particle FX and Sound FX. To assign something to these, you'll need to click the little circle to the right-hand side of the parameter names. First, we'll assign the MachineGunLvl2Effect child to the Particle FX entry. Next, we'll add the MG 1 sound effect under the Assets tab to the Sound FX entry. We also need to select Add Component and select Audio > Audio Source so the audio clip will have a source to play from.

We can then select the Play button on the toolbar to preview the turret behaviour in the Game window. You can try several different things that the above code supports; such as, if you have two or more targets, the gun will only aim for the closest. It will also not send a damage message if a wall or other object is blocking the line of sight. Once you're satisfied this is working, you can press Play again to exit the preview and continue development.

The next area we'll look at is making our turret deployable; we can implement this in a similar way to our projectile. The first set of changes is to prepare the MachineGunTower_1 prefab by selecting it in the Hierarchy; in the Inspector, select Add Component and then select Physics > Rigidbody. On the Rigidbody, we need to expand Constraints and check the options for Freeze Rotation on the X, Y, Z.

"If you have two or more targets, the gun will only aim for the closest"

We again select Add Component and then Physics > Box Collider, and then for the Center values change the Y value from 0 to 0.5. This will make the wireframe box appear more central on the turret. Finally, look for the word Prefab along the top of the Inspector. We should select the Overrides option, then select Apply All to confirm the latest changes we made. Then we ➔

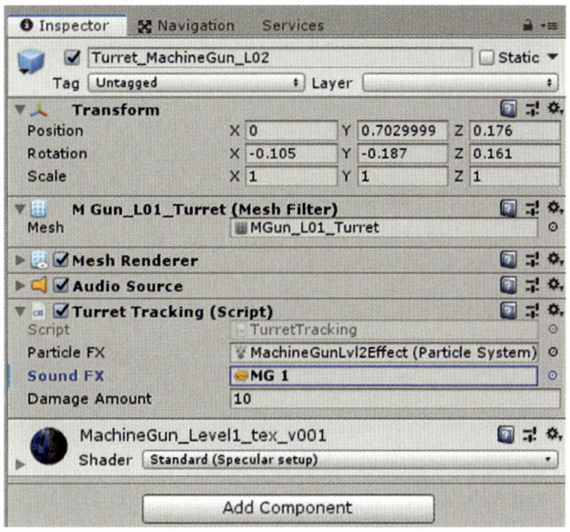

To ensure you get the full effect of the turret in action, make sure you have correctly assigned your particle and sound effects, and also that you have assigned an audio source to the game object. For more on sound, turn to page 70.

DAMAGE

Remember, the TargetDamage script will need to be on each target to make the turret fire at it. To speed things up, we can always set up a prefab of the current completed object by dragging this into the Project panel. We can then reuse the prefab anywhere in our scene.

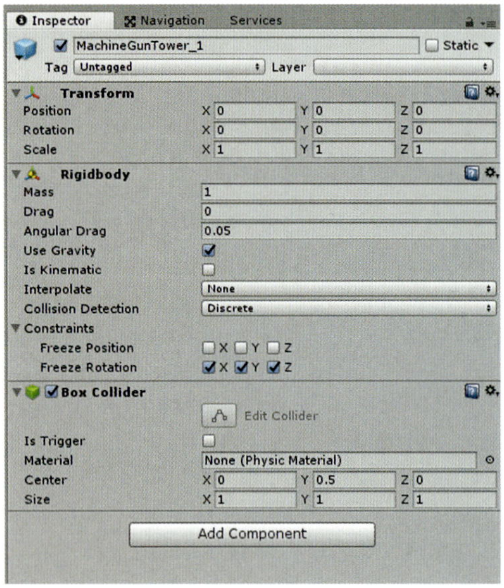

> Make sure you've set the rotation constraints on your turret, otherwise when it's thrown out and deployed, you'll get all sorts of odd behaviours.

can delete the turret in the Hierarchy, as we'll spawn it later for the Project files.

The next area for change is the Player prefab that we added. We need to expand it in the Hierarchy and select the Main Camera object, then right-click and select Create Empty. With the new object selected, move to the Inspector and rename this as 'LaunchPoint'. I would also move this forward of the character, so about 0.7 in the Z direction. If we don't make this change, the turret will be spawned inside the character – not ideal, I'm sure you'll agree.

Next, we'll add another script to this object, so select Add Component, then New Script – we can name this TurretLauncher – and select Create and Add. Finally, double-click the new script to open it in the script editor ready for adding our code.

```
using System.Collections;
using System.Collections.Generic;
using UnityEngine;

public class TurretLauncher : MonoBehaviour
{
    public GameObject spawn;
    public float kickDistance = 300.0f;
    private bool spawned;


    // Update is called once per frame
    void Update()
    {
        if (Input.GetButtonDown("Fire2") &&
spawned == false)
        {
            spawned = true;
            var clone = Instantiate(spawn,
gameObject.transform.position, gameObject.
transform.rotation);
            clone.GetComponent<Rigidbody>().
AddForce(transform.forward * kickDistance);
        }
    }
}
```

Save the script and then select the LaunchPoint we created. The script should have two values in the Inspector; one should be named Spawn and be empty. We need to assign

"By using a right-mouse click or left ALT key, we can deploy our turret"

the MachineGunTower_1 prefab from the Assets tab to the Spawn entry. The other value can be used to set how far our turret will be 'kicked' on pressing the secondary fire button. We can now preview this again by using the Play button and then, by using a right-mouse click or left **ALT** key, we can deploy our turret.

TESTING THE TURRET

We also want to test that the damage is working. We aren't going to do too much with this as we're only testing that the turret damage system works. We could easily expand on this to show some sort of damage on the enemies and

> With everything set on our FPS character, and the turret prefab assigned, we should be able to deploy our turret by selecting the appropriate key bindings.

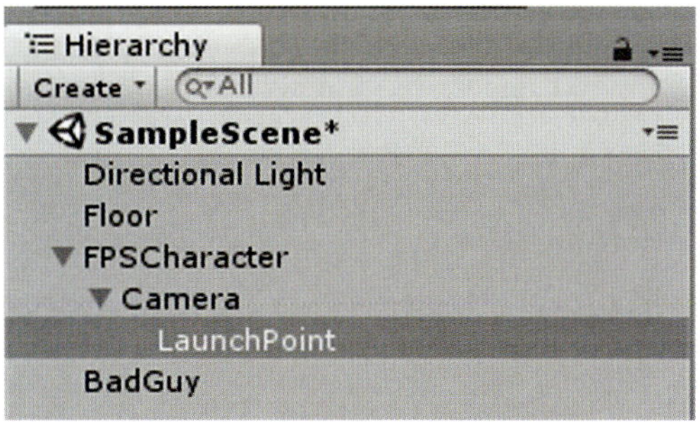

We need to add the LaunchPoint as a child of the camera, so that the turret will end up launched in the direction in which the player is looking.

While we're prototyping, we can check that the damage feedback is working by looking for debug information in the Unity console. This is a common way to debug a feature that hasn't been completely hooked up.

have a more convincing 'death' sequence. For now, we're going to display the damage values to the Unity console and then hide the target when it's destroyed.

Keen-eyed readers may note that this is very similar to how we had our enemies reduce the player's health. First, we need to select one of the Spheres we added to represent the targets. We then need to go to our Inspector and select Add Component and then select New Script. We'll name this TargetDamage, then select Create and Add. We can open this new script and start adding the code shown below

```
using UnityEngine;

public class TargetDamage : MonoBehaviour
{
    //Sets default health to 100
    public int health = 100;

    void ApplyDamage(int damage)
    {
        //Checks our health is greater than 0
        if (health > 0)
        {
            //Stores the current health and
subtracts the damage value
            health = health - damage;
            //Shows the health in the log.
            Debug.Log("Health: " + health);
        }
        else
        {
            //Log a message to show it's
destroyed
            Debug.Log("Destroyed!");
            //Disable object so it's not
visible.
            gameObject.SetActive(false);
        }
    }
}
```

As usual, we can save the script we just created. Before we preview the result of the damage script, we should enable the Unity console. This can be found in the toolbar under Window > General > Console (**CTRL+SHIFT+C**). Personally, I dock this next to or alongside the Project window. I always have this open to look for errors, but in our case, we can use it to look for our debug damage logs. Run the preview by selecting the Play button; as the relevant target gets hit, you can see the current health in our console, and the object will be 'destroyed' when it reaches zero health.

We now pretty much have a fully working deployable turret. There are a few improvements we can make: the turret could ignore targets that are in cover, and we could allow the turret to take damage itself. Additional mechanics could then be added, such as being able to repair or upgrade the turret. Remember, this project is meant as a starting point and it's up to you to take the turret mechanics in the direction you want for your game!

In *Borderlands*, Roland's turret not only targets the fauna, but can also be upgraded to heal his team members.

Creating a Blink ability in Unity

Want to teleport around levels like Tracer in Overwatch? Stuart shows you how to recreate the mechanic

AUTHOR
STUART FRASER
Stuart is a former designer and developer of high-profile games such as *RollerCoaster Tycoon 3*, and also worked as a lecturer of games development.

PACKAGES

Unity now provides additional tools and features via their package manager, this can help with everything from blockout for levels to augmented reality. The package manager can be accessed via Window > Package Manager in the editor toolbar.

We're going to look at creating a game mechanic that will allow the player to instantaneously teleport a short distance. This is commonly called a blink mechanic, and can be seen in single-player shooters like *Dishonored* – it's one of the skills that the player can unlock when playing as Corvo – or in online, competitive games like *Overwatch* with Tracer's ability to shift from point to point.

As with our earlier tutorials, we can use Unity's tools and C#a to create a prototype of this mechanic.

EXPANDING OUR PROTOTYPE

To start, we'll open the first-person project we worked on earlier. While we're working on this, we should create a new scene for prototyping our blink mechanic before we integrate it into a larger level. When you've loaded up your Unity project, we'll select File > New Scene to create our new level for test purposes.

We also need to drag our Player prefab from the Project panel into the Hierarchy so it appears in the level. We should then delete the Main Camera in our level – this is because we already have one in our Player prefab.

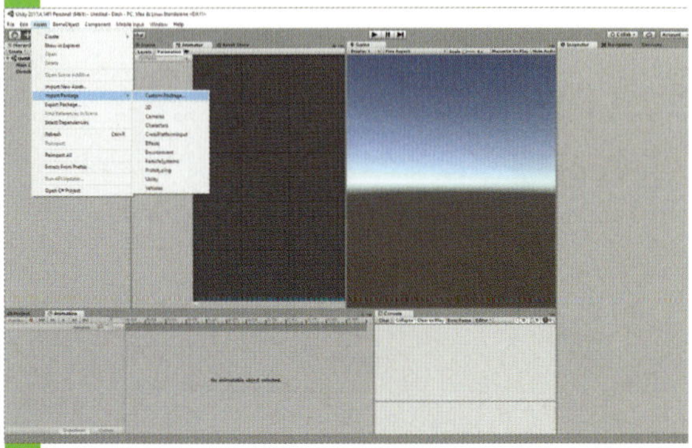

> Unity has a bunch of useful assets that come as standard in the installation. You can always add them to help you to prototype levels or mechanics.

CHECKING THE DESTINATION

Before we implement the mechanic, we need to do some groundwork. In our example, we're going to first do something like the *Dishonored* blink ability, where you can set a destination and teleport there.

We'll use a raycast, which is something we used in our code for an earlier tutorial. Effectively, we'll shoot out an invisible beam to see if these destinations are possible to reach before we blink between them. Ideally, we want a surface such as a floor or walkable slope to be valid to blink to; meanwhile, a wall should be invalid as we would end up inside it. We can differentiate these two types by looking at the normal directions of where the ray hits.

So that we can test this, we'll also build out a level using some basic cubes. First, we need a floor, so select GameObject > 3D Object > Plane. In the Inspector window, set the Y value for the Scale to 2. We want to move this cube object so it's not in the same space as our Player

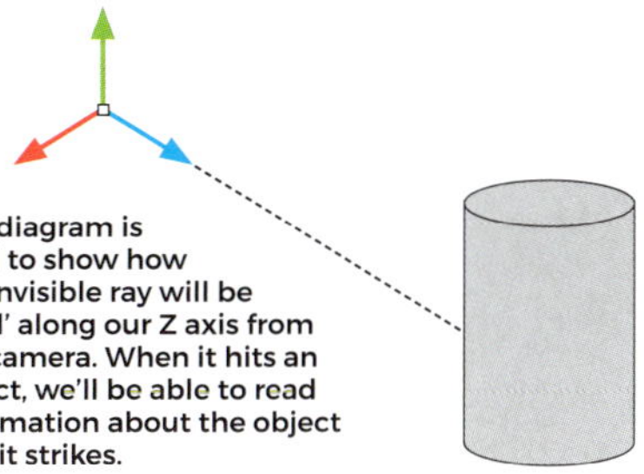

> This diagram is used to show how the invisible ray will be 'fired' along our Z axis from the camera. When it hits an object, we'll be able to read information about the object that it strikes.

object and also that it's touching, but not in, the ground. If we hold the **CTRL** key and then click the left mouse button while selecting one of the transform arrows on our cube object, we can accurately snap our cube object into a suitable position.

We'll now make a slope by duplicating our cube by selecting Edit > Duplicate. We then move to the Inspector and change the X value for the Rotation to around 65 degrees. Using the positioning tools again, we use the **CTRL** key and select the red arrow (X) to move this cube so it's next to the first.

We can then release the **CTRL** key and manually move this using the green arrow (Y) so that a slope is formed by effectively submerging the cube in the ground.

"We'll send out an invisible beam to see if destinations are possible to reach"

Next, we'll create our initial script on the player camera object. In the Hierarchy, look for the Player and select the arrow next to it. This will expand, and you should then see an object called MainCamera. Select this object, and then in the Inspector look for the Add Component button. Now scroll down the list and select New Script; we can call this Blink, and then select Create and Add. We can now add our code to preview the logic of our blink ability by replacing the template code with our own. We do this by double-clicking on the script name to open our script editor.

```
using UnityEngine;

public class Blink : MonoBehaviour {

        // Update is called once per frame
        void Update () {
        if (Input.GetMouseButton(0))
```

```
        {
            RaycastHit hit;
            Ray ray = Camera.main.
ScreenPointToRay(Input.mousePosition);

            if (Physics.Raycast(ray, out hit))
            {
                // Draw debug lines to aid
visualisation.
                if (hit.normal.y > 0.5f)
                {
                    Debug.DrawLine(transform.
position, hit.point, Color.green);
                }
                else
                {
                    Debug.DrawLine(transform.
position, hit.point, Color.red);
                }
            }
        }
    }
}
```

Once we save this in the code editor and move back to Unity, we can preview this in the Scene view. For now, we don't want to shoot ➔

NORMAL DIRECTION

A normal direction is something that exists for all polygons in a game. It usually tells the renderer that a valid polygon should be drawn in a certain orientation. In 3D packages, it's often shown as a small line that points in an opposing direction to the rendered polygon face. We're using this knowledge to determine if our surfaces are valid for teleporting onto.

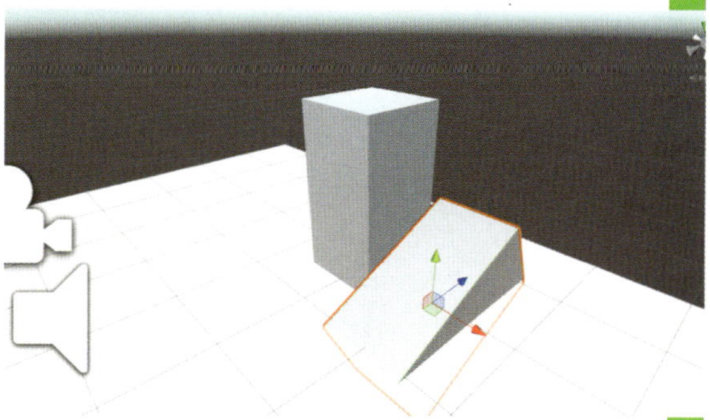

< You can easily create geometry by using the basic shapes in clever ways; level designers often do this to block out levels, which will be replaced later by artists.

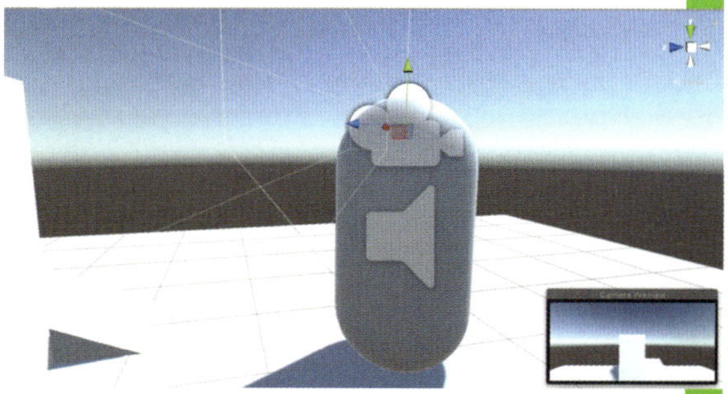

< We'll add an extra script to the imported first-person character prefab created by Unity. As we want to blink to a point we are looking at, we attach the script to the player camera.

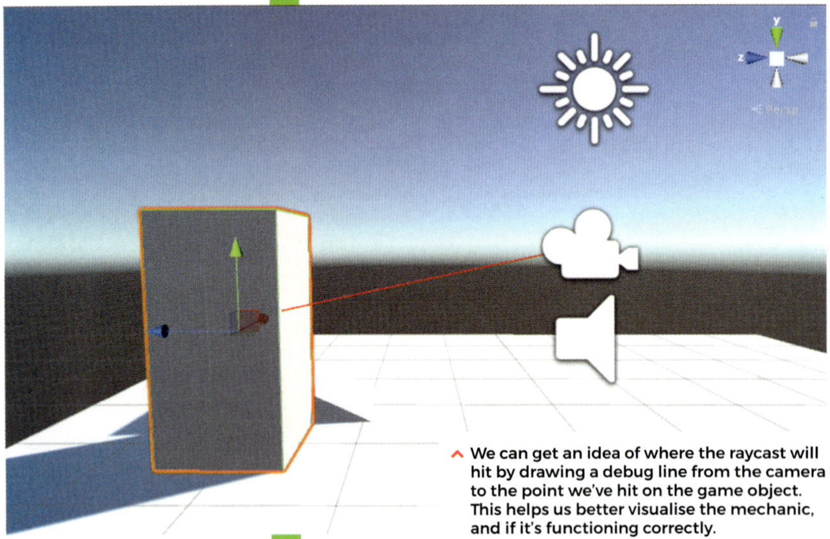

We can get an idea of where the raycast will hit by drawing a debug line from the camera to the point we've hit on the game object. This helps us better visualise the mechanic, and if it's functioning correctly.

PREVIEWING RAYCASTS

Raycasts are usually invisible. We can preview this in the Scene view by using built-in Unity functions for debugging raycasts. This is one of the many useful debug functions that are available in Unity, and typical in most game engines.

and use our teleport, so expand the Player and the Main Camera objects and look for the Weapon object. In our Inspector, select the active checkbox next to the word Weapon and this will disable this object. We need to make sure both the Scene and Game are both visible to achieve this. If you haven't done this already, undock the Game tab by left-clicking and dragging this to the right. This will allow you to dock with another empty area of the editor interface.

Press Play now and, as the FPS character, go find your cube objects in the level. If you hold the left mouse button, you will see that the raycast will be drawn. In our code, the valid locations are a green debug line, while invalid locations are red.

With this tested, we can stop the preview and add our basic blink mechanic.

BLINKING BETWEEN LOCATIONS

As the debug lines aren't drawn, and our goal is to emulate the mechanics from popular games, we want some sort of visualisation of the location where the player will end up. To achieve this, we'll use some of the ready-made particle assets in Unity, and use this to preview the end location.

We need to open the Store by selecting Window > Assets Store from the toolbar. You can use the search to find the Standard Assets or use the following link: **wfmag.cc/asset-pack**. We simply download the assets and then select Import. Although we don't need all the assets, there are many dependencies between them, so it makes sense to download them all.

Our next step is to update our script to include the mechanic: select the blink script in the Project window, and double-click to open it. We can simply replace the current script with the updated one below.

```
using UnityEngine;

public class Blink : MonoBehaviour {
    public GameObject particlePrefab;
    GameObject particleFX;
    Vector3 destination;
    bool FXVisible=false;

    private void Start()
    {
        particleFX =
Instantiate(particlePrefab);
    }

    // Update is called once per frame
    void Update () {
        if (Input.GetMouseButton(0))
        {
            RaycastHit hit;
            Ray ray = Camera.main.
ScreenPointToRay(Input.mousePosition);

            if (Physics.Raycast(ray, out hit))
            {
                // Draw debug lines to aid
visualisation.
                if (hit.normal.y > 0.5f)
                {
                    Debug.DrawLine(transform.
position, hit.point, Color.green);
                    destination = hit.point;
                    FXVisible = true;
                }
                else
                {
                    Debug.DrawLine(transform.
position, hit.point, Color.red);
                    destination = transform.
position;
                    FXVisible = false;
                }
            }
```

```
            else
            {
                destination = transform.
position;
                FXVisible = false;
            }
        }
        if(Input.
GetMouseButtonUp(0)&&transform.
position!=destination)
        {
            destination.y += 0.5f;
            transform.parent.position =
destination;
            FXVisible = false;
        }
        if(FXVisible)
        {
            particleFX.transform.position =
destination;
            particleFX.SetActive(true);
        }
        else
        {
            particleFX.SetActive(false);
        }
    }
}
```

Save the script and return to the Unity editor. We're now going to make some final tweaks before we try out the mechanic. First, select the

"We want some sort of visualisation of where the player will end up"

Main Camera game object in the Hierarchy, and then in the Inspector, look for your script. You should see a new slot named Particle Prefab – this is where we can assign our particle. If we look in the Project window and navigate to Standard Assets > Particle Systems > Prefabs, we have several effects at our disposal.

I suggest we use the Flare effect, and drag this onto the Particle Prefab slot in the Inspector. A final change, which allows us to easily see the particle effect, is to change the light colour. Select the Directional Light in the Hierarchy, and then in the Inspector, set the colour to something other than white; my suggestion is blue.

We can now try out the mechanic. Press the Play button to preview, and then hold the left mouse button; you'll see the particle effect appearing on valid surfaces, and disappearing when this is not the case. We can also teleport to these locations if we release the left mouse button. Once you've finished testing this out, remember to click the button to stop playing the game preview.

A blink ability was among the many powers at Corvo's disposal in *Dishonored*.

EXPANDING THE BLINK MECHANIC

Now, let's think about how we can change this to make the blink mechanic work more like it does with Tracer in *Overwatch*.

To do this, we can simply use the same setup and make a few modifications to the code. Note that with this code there is no test for the ground surface – this is because Tracer will attempt to blink forward regardless of obstacles. If you wanted to, you could make a new script so you could easily switch between both versions; or you can modify the existing blink script with the updated code below.

```
using UnityEngine;

public class Blink : MonoBehaviour {
    public float maxDistance = 4.0f;
    public GameObject canvas;
    Vector3 destination;
    Animator anim;

    private void Start()
    {
        if (canvas != null)
        {
            anim = canvas.GetComponentInChildr
en<Animator>();
            anim.enabled = false;
        }
    }
```

Our particle will render on the position that is hit by our raycast - this gives the player a good indication of where they will be moved to when they use the blink mechanic.

PARTICLES AND SOUND

You can always consider making your own particle effect, or even adding a sound when you're using the blink mechanic. These are elements that can be fleshed out as you iterate on your design.

```
    // Update is called once per frame
    void Update ()
    {
        if (Input.GetMouseButton(0))
        {
            RaycastHit hit;
            Ray ray = Camera.main.
ScreenPointToRay(Input.mousePosition);

            if (Physics.Raycast(ray, out hit,
maxDistance))
            {
                destination = hit.point;
            }
            else
            {
                destination = transform.
position+transform.forward*maxDistance;
            }
        }
        if(Input.
GetMouseButtonUp(0)&&transform.
position!=destination)
        {
            destination.y += 0.5f;
            transform.parent.position =
destination;
            if (anim != null)
            anim.enabled = true;
        }
        if(anim==null)
        {
            return;
        }
        if (anim.
GetCurrentAnimatorStateInfo(0).
normalizedTime>=1)
        {
            anim.Rebind();
            anim.enabled = false;
        }
    }
}
```

In the case of Tracer, she has a full-screen effect that appears when she blinks, which is designed to represent speed lines. A cheap alternative we can add is to quickly fade out the alpha on a white overlay. We've previously used a canvas in other tutorials, but this time we'll animate it to simulate this effect. I've also built in the trigger for it in our code above, but the mechanic will still work regardless.

If you want to add this effect, then create a new canvas by selecting GameObject > UI > Canvas from the taskbar. We can then select the Canvas in the Hierarchy, and then right-click and select UI > Panel. The panel is the actual object that will display our white flash, so with this still selected, move to the Inspector.

In the Inspector, you'll see the Image (Script) and a parameter called Source Image. We want to select the circle to the right of this entry and change the Source Image to None. You'll have probably noticed there seems to be a white tint on the whole scene. The reason is that the panel image always gets set to around 50% opacity. We can change that by selecting the white box to the right of the Color parameter. You should see a standard colour palette where we can adjust the value to the right of the letter A to be 0.

We're also going to make a very short animation to create the fade from white to transparent on this panel. We can achieve this by going to the Project window, then right-clicking and selecting Create > Animation. I would simply rename the new Animation to Blink, so we know what it will be used for. We then select the Panel in the Hierarchy and drag our Blink animation onto the objects Inspector.

At this stage, we might need to make the Animation window visible. For this, just select Window > Animation and dock the new window suitably. We then select the Panel in the Hierarchy and then select the button Add Property in the

Tracer's blink ability makes her one of the more mobile characters in *Overwatch*.

SPECIAL EFFECTS

A standard canvas element will always be rendered on top of the game scene – this means we can add full-screen effects like player damage, colour tints, and fades to our player camera to enhance the experience.

Animation window. You should then drop down the arrow next to the listing for Image (Script) and select Color from the further options by clicking the + symbol.

In the Animation window, you should see an entry labelled Panel : Image Color, and again, we expand this by clicking the arrow. You should see the entries for the Red, Green, Blue, and Alpha channels (RGBA), and a timeline with keyframes on. The keyframes will look like diamonds on the timeline. Next to the text that shows color.a, you should see a value; this is probably 0 in our case. We select this and change it to 1. We then scrub the timeline to the end of the animation. This is achieved by placing the mouse at the very top of the Animation window along the bar with the time value visible. We select the white vertical line and drag it to the right until we have the next set of keyframes selected. We can now make sure that the value for the color.a entry is 0, and if it isn't, alter it to this value.

Finally, we can select our Main Camera in the Hierarchy and drag the Canvas object onto the slot in our script, labelled as Canvas. When we play the game, we should be able to blink in the direction our character faces. We'll have similar limitations as before, but be able to traverse forward a short distance if there's nothing that would block the player's path.

"We should be able to blink in the direction our character faces"

We should also see our blink screen effect show up – you can easily tweak the animation timings for yourself if you like.

Another option is that we could limit the number of blinks the character can attempt within a timeframe, as with the real Tracer character. For now, though, we've successfully developed two different ways of handling a blink mechanic – feel free to experiment with it, and see how you can tailor the movement for your own game.

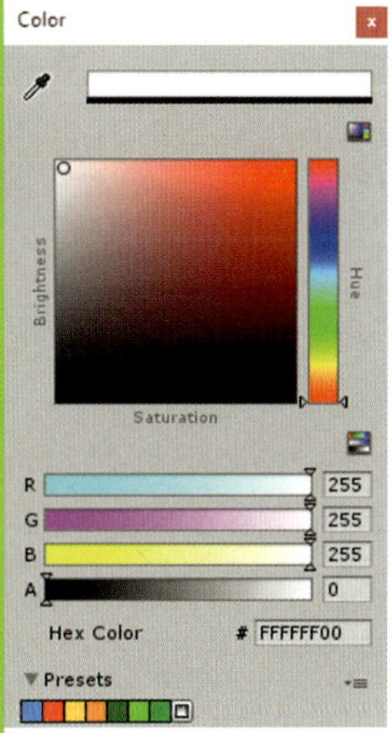

Adjust the alpha value so that it's fully transparent – or, in other words, has no opacity.

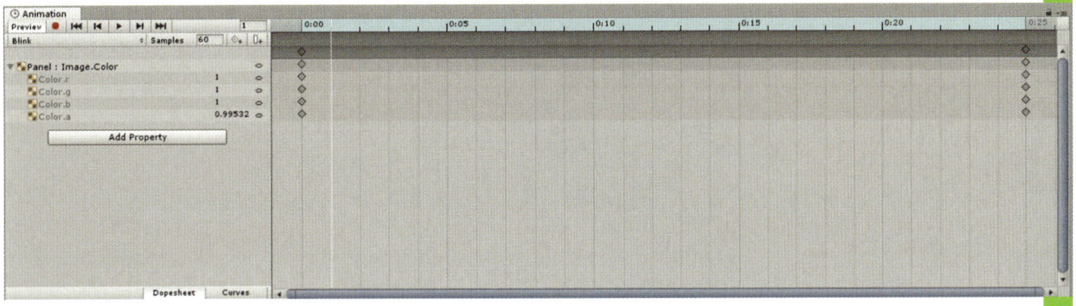

The animation timeline lets us set keyframes, which in turn let us set specific values during the animation playback.

Developing wall running in Unity

Let your players defy gravity and dodge enemies with a fleet-footed wall-running mechanic

AUTHOR
STUART FRASER

Stuart is a former designer and developer of high-profile games such as *RollerCoaster Tycoon 3*, and also worked as a lecturer of games development.

We're going to look at how to create a wall-running mechanic in Unity. You can see this mechanic in action in games such as *Titanfall* and *Mirror's Edge*; the mechanic will allow you to run along a wall in a gravity-defying motion. We are going to use the existing first-person blueprint provided by Unity and extend the code to achieve what we want.

SETTING UP

As always, the first thing to do is open your first-person character project. We'll create the prototype in a new scene so we can try out this new mechanic in isolation. We need to select File > New Scene – we can go ahead and delete the Main Camera. We then select the Player prefab from the Project panel and drag this into the Hierarchy view.

BUILDING OUR LEVEL

Before we can even think about creating a detailed level, we'll have to build some geometry for our character to stand on and wall-run along. We're going to use the basic 3D shapes in Unity to whitebox our level. First, we'll select GameObject > 3D Object > Cube. This will appear in the Scene viewport and be listed in our Hierarchy window. We can now use the Inspector to position and scale our object. On the right-hand side of the Unity editor, you'll find the Inspector panel, which has details about the selected object. With the cube still selected, set the X,Y,Z Position to 0 and the Scale values for the X to 20, Y to 0.5, and Z to 10. We should have something that we can use to make a floor. You may need to move your player character up in the Y direction so it's on top of the floor. I'd then duplicate this shape by selecting Edit > Duplicate from the toolbar. We can then set the X Rotation in the Inspector to 90.

We're going to build our wall with this piece, but we want this to snap to an edge of our floor. To achieve this, we'll select Edit > Snap Settings... and set the Move X,Y,Z values to 0.25 in each of the fields. We can then hold the **CTRL** key and in the Scene viewport, we can use our transform

We're going to create our very own parkour or wall-running mechanic, as can be seen in games like *Mirror's Edge Catalyst*.

widget to position our duplicate wall shape next to our floor. Duplicate this again, and then move this new duplicate in the X position to have a wall that is positioned forwards of our previous floor and wall. It's a little up to you how you want to build your level out. I duplicated both my original floor and wall again, and put them to the other side of the free-standing wall, so we can use our wall-running technique to traverse between the gaps in the floor.

SETTING UP OUR CHARACTER

The next thing we're going do is add some tags. We've looked at these in previous projects, but tags allow us to mark up certain objects with a label. We can then use these to give objects specific rules – in our example, the character will behave differently when colliding with the walls we're about to tag.

We can do this by selecting one of the game objects that make up our wall pieces; in the Inspector panel, we can select the Tag drop-down and then select the Add Tag... option. We can then simply select the + icon and type in Walls for our tag and Save. To apply this, select

"You can see this mechanic in action in games such as *Titanfall* and *Mirror's Edge*"

all our wall pieces and once again select the Tag drop-down – this time we can apply the Walls tag we created.

We'll need to edit some of our original scripts to handle what we'll be able to wall-run on. There are no massive changes to make, but all the code including the modifications has been provided below. The first script we have to modify is the CharacterMovement script. You can just open this in your code editor and modify it to match the following code:

```
using UnityEngine;

public class CharacterMovement : MonoBehaviour
{
    public float speed = 5;
    public float jumpPower = 4;
    public bool Grounded;
    private Rigidbody rb;
    private CapsuleCollider col;
    private float Horizontal;
    private WallRunning wr;

    // Use this for initialization
    void Start()
    {
        Cursor.lockState = CursorLockMode.
Locked;
        rb = GetComponent<Rigidbody>();
        col = GetComponent<CapsuleCollider>();
        wr = GetComponent<WallRunning>();
    }

    // Update is called once per frame
    void Update()
    {
        Grounded = isGrounded();
        //Get the input value from the
controllers
        float Vertical = Input.
GetAxis("Vertical") * speed;
        if (!wr.isWall)
        {
            Horizontal = Input.
GetAxis("Horizontal") * speed;
        }
        Vertical *= Time.deltaTime;
        Horizontal *= Time.deltaTime;
        //Translate our character via our
inputs.
        transform.Translate(Horizontal, 0, Ver
tical);
```

GEOMETRY

It's a good idea to name the geometry that makes up your level so it's easier to find in the Hierarchy view. You can easily do this by typing a new name into the top of the Inspector panel for that game object.

We can block out a quick level to test that our wall-running mechanic is functioning as we expect it to. This is a common thing to do when you're a developer and want to quickly iterate on a design.

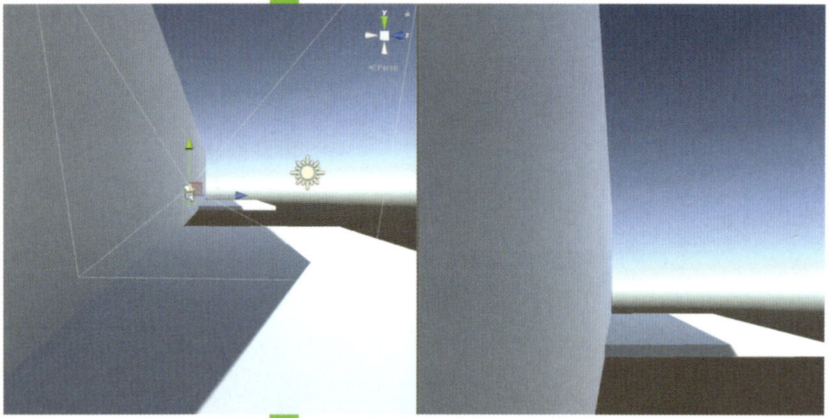

Don't forget to keep testing out the mechanic as you build out your level, to make sure the gameplay feels satisfying.

```
        if (isGrounded() && Input.
GetButtonDown("Jump"))
        {
            //Add upward force to the rigid
body when we press jump.
            rb.AddForce(Vector3.up *
jumpPower, ForceMode.Impulse);
        }

        if (Input.GetKeyDown("escape"))
            Cursor.lockState = CursorLockMode.
None;
    }

    private bool isGrounded()
    {
        //Test that we are grounded by drawing
an invisible line (raycast)
        //If this hits a solid object e.g.
floor then we are grounded.
        return Physics.Raycast(transform.
position, Vector3.down, col.bounds.extents.y
+ 0.1f);
    }
}
```

Once you've saved the above, we'll then open our MouseLook script so we can make the following additional modifications:

```
using UnityEngine;

public class MouseLook : MonoBehaviour
{
    private GameObject player;
    private float minClamp = -45;
    private float maxClamp = 45;
    [HideInInspector]
    public Vector2 rotation;
    private Vector2 currentLookRot;
    private Vector2 rotationV = new Vector2(0,
0);
    public float lookSensitivity = 2;
    public float lookSmoothDamp = 0.1f;
    //Required if we are using the camera to
freelook.
    private CharacterMovement cm;
    private bool resetRotation = false;

    void Start()
    {
        //Access the player GameObject.
        player = transform.parent.gameObject;
        cm = player.GetComponent<CharacterMov
ement>();
    }

    // Update is called once per frame
    void Update()
    {
        //Player input from the mouse
        rotation.y += Input.GetAxis("Mouse Y")
* lookSensitivity;
        //Limit ability look up and down.
        rotation.y = Mathf.Clamp(rotation.y,
minClamp, maxClamp);
        //Rotate the character around based on
```

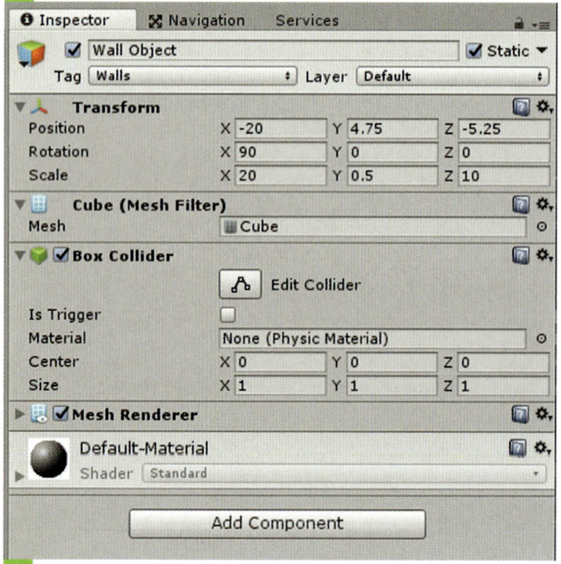

Make sure that all the walls are tagged correctly in the Inspector panel, else the wall-running ability will not work correctly.

```
the mouse X position.
        //Unless we are not grounded or for
the one frame where we set the player to match
the camera.
        if (cm.Grounded)
        {
            if (resetRotation)
            {
                resetRotation = false;
                player.transform.
localEulerAngles += new Vector3(0,
currentLookRot.x, 0);
                currentLookRot.x = 0;
            }
            else
            {
                player.transform.
RotateAround(transform.position, Vector3.up,
Input.GetAxis("Mouse X") * lookSensitivity);
            }
        }
        else
        {
            resetRotation = true;
            //Free look in the Y rotation
based on mouse.
            currentLookRot.x += Input.
GetAxis("Mouse X") * lookSensitivity;
        }
        //Smooth the current Y rotation for
looking up and down.
        currentLookRot.y = Mathf.
SmoothDamp(currentLookRot.y, rotation.y, ref
rotationV.y, lookSmoothDamp);
        //Update the camera X, Y rotation
based on the values generated.
        transform.localEulerAngles = new
Vector3(-currentLookRot.y, currentLookRot.x,
0);
    }
}
```

Once you've saved this script, we should have all the modifications we need to continue.

Our next task is to add a new C# script to allow for our new wall-running ability. First, select the Player prefab in the Hierarchy panel. We then look in the Inspector panel and select the Add Component > New Script options, and then in the Name field, type WallRunning as our script name. We then select the Create and Add button to generate the script and attach it to our game object. To edit our script, double-click on the script name. We can then add the script below in our code editor of choice:

```
using System.Collections;
using System.Collections.Generic;
using UnityEngine;

[RequireComponent(typeof(AudioSource))]
public class WallRunning : MonoBehaviour
{
    public AudioClip audioClip;
    private CharacterMovement cm;
    private Rigidbody rb;
    private bool isJumping;
    public bool isWall;
    private bool playAudio;
    private AudioSource audioSource;


    private void Start()
    {
        //Get attached components so we can
interact with them in our script.
        cm = GetComponent<CharacterMoveme
nt>();
        rb = GetComponent<Rigidbody>();
        audioSource =
GetComponent<AudioSource>();
    }

    private void FixedUpdate()
    {
        bool jumpPressed = Input.
GetButtonDown("Jump");
        float verticalAxis = Input.
GetAxis("Vertical");
        //Check if the controller is grounded.
        if (cm.Grounded)
        {
            isJumping = false;
            isWall = false;
        }
        //Has the jump button been pressed.
        if (jumpPressed)
        {
            StartCoroutine(Jumping());
```

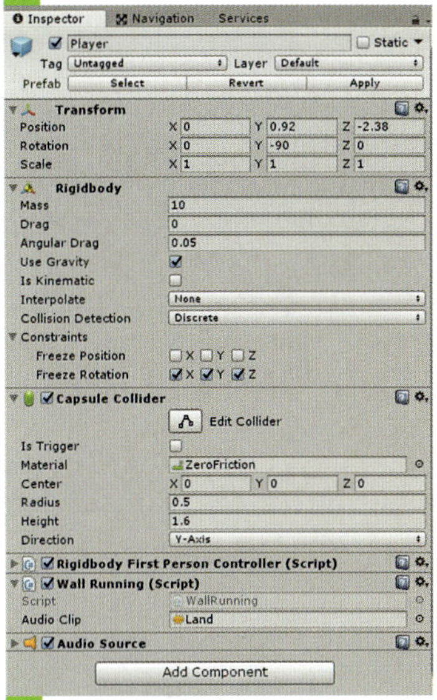

With our script attached and compiled, we can easily drop in a suitable audio clip for when we begin our wall-run.

Titanfall allows the player to use boosted jumps and the player's momentum to keep moving between buildings.

ENERGY

The value for the energy limit should let us just about clear the gap we created earlier. However, you can always make this longer or shorter by making the float value bigger or smaller.

```
        }
        //If we are pushing forward, and not
grounded, and touching a wall.
        if (verticalAxis > 0 && isJumping &&
isWall)
        {
            //We constrain the Y/Z direction
to defy gravity and move off the wall.
            //But we can still run forward as
we ignore the X direction.
            rb.useGravity = false;
            rb.constraints =
RigidbodyConstraints.FreezePositionY |
RigidbodyConstraints.FreezePositionX |
RigidbodyConstraints.FreezeRotation;
            //We also telegraph to the player
by playing a sound effect on contact.
            if (audioClip != null && playAudio
== true)
            {
                audioSource.
PlayOneShot(audioClip);
                //We block more audio being
played while we are on the wall.
                playAudio = false;
            }
        }
        else
        {
            //We need to make sure we can play
audio again when touching the wall.
            playAudio = true;
            rb.useGravity = true;
            rb.constraints =
RigidbodyConstraints.FreezeRotation;
        }
    }


    void OnCollisionEnter(Collision other)
    {
        //Are we touching a wall object?
        if (other.gameObject.tag == "Walls")
        {
            isWall = true;
        }
    }

    void OnCollisionExit(Collision other)
    {
        //Did we stop touching the wall
object?
        if (other.gameObject.tag != "Walls")
        {
            isWall = false;
        }
    }


    IEnumerator Jumping()
    {
        //Check for 5 frames after the jump
button is pressed.
        int frameCount = 0;
        while (frameCount < 5)
        {
            frameCount++;
            //Are we airborne in those 5
frames?
            if (!cm.Grounded)
            {
                isJumping = true;
            }
            yield return null;
        }
    }
}
```

Once we've completed the script, we can save this in the code editor and move back to the Unity editor. As part of the script, we have an option to play a sound effect when we jump and make contact with the wall – this will telegraph to the player that the action was successful.

For this to work, we need to assign an audio file to the new variable we have exposed on our script. This can be located if we look at the script in the Inspector panel. If you select the circle icon to the right of the words Audio Clip, you should be able to select a suitable sound effect – something that makes it sound like the player is landing on a surface. If you don't have any Audio Clips listed, you can always import any suitable audio effect as a common audio file – MP3 or WAV, for example. If you find there's an error due to a missing AudioSource, you can select Add Component and manually add one.

We can now test the new wall-running mechanic by selecting the Play button.

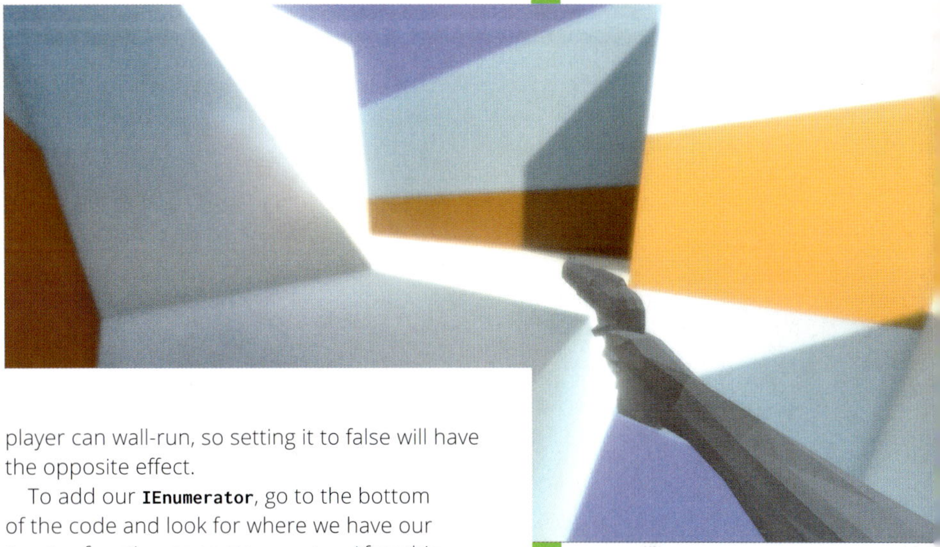

^ By expanding our test level and adding some prototype assets from Unity, we can start to create the look and feel of the games we're trying to emulate.

You should be able to jump as before by tapping the **SPACE** bar, but if we jump at a wall and push forward at the same time, we should be able to wall-run along it until we stop pushing forward. At this stage, it's worth making sure you apply the script to the Player prefab.

LIMITED RUN

Finally, we're going to complicate the mechanic a little by adding limited energy, so the player can only wall-run for a certain length of time. Once the player's energy is depleted, their character will lose their grip and fall.
To get this working, we're going to make some edits to the code already in place. I would only suggest attempting this if you're comfortable with being able to make these changes.

The first thing to do is open the Wallrunning script and look for our initial variables – we can add the following code on the line above the `audioclip` variable we defined earlier:

```
public float energyLimit = 3.5f;
```

The next thing to do is make sure that we trigger our energy to start depleting. We're going to call an `IEnumerator` as a way of timing our ability – we already used one of these to test if we're off the ground when we're jumping.

In this case, we need to start this counting down when we're wall-running and stop it when we're not. We'll use the functions of `StartCoroutine` and `StopCoroutine` to achieve this. First, look for the statement where we test if we're touching a wall – it should be easy to find from the code comments. Then, inside the parentheses, add the following code:

```
StartCoroutine(Energy());
```

As stated, we stop this when we aren't wall-running, so look for the `Else` statement and, in the parentheses, add the following code:

```
StopCoroutine(Energy());
```

We've finished all the setup. Now we need to set the time we can wall-run for and then, after this, disengage it.

An effective way to handle this is to reuse the Boolean we set when the player character makes contact with tagged objects, and set this to false. The Boolean has to be true before the player can wall-run, so setting it to false will have the opposite effect.

To add our `IEnumerator`, go to the bottom of the code and look for where we have our `Jumping` function as an `IEnumerator`. After this, but before our closing parenthesis, add the following code:

```
IEnumerator Energy()
{
    yield return new
WaitForSeconds(energyLimit);
    isWall = false;
}
```

Note that the yield uses a function call: `WaitForSeconds`; the `energyLimit` variable contains that wait time. Because we've made the `energyLimit` a public variable, we can tweak this for the Player game object in the Inspector. Now we can save the code changes and go back to Unity. Hopefully, your log will be free of errors – if not, read what the errors are, and they should give you an idea of what you need to fix the issue.

We can now press Play and test out our limited wall-run. If we jump on the wall too soon, then we'll end up losing our energy and fall off the wall.

By now, you should have the base mechanic working and be able to run along walls to avoid pitfalls. There are some limitations with this implementation due to it locking movement to one axis – rotating the walls, for example, may cause undesirable effects. This is something you can fix by detecting the angle of the wall the Player game object is touching and changing the movement logic accordingly.

You could also expand the mechanic by adding a boost jump between walls, or you could add power-ups that have to be collected to top up your energy. As always, feel free to experiment with what you've developed so far.

Saving and loading game data in Unity

Learn how to give players the ability to save and load their progress

AUTHOR
RYAN SHAH
An avid developer with a strong passion for education, Ryan Shah moonlights as KITATUS – an education content creator for all things game development.

Unity provides us with a number of solutions for saving and loading data. From asset store packs to serialisation and PlayerPrefs, let's take a moment to break apart what this means for our game, and how we can use Unity's built-in systems to efficiently create a save game system.

Unity provides two core solutions for saving and loading data: Serialization or PlayerPrefs. We'll dive into each one in depth, but a general overview is as follows: PlayerPrefs is a saving system in Unity that can only support strings (lines of text), integers (whole numbers such as 1,2,3), and floats (numbers with decimal places such 1.02, 2.423, 3.1). Serialization allows you to save any object or piece of data to a file by turning an object into data that can then be sent, deserialised, (turned back into an object), or received.

So how do we know which save/load system to use for our projects? To answer that question, let's create a system with PlayerPrefs before moving onto a system created with Serialization to help gain an insight into what system you might prefer to use in your own projects.

To get started, we're going to need data to save and load. In the interest of the theme of a shooting game, we're going to save the player's current health and ammunition count. To do this, we need to create a new C# script. We'll create this script in a folder titled SaveGame and call the script PlayerPrefExample.

Once you've created the script, we need to add code inside. Double-click the file to load up the file in your code editor of choice, ready for us to implement our functionality. For our example, we need two functions in this class to save and load our data. One of these functions will save our data and the other will load it.

We'll name these functions `PlayerPrefSave` and `PlayerPrefLoad` respectively. When you create a new C# script in Unity, you'll notice that two functions are auto-generated; `void Start()` and `void Update()`. These functions aren't needed in the scope of our example, so we can either remove them and create our own functions or rename these functions to suit our needs (don't forget to remove the comments if you do this).

Go ahead and create the two functions now; `public void PlayerPrefSave()` and

The Unity Asset Store has a library of content that allows you to add code, content, and tools to your projects.

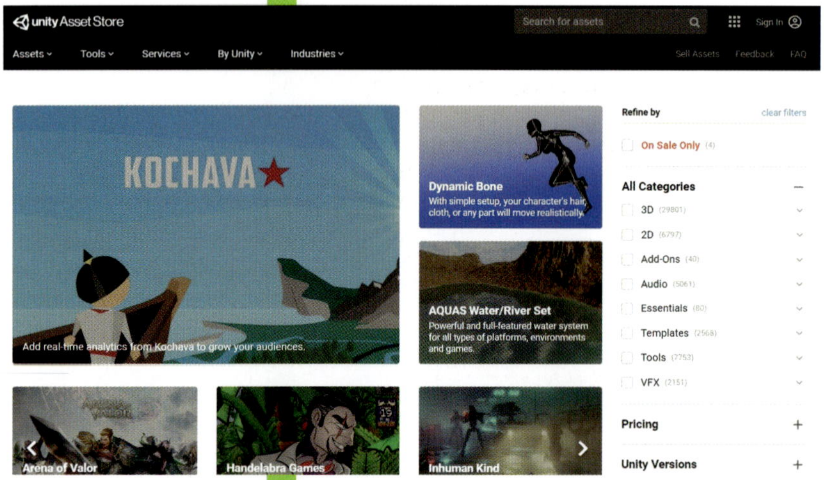

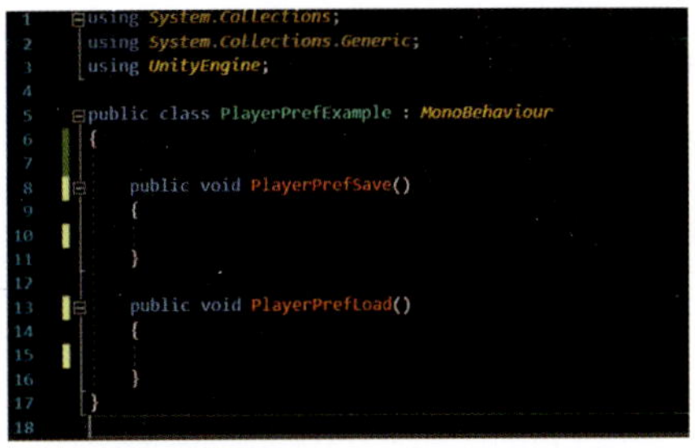

When replacing the `Start()` and `Update()` functions auto-generated by Unity, it's good practice to remove the comments from the file as they're no longer applicable.

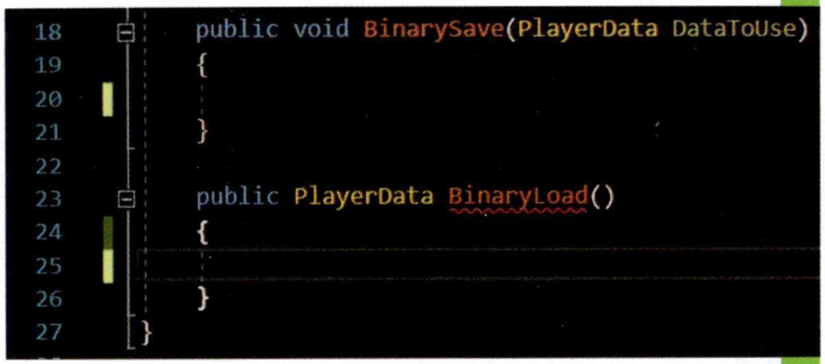

When you don't use voids in your functions and you're returning a variable, your code editor should warn you with red squiggly lines when you're not returning a value. You can fix this for now by adding `return new PlayerData;` to your function.

`public void PlayerPrefLoad()`. We can use the `PlayerPrefLoad` function to load our data. To do so, head inside the function and add `PlayerPrefs.GetInt("currentAmmo");` and `PlayerPrefs.GetFloat("currentHealth");`.

```
public  void PlayerPrefLoad()
  {
      PlayerPrefs.GetInt("currentAmmo");
      PlayerPrefs.GetFloat("currentHealth");
  }
```

These two lines of code load the integer (whole number) `currentAmmo` and the float (number with decimal place) `currentHealth`. You might notice that these variables don't exist yet and we're not doing anything with the loaded data. We'll fix that shortly.

Our `PlayerPrefSaveGame()` function needs to save the data. As we used `GetInt` and `GetFloat` in the load data function (which *gets* data), we can use `SetInt` and `SetFloat` to *set* the data. As we're setting data, these calls will want a value attached to them. For now, `currentAmmo` should equal 1 and `currentHealth` should equal 50.0. You can add these values to these calls by adding a comma alongside the value after the quotation marks.

"We're going to save the player's current health and ammunition count"

```
public void PlayerPrefSave()
  {
      PlayerPrefs.SetInt("currentAmmo", 1);
      PlayerPrefs.SetFloat("currentHealth",
50.0f);
  }
```

We now have code that saves and loads data for `currentAmmo` and `currentHealth`. This is currently all it does, which creates two issues: every time we fire `PlayerPrefSave`, it's saving our Ammo value as 1 and our Health as 50. So, every time we load this data, our Ammo and Health will always be the same. The second issue is that once we've loaded the data, we're not storing the loaded data anywhere. Essentially, our data is being thrown into the void and never used. Let's fix these issues.

Looking at `PlayerPrefLoadData()` first, we need a way to give this function the variables for Health and Ammo, so we can tell whatever has called this function the returned Health and Ammo values. In Unity, we have a tool that can help us achieve this. We're about to change the header of our function, which tells us what data to pass in. When we do this, we can tell our compiler that we intended to make changes to the data we're sending into this function.

Normally, when you send data into a function, Unity makes a copy instead of sending the actual data. This is so that we don't accidentally make changes to the data and cause issues for other parts of our code.

A normal function header with data might look something like this: `void CoolData (int iDataToUse)`. This means that whenever we call this function, we need to supply an integer which our function will call `iDataToUse`. If we were to write code that dynamically set `iDataToUse`, such as using a pre-existing variable called `iOriginalData`, our call might look something like this: `CoolData(iOriginalData)`. This would be sending in the value of `iOriginalData` but not sending in the variable itself, because making changes to the variable could be dangerous to the other code in our project.

There are some cases where you intend to make changes to a variable inside a function and you're intentionally sending data into the function to change the value. This is where the `ref` keyword comes in. `ref` lets Unity know that we don't want a copy of the data, we want the actual data because we intend to change its value inside our function. An example of this would be `void CoolData(ref int iDataToUse)`. This means that whatever →

You can create and keep track of all of your projects in Unity's new Hub application.

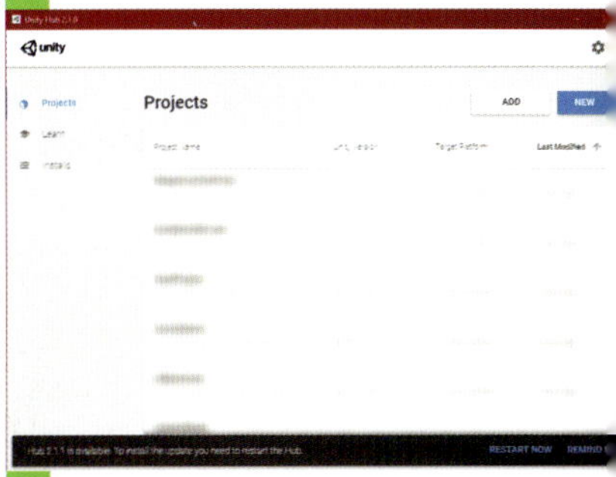

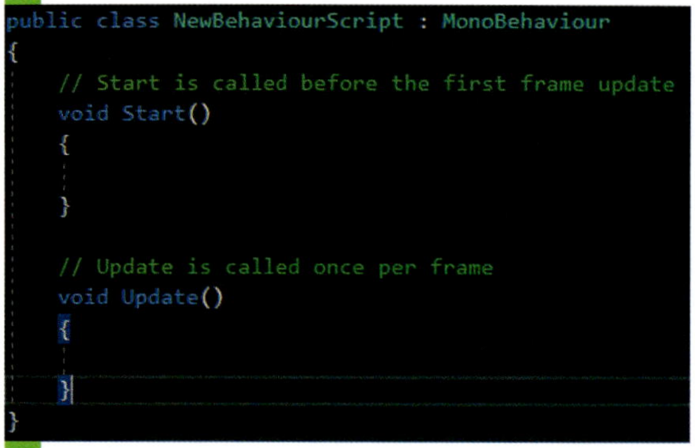

› Editing MonoBehaviours – this is where all the magic happens in Unity.

integer we send has the power to be changed by our function.

As our plan is to load our data and set our Ammo and Health, go to the `PlayerPrefLoad` function and change the function's header from `public void PlayerPrefLoad()` to `public void PlayerPrefLoad(ref int iAmmoToUse, ref float fHealthToUse)`. Now inside the function, we can say that our Ammo value is what we've loaded from the PlayerPrefs and our Health value is what we've loaded. We can do this by typing this out: `iAmmoToUse = PlayerPrefs.GetInt("currentAmmo");` and `fHealthToUse = PlayerPrefs.GetFloat("currentHealth");`.

With our header and function body combined, we're asking that if you're going to fire this code, you need to supply an integer for the Ammo value and a float for the Health value. We then take these values and tell the variables that their new value is whatever data we've loaded from PlayerPrefs. In our case, we've loaded the saved Ammo and Heath values. We load this data and then set the variables to the data we've loaded.

```
public void PlayerPrefLoad(ref int iAmmoToUse, ref float fHealthToUse)
    {
        iAmmoToUse = PlayerPrefs.GetInt("currentAmmo");
        fHealthToUse = PlayerPrefs.GetFloat("currentHealth");
    }
```

We still have the problem that we're saving an Ammo value of 1 and a Health amount of 50. We want to be able to save whatever values the Ammo and Health values are instead of these hard-coded numbers. In order to do this, we simply change the function header of our `PlayerPrefSave` from `public void PlayerPrefSave();` to `public void PlayerPrefSave (int iAmmoToSave, float fHealthToSave);`. Now replace the values inside the function body with our variables, and our function will use the data sent in instead of the previous hard-coded values.

```
public void PlayerPrefSave(int iAmmoToSave, float fHealthToSave)
    {
        PlayerPrefs.SetInt("currentAmmo", iAmmoToSave);
        PlayerPrefs.SetFloat("currentHealth", fHealthToSave);
    }
```

We've now created a working Saving and Loading system in Unity using the PlayerPrefs system that can load saved data or save data to the user's hard drive.

If you want to test the functionality of your created code, you can save it and head back into Unity. From here, you can attach your code onto any object in the scene by dragging the code file and dropping it into the blank area of any properties page. You can then write another class that calls the functions whenever you want to save and load the data. An example class would be:

```
using System.Collections;
using System.Collections.Generic;
using UnityEngine;
// Putting this before our class makes sure that we can't fire this code without our PlayerPrefExample code attached.
[RequireComponent(typeof(PlayerPrefExample))]
public class ExampleSaveLoadScript : MonoBehaviour
{
    PlayerPrefExample ourSaveScript;
    int iCurrentAmmo;
    float fCurrentHealth;
    // Start is called before the first frame update
    void Start()
    {
        // Find our Save Game Script
        ourSaveScript = GetComponent<PlayerPrefExample>();
        // Fire the function using our ammo and health values
        ourSaveScript.PlayerPrefLoad(ref iCurrentAmmo, ref fCurrentHealth);
```

INTEGERS AND FLOATS

Sometimes, our compiler (the tool that turns our code into something readable by Unity) can't tell the difference between an integer and a float. It's good practice to force the compiler to read float values as floats by adding an 'f' immediately after the number. This will tell the compiler this value is a float and not an integer.

```
        //Write our values to the log, so we
can see if they were correctly loaded.
        Debug.Log("Our current Ammo = " +
iCurrentAmmo + ", and our health value = " +
fCurrentHealth);
    }
    void PickedUpAmmo(int iAmountOfAmmoPickedUp)
    {
        iCurrentAmmo += iAmountOfAmmoPickedUp;
    }
    void PickedUpHealthPack(float fHealthToAdd)
    {
        fCurrentHealth += fHealthToAdd;
    }
    private void OnApplicationQuit()
    {
        // Find our Save Game Script
        ourSaveScript = gameObject.GetComponent
<PlayerPrefExample>();

        //Write our values to the log, so we
can see if they were correctly loaded.
        Debug.Log("We are saving the ammo value
of = " + iCurrentAmmo + " and the health value
of = " + fCurrentHealth);
        // Fire the function using our ammo and
health values
        ourSaveScript.
PlayerPrefSave(iCurrentAmmo, fCurrentHealth);
    }
}
```

This example code will load our file and the values when the game starts; and, when the game ends, it will save our values to a file. There are also two functions in there to change the values while the game is being played. Using what you've learned this far, you should be able to trigger these functions in your example game.

Now that we have a working saving and loading system working in Unity, it's time to create another saving and loading system – this time using the Serialization tools. This will give us a deeper understanding of what each system does and why you'd use Serialization in some situations and PlayerPrefs in others.

Create another C# script file and call this one BinarySaveLoad – place it in the same location (the folder named SaveGame) and open it up in your code editor. As we did before, remove the **`Start`** and **`Update`** functions, replacing them with your own **`void BinarySave();`** and **`void BinaryLoad();`** functions. We won't be using the same function headers as we did before because this time, we want to deal with a lot more data.

Functions have been added, so now we can get to writing all of the fun test stuff.

```
using System.Collections;
using System.Collections.Generic;
using UnityEngine;
public class BinarySaveLoad : MonoBehaviour
{
    public void BinarySave()
    {
    }
    public void BinaryLoad()
    {
    }
}
```

To show you how to use Serialization, we're going to use a structure. To put it very simply for the purposes of this tutorial, a structure (or struct) is essentially a data type that can store more than one variable inside, so we'll be creating and using one to store our player information for our Serialization save-load system.

To do this, create a new function just before **`BinarySave()`** – the function header should be **`public Struct PlayerData`**. Inside, we need to add our variables.

To show off the power of Serialization, we're going to add various types of variables to this struct. We need to add a string (text) for the player's name (**`sPlayerName`**), an integer (whole number) for the current ammo (**`iCurrentAmmo`**), a float (number with decimal place) for the player's current health (**`fCurrentHealth`**) and a bool (true or false) value for if the player has achieved a certain goal (**`bHasPlayerDoneSomething`**). We will implement these variables into our struct before moving on. →

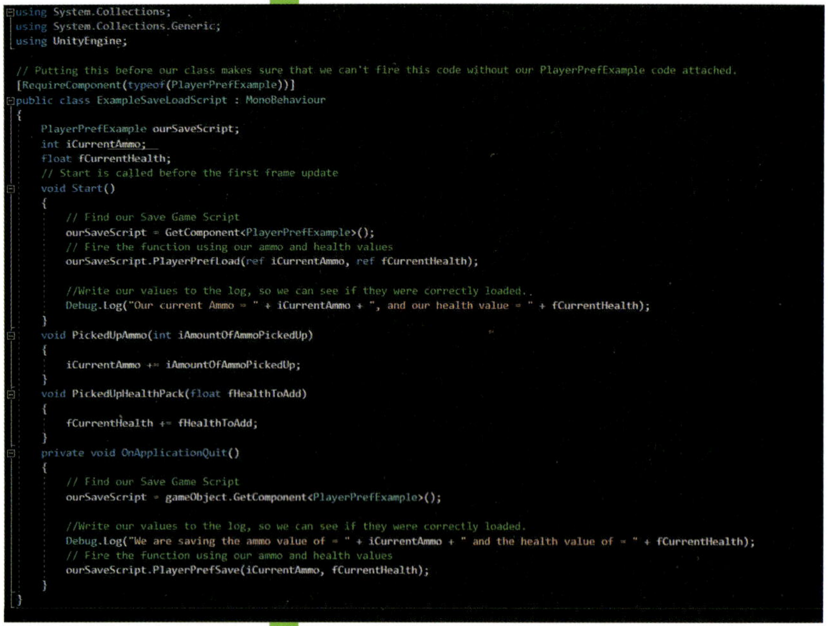

```
using System.Collections;
using System.Collections.Generic;
using UnityEngine;

// Putting this before our class makes sure that we can't fire this code without our PlayerPrefExample code attached.
[RequireComponent(typeof(PlayerPrefExample))]
public class ExampleSaveLoadScript : MonoBehaviour
{
    PlayerPrefExample ourSaveScript;
    int iCurrentAmmo;
    float fCurrentHealth;
    // Start is called before the first frame update
    void Start()
    {
        // Find our Save Game Script
        ourSaveScript = GetComponent<PlayerPrefExample>();
        // Fire the function using our ammo and health values
        ourSaveScript.PlayerPrefLoad(ref iCurrentAmmo, ref fCurrentHealth);

        //Write our values to the log, so we can see if they were correctly loaded..
        Debug.Log("Our current Ammo = " + iCurrentAmmo + ", and our health value = " + fCurrentHealth);
    }
    void PickedUpAmmo(int iAmountOfAmmoPickedUp)
    {
        iCurrentAmmo += iAmountOfAmmoPickedUp;
    }
    void PickedUpHealthPack(float fHealthToAdd)
    {
        fCurrentHealth += fHealthToAdd;
    }
    private void OnApplicationQuit()
    {
        // Find our Save Game Script
        ourSaveScript = gameObject.GetComponent<PlayerPrefExample>();

        //Write our values to the log, so we can see if they were correctly loaded.
        Debug.Log("We are saving the ammo value of = " + iCurrentAmmo + " and the health value of = " + fCurrentHealth);
        // Fire the function using our ammo and health values
        ourSaveScript.PlayerPrefSave(iCurrentAmmo, fCurrentHealth);
    }
}
```

Now that our test stuff is working, you can freely save and load your ammo and HP for your player.

```
using System.Collections;
using System.Collections.Generic;
using UnityEngine;
public class BinarySaveLoad : MonoBehaviour
{
    public struct PlayerData
    {
        public string sPlayerName;
        public int iCurrentAmmo;
        public float fCurrentHealth;
        public Vector3 vPlayerLocation;
        public bool bHasPlayerDoneSomething;
    }

    public void BinarySave()
    {
    }
    public void BinaryLoad()
    {
    }
}
```

We have our struct and functions, but before we dive in and begin saving and loading our data, we need to make two slight changes to our functions. When we load our data, we don't want to have to already have this data to hand. We want our function to return the loaded struct. To do this, we'll simply change **`Public Void BinaryLoad()`** to **`Public PlayerData BinaryLoad()`**. This is because the first variable declared in a function header is what the variable will return. Before this, we used **`void`** – which is a keyword for saying that the function doesn't return any value. By putting **`PlayerData`** in place of **`void`**, we're telling Unity that this function will return a **`PlayerData`** variable. The second change we need to make is to **`BinarySave`**. We want to be able to pass in the data to save, so go ahead and alter the **`BinarySave()`** function header from **`Public Void BinarySave()`** to **`Public Void BinarySave(PlayerData DataToUse)`**. We learned about sending variables into our functions earlier, so by now you should be quite comfortable with parsing variables into and out of functions.

Before we implement our Serialization save/load code, we have to add two includes to this file. An include is a statement that tells Unity that this code needs to talk to the specified file, to retrieve the functions and variables and perform the tasks we need. To add the includes, go to the top of your file and after the last Include statement, add **`using System.Runtime.Serialization.Formatters.Binary;`** and **`using System.IO;`**. These are the includes we need to read and write data from a file:

```
using System.Collections;
using System.Collections.Generic;
using UnityEngine;
using System.Runtime.Serialization.Formatters.
Binary;
using System.IO;
public class BinarySaveLoad : MonoBehaviour
```

Now that we have the power to read and write to a file, the time has come to do exactly that. Within our **`public PlayerData BinaryLoad()`** function, we need an **`if`** statement.

"The data is now loaded and the PlayerData has been extracted from the file"

This **`if`** statement should read: **`if(File.Exists (Application.persistentDataPath + "/BinaryData.save"))`**. This line of code is checking the path where data is saved and looking for the file called BinaryData.save. If this is true, we need to tell Unity what to do, so add a **`{`**, and we're going to create a BinaryFormatter – a built-in C# utility for serialising and deserialising objects.

To create a new variable inside a function, we declare the variable type, give it a friendly name and then fill it with data. To create a BinaryFormatter variable, we're going to add this line to our code: **`BinaryFormatter tempFormatter =`**

```
using System.Collections;
using System.Collections.Generic;
using UnityEngine;
using System.Runtime.Serialization.Formatters.Binary;
using System.IO;

public class BinarySaveLoad : MonoBehaviour
{
    public struct PlayerData
    {
        public string sPlayerName;
        public int iCurrentAmmo;
        public float fCurrentHealth;
        public Vector3 vPlayerLocation;
        public bool bHasPlayerDoneSomething;
    }

    public void BinarySave(PlayerData DataToUse)
    {
        FileStream tempStreamToUse;
        BinaryFormatter tempFormatter = new BinaryFormatter();
        string sPathToUse = Application.persistentDataPath + "/BinaryData.save";

        if (File.Exists(sPathToUse))
        {
            tempStreamToUse = File.OpenWrite(sPathToUse);
        }
        else
        {
            tempStreamToUse = File.Create(sPathToUse);
        }
        tempFormatter.Serialize(tempStreamToUse, DataToUse);
        tempStreamToUse.Close();
    }

    public PlayerData BinaryLoad()
    {
        if (File.Exists(Application.persistentDataPath + "/BinaryData.save"))
        {
            BinaryFormatter tempFormatter = new BinaryFormatter();
            FileStream tempStreamToUse = File.OpenRead(Application.persistentDataPath + "/BinaryData.save");
            PlayerData tempData = (PlayerData)tempFormatter.Deserialize(tempStreamToUse);
            tempStreamToUse.Close();
            return tempData;
        }
        return new PlayerData();
    }
}
```

^ The full binary formatter script is quite complex, but it might provide what you need for your project.

`new BinaryFormatter();`. This will create the utility for us. Once this has been done, we then need to open the file. We can do this with a FileStream, another C# utility, this time for loading files. Add the code `FileStream tempStreamToUse = File.OpenRead(Application.persistentDataPath + "/BinaryData.save");`. This tells Unity to look at the file at the location specified and the `File.OpenRead` tells Unity to open said file.

We know what data this is going to be, so we're going to add this code next: `PlayerData tempData = (PlayerData)tempFormatter.Deserialize(tempStreamToUse);`. This line of code tells Unity to get the raw data from the file we fed in, deserialize it using the BinaryFormatter, and treat that data as a `PlayerData` struct. The (`PlayerData`) call in that line of code is a cast, which means 'treat whatever is after this as whatever variable is in the bracket', which in this case is our `PlayerData` struct.

The data is now loaded and the `PlayerData` has been extracted from the file. Now we need to tell the FileStream utility that we're finished, and we can do that with `tempStreamToUse.Close();`. We're still holding onto the data we collected from the BinaryFormatter and as we discussed before, this function gives the data over to whoever asked for it. To do this, add `return tempData;` to push the data. Now simply close this block with a `}` and we're almost finished with this function.

We've told Unity what to do if the file is found, but we need to tell it what should happen if it can't find the file specified. Inside our `if` check, we're returning data. The `return` keyword tells Unity to stop firing this function as we have what we came here for. This means that if the `if` check is successful, this function will only fire what is in that `if` check. This helps us, because after the `if` block, we can add `return new PlayerData();`. If the `if` statement isn't true, it's going to look for the next line of code outside the `if` statement – which is our new `PlayerData`.

```
using System.Collections;
using System.Collections.Generic;
using UnityEngine;
using System.Runtime.Serialization.Formatters.
Binary;
using System.IO;
public class BinarySaveLoad : MonoBehaviour
{
    public struct PlayerData
    {
        public string sPlayerName;
        public int iCurrentAmmo;
        public float fCurrentHealth;
        public Vector3 vPlayerLocation;
        public bool bHasPlayerDoneSomething;
    }
    public void BinarySave(PlayerData
DataToUse)
    {
    }
    public PlayerData BinaryLoad()
 {
        if (File.Exists(Application.
persistentDataPath + "/BinaryData.save"))
        {
            BinaryFormatter tempFormatter = new
BinaryFormatter();
            FileStream tempStreamToUse = File.
OpenRead(Application.persistentDataPath + "/
BinaryData.save");
            PlayerData tempData = (PlayerData)
tempFormatter.Deserialize(tempStreamToUse);
            tempStreamToUse.Close();
```

LIMITATIONS

PlayerPrefs has a number of limitations to consider. PlayerPrefs can only read and save floats, integers, and strings, and stores this data as a text file on the user's hard drive. PlayerPrefs shouldn't be used for data that isn't floats, integers, or strings, and should never be used to store any sensitive data you don't want the player to manipulate, such as progress, passwords, or anything that could lead to a player gaining an unfair advantage in your game.

```
            return tempData;
        }
        return new PlayerData();

    }
}
```

Here's what your PlayerPrefs saving prefab should look like in your Inspector.

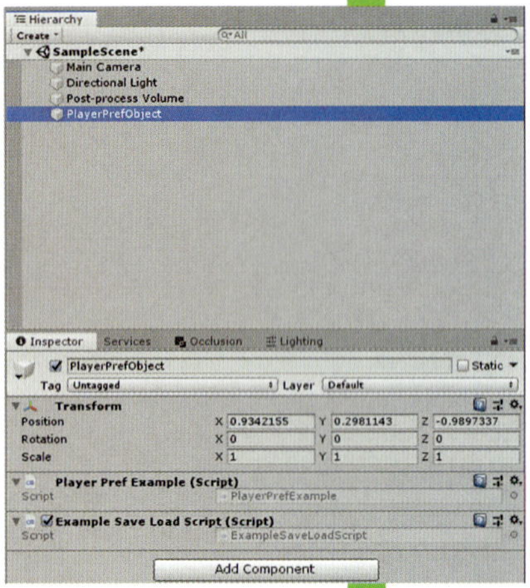

Now that we have file loading sorted, we need to fill out our **BinarySave** function. Luckily, it's quite similar to what we've already done. Head into the **BinarySave** function and create two variables. We need to store the FileStream and BinaryFormatter – all will become clear shortly. To create a new FileStream, add the code **FileStream tempStreamToUse;** and to create the BinaryFormatter, add **BinaryFormatter tempFormatter = new BinaryFormatter();**. The function we're about to write is going to reference the file path a number of times with **string sPathToUse = Application.persistentDataPath + "/BinaryData.save";**. That line of code lets us write **sPathToUse** instead of having to type out the whole string every time.

We now need an **if** statement to check if the file exists as we can't save data into thin air. Create a new **if** statement that says **if (File.Exists(sPathToUse))**. Notice how we didn't have to write that long string this time?

If the file exists, we open the file by adding the **{** and then **tempStreamToUse = File.OpenWrite(sPathToUse);** – this fills in our FileStream variable with the data loaded from the file we've just opened for writing data to. Once you've added that line, close off this block with a **}**. Unlike last time, we need to perform a task if the file doesn't exist, as again, we can't save data into thin air. To do this, we can use an **else** statement. **else** statements are similar to **if** statements, but they're used when something is false instead of true. Go ahead and add **else {**. Inside this block, we need to create the file. This can be done with **tempStreamToUse = File.Create(sPathToUse);**. We're creating the file at the location and storing this new data inside our FileStream variable. Once done, we can close off this block with **}**.

Once in the Inspector, your binary formatter saving prefab should look like this.

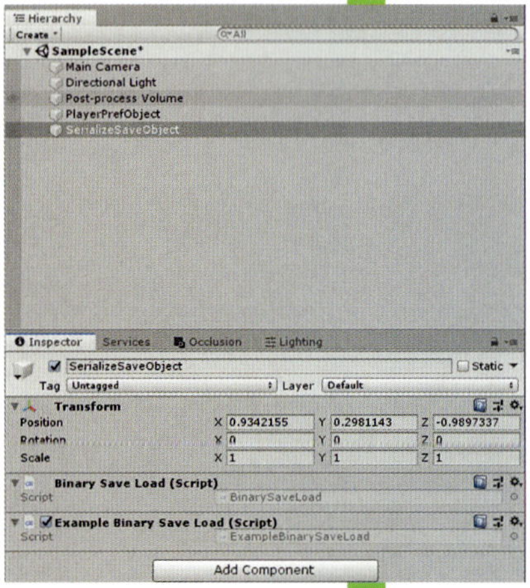

So far, we've either loaded the file ready to write to it or we've create a brand new file ready for data. We now have to add our data to the file, which can be done with **tempFormatter.Serialize(tempStreamToUse, DataToUse);**. This function serialises our data to the FileStream we've specified using the data we've fed into the function call. We then tell Unity we've finished editing the file by calling **tempStreamToUse.Close();**.

```
using System.Collections;
using System.Collections.Generic;
using UnityEngine;
using System.Runtime.Serialization.Formatters.
Binary;
using System.IO;
public class BinarySaveLoad : MonoBehaviour
{
    public struct PlayerData
    {
        public string sPlayerName;
        public int iCurrentAmmo;
        public float fCurrentHealth;
        public Vector3 vPlayerLocation;
        public bool bHasPlayerDoneSomething;
    }
    public void BinarySave(PlayerData DataToUse)
    {
        FileStream tempStreamToUse;
        BinaryFormatter tempFormatter = new
BinaryFormatter();
        string sPathToUse = Application.
persistentDataPath + "/BinaryData.save";

        if (File.Exists(sPathToUse))
        {
            tempStreamToUse = File.
OpenWrite(sPathToUse);
        }
        else
        {
            tempStreamToUse = File.
Create(sPathToUse);
        }
        tempFormatter.Serialize(tempStreamToUse,
DataToUse);
        tempStreamToUse.Close();
    }
```

```
    public PlayerData BinaryLoad()
    {
        if (File.Exists(Application.
persistentDataPath + "/BinaryData.save"))
        {
            BinaryFormatter tempFormatter = new
BinaryFormatter();
            FileStream tempStreamToUse = File.
OpenRead(Application.persistentDataPath + "/
BinaryData.save");
            PlayerData tempData = (PlayerData)
tempFormatter.Deserialize(tempStreamToUse);
            tempStreamToUse.Close();
            return tempData;
        }
        return new PlayerData();
    }
}
```

Now we have the power of saving and loading using the Serialization features of C#. To test this out, you can create another script like we did to test the functionality of the PlayerPrefs system.

```
using System.Collections;
using System.Collections.Generic;
using UnityEngine;

// Putting this before our class makes sure
that we can't fire this code without our
PlayerPrefExample code attached.
[RequireComponent(typeof(BinarySaveLoad))]
public class ExampleBinarySaveLoad :
MonoBehaviour
{
    BinarySaveLoad ourSaveScript;
    BinarySaveLoad.PlayerData ourPlayerData;

    // Start is called before the first frame
update
    void Start()
    {
        // Find our Save Game Script
        ourSaveScript =
GetComponent<BinarySaveLoad>();
        // Fire the function to get our data
values.
        ourPlayerData = ourSaveScript.
BinaryLoad();

        //Write our values to the log, so we
can see if they were correctly loaded.
        Debug.Log("Our current Ammo = " +
ourPlayerData.iCurrentAmmo + ", and our health
value = " + ourPlayerData.fCurrentHealth);
    }

    void PickedUpAmmo(int iAmountOfAmmoPickedUp)
    {
        ourPlayerData.iCurrentAmmo +=
iAmountOfAmmoPickedUp;
    }

    void PickedUpHealthPack(float fHealthToAdd)
    {
        ourPlayerData.fCurrentHealth +=
fHealthToAdd;
    }

    private void OnApplicationQuit()
    {
        // Find our Save Game Script
        ourSaveScript = gameObject.
GetComponent<BinarySaveLoad>();

        //Write our values to the log, so we
can see if they were correctly loaded.
        Debug.Log("We are saving the ammo
value of = " + ourPlayerData.iCurrentAmmo + "
and the health value of = " + ourPlayerData.
fCurrentHealth);

        // Fire the function using our ammo and
health values
        ourSaveScript.BinarySave(ourPlayerData);
    }
}
```

There we have it: you've created a full save/load game system in both PlayerPrefs and using the Serialization utilities. As you can see, PlayerPrefs gives us quick, lightweight access to our integers, floats, and strings, whereas Serialization gives us a lot more options, control, and security. Once you've wrapped your head around the concepts, it really is quite simple to load and save player data within Unity. From here, you can start to add functions to the example scripts (such as only letting the player save at certain points in the game). The possibilities are nearly endless.

LOOK SHARP

C# has a near limitless amount of helpful functions, utilities, and features that can help us in our game development adventure. Be wary, though: not all of these features will work out of the box on consoles or mobile platforms.

By changing the skybox and lighting in our level, we're able to make the boss feel moody and menacing when players eventually meet it.

Developing a boss battle

Want to end your level with a formidable boss encounter? Here's how to create one

AUTHOR
STUART FRASER

Stuart is a former designer and developer of high-profile games such as *RollerCoaster Tycoon 3*, and also worked as a lecturer of games development.

Boss battles are a major staple of any modern action game. These usually happen at the end of a level, and challenge the player to demonstrate all the skills they've honed up to that point. A common idea is that the boss has devastating but telegraphed attacks, which the player must learn how to avoid to survive, while at the same time hitting the boss's weak points to whittle down its energy. Good examples of these sorts of set-pieces can be seen in games like *God of War* and *Devil May Cry*, which are famous for their striking character designs and challenging attack patterns.

To start building a boss fight of our own, we first need to find a suitable 3D model with a specific set of animations that we can use to build our encounter. Luckily for us, there's a free service by Adobe called Mixamo that allows us access to models and animations in one convenient package.

To get started, head over to **mixamo.com** and then create an Adobe account if you don't already have one. You can then log in, at which point you'll be presented with a web-based browser that has both characters and animations to pick from.

We want to grab a character first, so select the Characters heading along the top, and then search for the word Mutant to find the character you can see in the image at the top of this page. Select this, and there should be a Download button on the right-hand side of the page.

When you select this, you'll then see a window that has several drop-down options. Set the Format to Collada (.dae) and check that the Pose is set to a T-Pose.

The *God of War* series is well known for its superb bosses that tower over the protagonist.

Next, we can jump to the Animations heading. We then need to search for Mutant – this returns all specific animations for this character. We're looking for the Creature Pack, since this bundle contains all the animations together. Select this as before, and then select the Download button on the right-hand side of the page. We want to set the Format to FBX for Unity and check that the Pose is set to T-Pose, then download it.

We're going to open our existing first-person shooter project, and then we can select File > New Scene to create a new level. Initially, we can delete the Main Camera from the Hierarchy as we don't need it in our scene.

We then need to find our Mixamo assets in Windows, then unzip both downloads. Starting with the initial character download, we can drag both unzipped folders into the Project panel in Unity. You may get a message about normal map settings – just select the Fix Now option. You can go ahead and delete the mutant.dae mesh from the mutant folder that appears in the Project panel, as it's no longer required.

Now select the Player prefab from your Project panel and drag it into the Hierarchy panel. An important step is to add a floor for the boss battle to take place on; my favoured way of doing this is to go to the toolbar and select GameObject > 3D Object > Plane. We can then set the X and Z scale values to around three units each in our Inspector. In the Project panel, select the Creature Pack folder – this contains our animations and the mutant mesh. Drag the mutant mesh from the folder into the Hierarchy panel. We may need to use the transform tools in Unity to place both the player character and mutant mesh on our floor. We should make sure there's some distance between the two – say about eight units. We also want to delete any additional cameras in the scene that don't belong to our player character.

"Boss battles are a major staple of any modern action game"

We can now work on making our boss seem more menacing, and start adding our animations – later, we'll add some C# code to make the boss character have some basic AI behaviours.

The first quick change we can make is select the mutant game object in the Hierarchy and then in the Inspector set the X, Y, Z scale to 2. This instantly makes the mutant feel more menacing as it towers above our player.

We now want to move to the Project panel and then right-click and select Create > Animator Controller. This will allow us to build up a set of animations that we can then switch between by using a finite state machine – just think of it like a flow chart which we can trigger. We should ➔

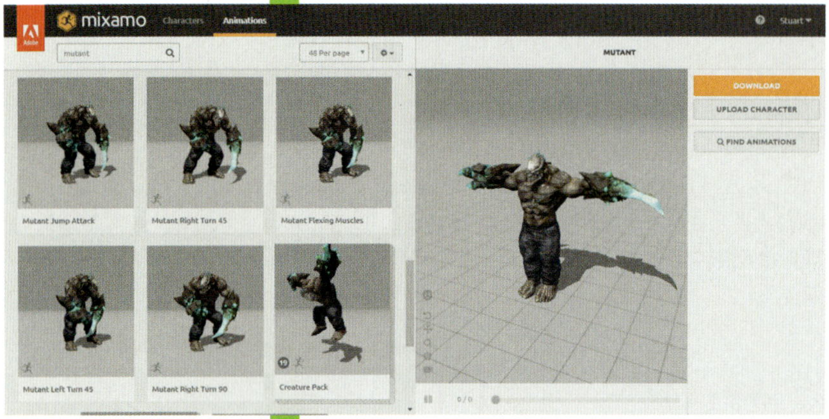

^ Mixamo is an excellent tool for adding animations to rigged characters. In our case, we're going to download one of the many animation packs and one of their pre-made characters.

rename the Animator Controller by clicking the name and then typing in BossAnimator. We can then double-click the icon, and this should open the Animator panel. We then navigate to the Creature Pack folder in the Project view, as we want to drag animations over to the Animator panel. The first animation to locate is the Mutant Roar animation; drag this into the Animator Controller and you should see it's linked to the Entry node.

To make it easier to differentiate between each animation, rename this new animation Roar in the Inspector panel. We'll then drag over several additional animations and ideally rename them as we did with the Roar. The animations you need to drag into the Animator are: mutant run, mutant swiping, mutant jump attack, and mutant punch. These give the boss some basic movements, such as the run, as well as a few attack moves.

GETTING ANIMATED

While we're here, we should also add transitions to each animation and a transition back to Roar. As an example, let's select the Roar animation and then right-click and select Make Transition. Select the Run animation, and you should see both are linked by a line with an arrow that points at the Run animation. We now need to select the Run animation and right-click it again. Choose Make Transition, this time selecting the Roar animation. With that one done, we can now repeat for the other animations.

Once all the transitions have been made, we need to make some parameters for us to trigger the correct animations. We can do this by selecting the Parameters tab in the Animator. We then select the + icon and choose Bool, and change the New Bool name to isRunning. Next, select the + icon again and choose Int; this time, set the New Int name to isAttacking.

We want to set up these parameters on our transitions. Starting with our Roar to Run transition, select the transition and then in the Inspector, deselect the checkbox for Has Exit Time, and then look for the Conditions entry. Select the + icon to the right-hand side of this word and choose isRunning and leave this set to true. We'll repeat this for the transition that is the opposite: it goes from Run to Roar. However, we need to change the drop-down for the isRunning to false, and remember to deselect Has Exit Time.

"We can play a satisfying animation to make it clear we've beaten our foe"

With the other animations, we only need to set our parameters on the transition from Roar to each of our attack animations. The reason for this is that we want the animations to play out completely, and the option Has Exit Time will handle this for us. If we focus on the Swiping attack as an example, we should select the Roar to Swiping transition. Next, uncheck Has Exit Time and in our Conditions, select the + icon and set the parameter isAttacking – set the middle drop-down to Equals, and the numeric value to 1. We can repeat the process with the other transitions and just increment the number value, so our Jump Attack may have the parameter values as isAttacking Equals 2, and so on.

We're going to add one more animation, a single one-way transition, and an additional parameter. Select the mutant dying animation from the Project folder and drag it onto the animator. As with the other animations, rename this to something meaningful in the Inspector: e.g. Dying. Select the Roar animation and right-click on it, then set the Make Transition to the new Dying animation. We need to enter the Parameters panel and select the + icon, then choose Bool. We will name this isDead and then select our

v We have the fully rigged mutant mesh and a set of suitable animations that we can pick from. We can implement these to make our boss come to life.

^ The stage is set for an epic boss fight. Or it would be with some additional artwork and level design.

transition to the Dying animation. In the Inspector, uncheck the Has Exit Time option, and set our Conditions by selecting the + icon and set the condition to isDead. This will mean that when the boss loses all of its health, we can play a satisfying animation to make it clear that we've beaten our abominable foe.

Once we have this set up, we can add a script that will trigger our boss behaviour. This can be achieved by selecting the mutant game object in the Hierarchy and then moving to the Inspector panel. In the Inspector, select Add Component > New Script, set the Name to BossController, and select Create and Add.

Once this script has been added, we can double-click on it to open it in a script editor and add the code below:

```
using UnityEngine;

public class BossController : MonoBehaviour
{
    public int attackRange = 3;
    private Transform player;
    private Animator anim;
    private int attackType;
    private bool setForce = false;
    private Vector3 direction;


    // Start is called before the first frame
update
    void Start()
    {
        player = GameObject.
FindGameObjectWithTag("Player").transform;
        anim = GetComponent<Animator>();
    }


    private void Update()
    {
        if (!anim.GetBool("isDead"))
        {
            //Find the direction
            direction = player.position -
transform.position;
            //If the boss is far enough away
from the player, rotate to look at the player.
            if (direction.magnitude > 2f)
            {
                transform.LookAt(new
Vector3(player.position.x, 0, player.
position.z));
            }
            //Set a random value between a
range we set to choose our attack type.
            if (!anim.GetBool("isRunning") &&
attackType == 0)
            {
                attackType = Random.Range(1,
attackRange+1);
            }
        }
    }


    // Update is called once per frame
    void FixedUpdate()
    {
        //If the boss is too far from the
player, run towards them.
        if (!anim.GetBool("isDead"))
        {
            if (direction.magnitude > 3f)
            {
                anim.SetBool("isRunning",
true);
                attackType = 0;
                anim.SetInteger("isAttacking",
0);
            }
            //If we are close enough, do an
attack.
```

ANIMATIONS

You can easily select other animations if you want to extend the range of movements or attacks the boss will have. Mixamo deals with making the animations work on any of the character skeletons, so you can try mixing and matching animations intended for other characters.

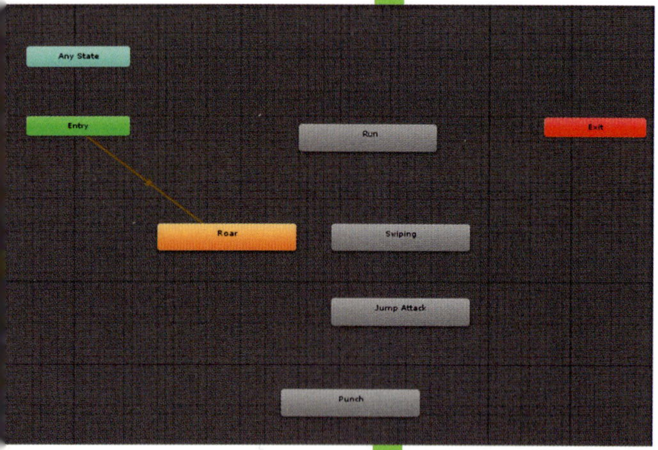

We must have a base set of animations in the animator so we can have the boss character stomp around and pull off some devastating attacks.

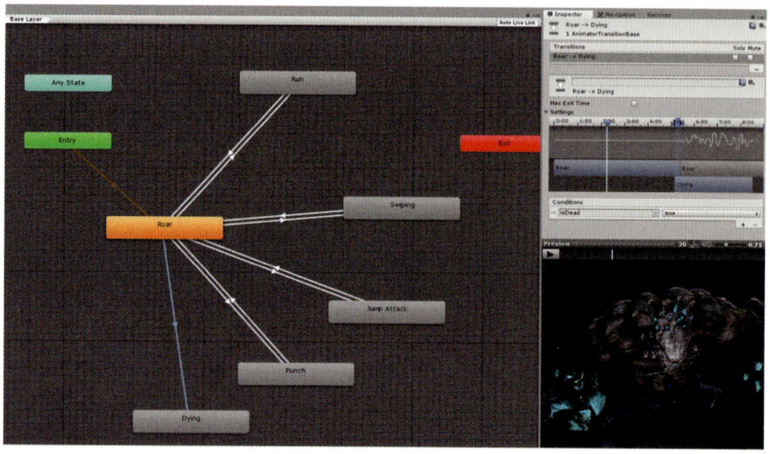

It's important to be sure that all the transitions have been made, and the parameters for triggering them are correct.

```
            else
            {
                anim.SetBool("isRunning",
false);
                anim.SetInteger("isAttacking",
attackType);
                if (anim.
GetCurrentAnimatorStateInfo(0).normalizedTime
< 0.1f)
                {
                    setForce = true;
                }
                //At the moment we trigger
damage at force when animation is about 50% for
all attacks.
                if (setForce && anim.
GetCurrentAnimatorStateInfo(0).normalizedTime
> 0.5f)
                {
                    //Add some knock back to
the player.
                    player.
gameObject.GetComponent<Rigidbody>().
AddExplosionForce(5.0f, transform.position,
6.0f, 4.0f, ForceMode.Impulse);
                    if (direction.magnitude <=
3f)
                    {
                        //We can replace this
with something that sends damage to the player.
                        Debug.Log("Damage
Player");
                    }
                    setForce = false;
                }
            }
        }
        else
        {
            anim.SetBool("isRunning", false);
            anim.SetInteger("isAttacking", 0);
        }
    }
}
```

Save the code, and then move back to Unity. We now need to do some additional setup in our project to make sure everything works as expected. The first thing to do is select your player object in the Hierarchy and check that the Tag drop-down is set to Player at the top left on the Inspector panel. Next, select the mutant object in the Hierarchy, and then in the Inspector, select Add Component > Physics > Capsule Collider. In the Capsule Collider, change the Y value for the Center to 0.9 and set the value for the Height to 1.8. Next, select the BossAnimator from the Project panel and drag it onto the mutant object in the Hierarchy.

The next step is to check our animations are set up correctly. First, select all files in the Creature Pack from the Project panel. We want to look in the Inspector and select the Rig tab and change the Animation Type to Humanoid and then Apply. Unfortunately, this shows an error, but we can easily fix this by selecting just the mutant animation file. We will select the button marked as Configure... and when prompted, we should select save. We now have a 2D view of a humanoid character. Notice that the right hand is highlighted red; select it and then scroll the optional bone list that is below this representation of our character.

DAMAGE

The code printed here doesn't deal with player damage, but this could easily be extended to allow for this. Eagle-eyed readers should see some comments and debug to allow you to hook this in easily.

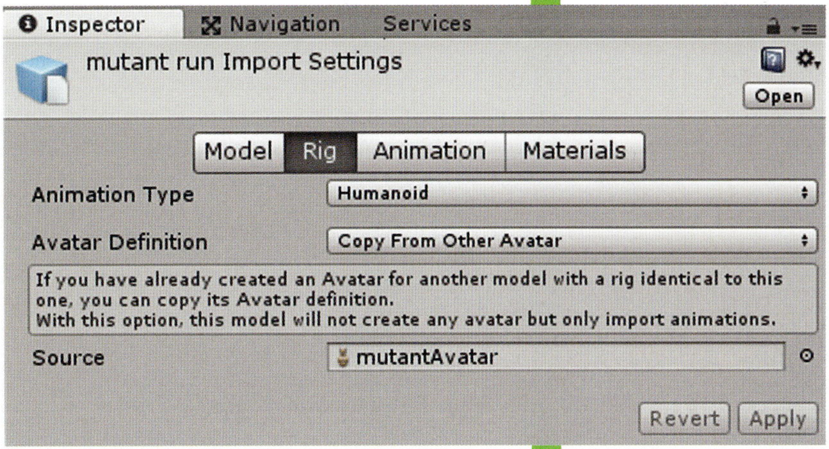

Make sure you have set up your base avatar and that you have set the option to copy this avatar to your animation set.

You should see that the left arm hasn't been set and shows None (Transform). We need to select it and set Mutant:LeftHand in the empty slot, then select Done and Apply.

We'll need to select all the other animations we're using in the Project panel. This can easily be achieved by holding the **CTRL** key and selecting the animations we're using. Next, look in the Inspector. In the Rig tab, change the drop-down for the Avatar Definition to Copy From Other Avatar, pick mutantAvatar as our Source, and Apply.

Next, select the mutant jump attack from the Project and then in the Inspector, you should select the Animation tab. We need to checkmark the following options – Loop Time, Loop Pose, and Bake into Pose – for Root Transform Rotation and Root Transform Position (Y). We'll have to repeat this process for the mutant run animation; however, we additionally need to set an Offset for the Root Transform Rotation to a value of -5.36.

We can now preview the scene by selecting the Play button from the toolbar. You should see the boss run toward the player and play one of the various attack animations. You should also see that we've added a knockback effect in our code.

HOW TO ADD WEAK SPOTS

Often in a boss battle, you'll get some feedback when you've successfully hit a weak spot. We're going to have a weak spot on each of our boss's hands, and we'll highlight the area to the player by using an emissive glow. This emissive glow effect is achieved by using a texture – anything black on the texture will be unlit, and anything white will be lit. We'll need to produce two new textures: we can use the mutant diffuse texture that's currently applied to the boss mesh to work out where we need to place our emissive hotspots. Using a photo editing package, open the Mutant_diffuse texture from the Unity Project. We'll save two copies of this with the names EmissiveLeft and EmissiveRight and then modify them as shown. I've created a diagram to show which areas to mask as white and what to paint as a solid black (**Figure 1**). Once these are done, we should save them into our Assets folder so they appear in our Project.

The next step is to create our own material. If we don't do this, then Unity will use its own default material and won't use our emissive channels. To make this new material, right-click in the Project panel and select Create > Material, then rename this MutantMat. In the Inspector we should see our material parameters; we need to set the Albedo to be the Mutant_diffuse texture provided by Mixamo. You will also need to set the Normal Map to be the mutant_normal that was also provided, and enable Emission via the checkbox. This material is now ready to use; we can simply drag it onto the mutant object in the Hierarchy.

"We're going to have a weak spot on each of our boss's hands"

We can now add a way to detect whether the player has managed to shoot our boss's weak spots. For this, we'll need to use colliders to check for the collision, and then a script to detect that they've been hit. This will work with a main boss health script to then calculate the damage.

The first step is to select the mutant object in the Hierarchy. We then need to navigate through the child objects. The objects we're looking for are buried and quite difficult to find, so expand mutant > Mutant:Hips > Mutant:Spine> Mutant:Spine1 > Mutant:Spine2 > Mutant:LeftShoulder > Mutant:LeftArm > Mutant:LeftForeArm and then select the Mutant:LeftHand. We can then right-click and select 3D Object > Capsule. →

Figure 1: For each of the new textures, we want to add white highlights to the areas that are used by the mutant mesh to render its hands. An example can be seen of the original diffuse texture and the emissive textures that have been created from it.

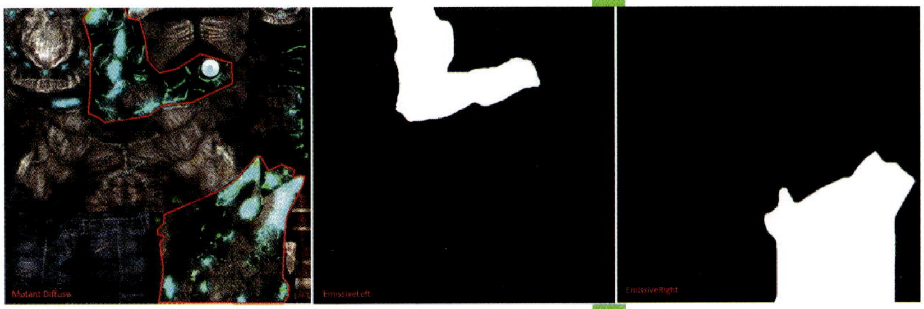

We should change the name in the Inspector to LeftHit for ease of use. The capsule is the wrong orientation and too big for the hand, so we need to rotate it 90 degrees in the Z axis and scale it down using the scale view.

We want to orient the capsule so the boss hand is just poking through its end. At this point, we can disable the Mesh Renderer component on our capsule, as we don't want it rendered in-game. We can then add the script by selecting Add Component > New Script and then setting our Name to WeakSpot and selecting Create and Add. We then need to double-click on the script and open it ready for editing with the following code:

```
using UnityEngine;


public class WeakSpot : MonoBehaviour
{
    private GameObject recGO;
    private BossHealth bossHealth;


    private void Start()
    {
        recGO = transform.root.gameObject;
        bossHealth = recGO.
GetComponent<BossHealth>();
    }


    public void OnCollisionEnter(Collision col)
    {
        string name = gameObject.name;
        bossHealth.ReceiveCollision(ref col,
ref name);
    }
}
```

Once complete, we can save the code and move back to Unity. The next stage is to repeat the process for the right hand. In this case, we need to go back to our Hierarchy panel and expand mutant > Mutant:Hips > Mutant:Spine > Mutant:Spine1 > Mutant:Spine2 > Mutant:RightShoulder > Mutant:RightArm > Mutant:RightForeArm and then select the Mutant:RightHand.

As before, right-click and create a capsule. This time, name it RightHit in the Inspector. Again, we need to rotate and rescale it and hide the render mesh. We may need to play about with the rotation as this hand is slightly offset from 90 degrees. There's no need for another script – we simply reuse the one we just made by dragging it from the Project panel to the Inspector.

We're nearly done. All we need to do is add our boss health script. Select the mutant in the Hierarchy; in the Inspector, you should be able to select Add Component > New Script and set the Name to BossHealth, and then select Create and Add.

As usual, open the script and add the following code to handle the boss's health:

```
using System.Collections;
using UnityEngine;


public class BossHealth : MonoBehaviour
{
    public int health = 5000;
    public GameObject mutantMesh;
    public Texture[] texture = new Texture[2];
    private int texRef;
    private Animator anim;


    // Start is called before the first frame
update
    void Start()
    {
        anim = GetComponent<Animator>();
    }


    public void Update()
    {
        if (health <= 0)
        {
            anim.SetBool("isDead", true);
        }
    }


    public void ReceiveCollision(ref Collision
col, ref string name)
    {
        if (col.transform.tag == "bullet")
        {
            health -= 250;
```

```
            Destroy(col.gameObject);
            if (mutantMesh != null && health >
0)
            {
                if (name == "LeftHit")
                {
                    StartCoroutine(HitFlash(0));
                }
                if (name == "RightHit")
                {
                    StartCoroutine(HitFlash(1));
                }
            }
        }
    }


    private void OnCollisionEnter(Collision
other)
    {
        if (other.gameObject.
CompareTag("bullet"))
        {
            health -= 1;
            Destroy(other.gameObject);
        }
    }


    private IEnumerator HitFlash(int num)
    {
        for (int i = 0; i < 5; i++)
        {
            mutantMesh.GetComponent<Renderer>().
material.SetTexture("_EmissionMap",
texture[num]);
            mutantMesh.GetComponent<Renderer>().
material.SetColor("_EmissionColor", Color.red);
            yield return new
WaitForSeconds(0.1f);
            mutantMesh.GetComponent<Renderer>().
material.SetColor("_EmissionColor", Color.
black);
            yield return new
WaitForSeconds(0.1f);
        }
        yield return null;
    }
}
```

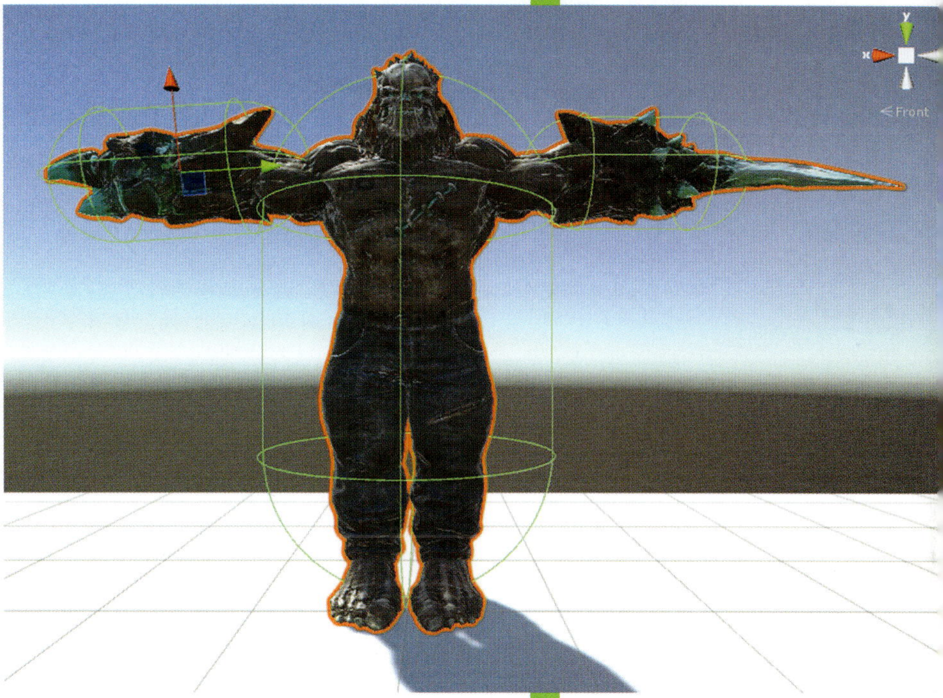

We should have colliders on the main body of the boss, as well as the two weak spot colliders we just set up on each hand. This is to help detect collisions, but specifically between the projectiles and the boss.

Save the script and move back to the mutant object in Unity. Once it's fully compiled, you should see a few new entries in the script on the Inspector that need us to assign some references. First, select the circle to the right of the words Mutant Mesh; search for MutantMesh in the window that appears and select it. You should also see the parameter called Texture; this needs to be expanded so you can see two slots. These slots are for the emissive textures we made earlier. We can easily drag these over from the Project view into these slots. Start with the EmissiveLeft texture in the first slot and the EmissiveRight texture in the second slot.

Now we can press the Play button from the Unity toolbar and try out our boss battle. You should see that we do the most damage to the boss by blasting the weak points, but you can still chip away at its energy by hitting the body. The range of attacks it uses is quite simple, so you could look at adding to those. You could also make a more bespoke boss mesh, add different weak spots, or even design a boss fight with multiple stages – shooting a weak spot on the boss's back could eventually expose a second vulnerable area on its chest, for example. There are all kinds of ways you could customise this tutorial to make an epic boss battle of your own.

Level design and inspiration

Find out more about the theory behind hitboxes, and glean some tips from the masters

System Shock 2 director Jon Chey and *Bulletstorm* level designer Steve Lee provide their insights into the process of making a great shooter.

Getting into FPS level design

Want to learn more about shooter level design? Then Half-Life 2 is a perfect place to start

AUTHOR
STEVE LEE

Steve Lee is a former designer at studios including Arkane and Irrational, and is now freelancing and consulting.
doublefunction.co.uk

I've been a designer in the games industry for about twelve years now, mostly working as a level designer on such triple-A games as *Bulletstorm*, *BioShock Infinite*, and *Dishonored 2*. The through-line that connects these titles is my love for the mix of action, storytelling, and exploration in first-person games. Like many designers of my generation, I started out making my own maps for *Doom*, back in the 1990s: one day, my older brother got hold of a *Doom* level editor called DoomCAD. As an eleven-year-old, it was a real watershed moment for me to learn that I could design levels myself.

The idea of learning game development at school or university basically didn't exist back then, but when *Doom* helped kick-start the mapping and modding scene, a number of later shooters included official level editors. I moved onto *Quake* level editing after *Doom* – another milestone, because it was one of the first truly 3D game engines that was deliberately designed to be modded – and later, *Half-Life 2*. You can still watch a video of the *Half-Life 2* level I made as my final project in university on YouTube (**wfmag.cc/steve-lee**). That level and video was my main portfolio piece when I applied for level design jobs in the industry.

Today, most people talk about Unity and Unreal 4 as the game engines of choice for would-be designers – but for getting into a first-person, single-player level design in 3D environments, I still recommend *Half-Life 2* as an ideal way to get started. It's modern enough that you can make things that look good, but also simple enough that it won't take you three years to finish a map on your own (which is an important thing to consider while you're learning).

Unity and Unreal 4 are obviously great at a lot of things, but they're largely a blank canvas for making games from scratch. This basically

Here's how Steve's Terminal level looks in Valve's Hammer Editor, the studio's Source engine map editor.

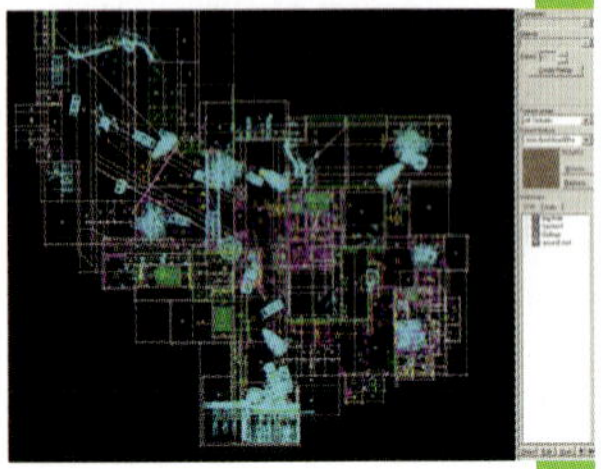

Steve Lee's Terminal level up and running in *Half-Life 2*.

A few tips for beginners:

1. Start with the smallest ideas and projects that you can think of. You'll learn far more by finishing a few small projects than starting one major project that's too ambitious to complete.
2. Focus on the player's experience. What can the player do, what are they thinking at any given time, and what happens if they perform a particular action?
3. Work efficiently to make something playable early on, in simple, rough form – then test it, analyse it, and build on it from there.
4. Get some friends or find people online to playtest your levels and give honest feedback throughout the process. Testing your own work is important, but the real acid test is when other people play it.

Placement of enemies is a key consideration in FPS level design.

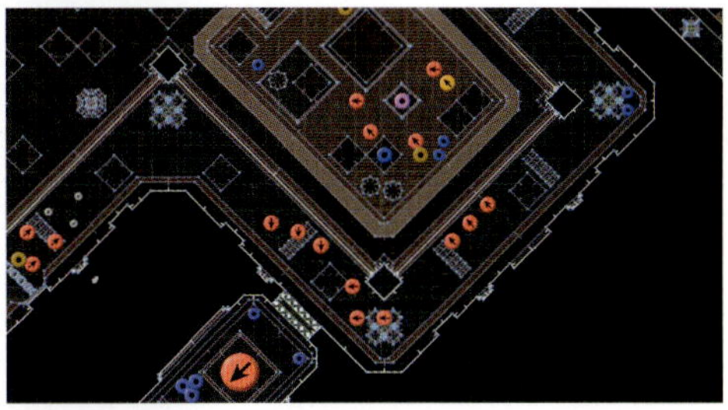

Doom Builder's top-down level editor is clean and intuitive.

Doom may be an antique, but Doom Builder is still an intuitive, fun map editor.

means that in order to do any level design with them, you have to make a whole game, too – exponentially multiplying the amount of work on your plate before you even start thinking about level design. If you know that it's specifically level design that you want to get into, I strongly recommend you approach it in a way that lets you focus on it as purely and efficiently as possible.

"What employers want to see is that you can make real, playable levels, with smart, interesting design"

I want to stress that to get a job as a level designer at a modern studio, you don't need to use the latest software or make levels for the latest, most complex games. My last job on a triple-A game was as a Senior Level Designer on *Dishonored 2* at Arkane Studios, and for my level design test, I made another, small *Half-Life 2* level to show that I knew my stuff and was a good fit for the team. This worked partly because I knew that Arkane have a history of using that engine, and that they like the kind of game *Half-Life 2* is: rich world-building and narrative, non-linear, systemic gameplay – all of that stuff.

What employers want to see is that you can make real, playable levels, with smart, interesting design, that are robust enough to deal with lots of different players let loose inside them. Knowing how to use a certain editor or tool a company uses is a plus, of course – but if you've made something good, they'll assume you can learn a new tool on the job.

So this first column is a call for you to go and seek out some level design software, look up the level design communities and tutorials online, and see what you can make. These projects take a lot of time, but stick with it and you might be surprised by what you can come up with, and where it leads you.

Half-Life 2: classic game, perfect for learning level design.

What if I don't like shooters?

Here are a few alternative approaches for you to consider, if you're keen to dip your toes into level design some other way:

- Make a small *Half-Life 2* level that tells a simple story without any action – perhaps through environmental storytelling, some simple interactions with other characters, and using the game's weapons to solve puzzles and navigate the area instead of engaging in combat.
- Find another kind of game that you like that comes with a level editor. *Portal*, *Super Mario Maker*, *TrackMania*, *Skyrim* – there are plenty of them to choose from.

6 tips for improving your level designs

Want to really make your stages stand out? Then here are six tips handy tips to follow

AUTHOR
STEVE LEE
Steve Lee is a former designer at studios including Arkane and Irrational, and is now freelancing and consulting.
doublefunction.co.uk

In the previous chapter, I talked about getting into level design the way I did – using the level editors for games you can get for free – and how I still recommend people get into it today using something like Hammer, the editor that comes with *Half-Life 2* (and *Portal*, *Team Fortress 2* and *Left 4 Dead*).

Here, I want to follow that up with a series of simple but important tips on how to approach the level design process, for any of you who are giving it a go. Sound good? Good.

1. Know your goals

This might sound obvious, but before you start doing things, it really helps to understand what you're trying to do. Yes, you're trying to make a level – but what kind of level? Which game is it for? What is it about? Is the focus on exciting, cinematic action gameplay? Mind-bending puzzles? Subtle, engaging interactive storytelling? What kind of experience do you want players to have? How is this level similar to what has come before, and how is it unique? Are you making the level to convince companies to hire you as a level designer, and if so, which ones?

These are questions that it's worth having answers to. Always have sensible and specific goals, and consciously design your project or level to achieve them.

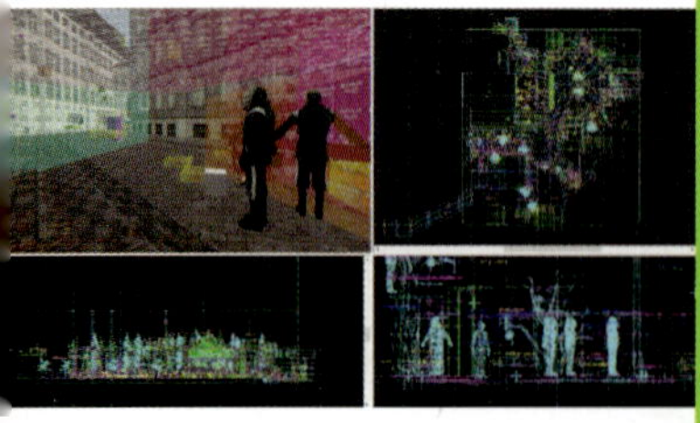

Half-Life 2 levels look like this, when viewed in Hammer, the Source Engine's level editor.

2. Keep your projects small

Speaking of sensible goals, try not to fall into the classic trap of being too ambitious with your project – especially if this is your first one. A common piece of advice in game development is to take your estimate of how long you think a project will take, and double it (at least).

Game dev and level design is hard, and it can take a long time to try ideas out, see which ones work, and which ones don't. By keeping your projects small, everything becomes faster, you increase the chances that you'll finish them, and you give yourself more time to not only make things, but make them really good.

3. Greybox first, get playable quickly

Another classic trap in game development is going overboard and being too wrapped up in making stuff, or polishing little things that don't really matter, forever – losing track of the bigger picture and how all things fit together (if they do at all). To avoid this, it's important to work broad strokes to begin with, blocking things out and prototyping in a quick and functional way early on, trying things out, and seeing what works (and just as importantly, what doesn't).

With 3D level design, this blockout phase is often done literally with big, simple boxes, covered in flat-colour development textures –

Levels for triple-A games can take several people months, even years, to make. Start simple and small!

Level designers work with simple shapes and textures to begin with, to be able to test, change and improve things quickly.

hence the term 'greyboxing' (or 'whiteboxing', 'orangeboxing', etc.). It's important to work like this so that shapes and layouts can be tested early, and also iterated on quickly, when testing reveals problems and changes that need to be made.

4. Focus on the player experience

When you're making levels, it can be tempting to get swept up in things like nice graphics, or deep, complex fiction that could fill a book, or cinematic presentation and bombastic events. All of these things can be good, of course, but the most important thing is always the player experience. It can be very easy to make something that seems superficially cool or impressive, but really, is kind of boring to play.

As level designers, we don't just care about what happens or what the players see and do – but what they're thinking, and how they feel about it. Are they really thinking about and understanding the things you want them to? Are they really having the experience you intended?

5. Playtest your map with others

It's important to remember that we're not designing levels just to play ourselves – they're for other people (and hopefully lots of them). Every player is different, and is going to experience a level in their own way. While you need to test your own work constantly while you're making it, the only real proof for whether a level is really working is when you see other people play it, and they give you honest opinions about their experience.

Everyone is too close to their own work to be able to see it from every angle. So if you want it to be good enough for lots of people to play, you have to let other people show you how it looks through their eyes, played by their hands.

6. Quality only comes from iteration

To paraphrase the novelist Ernest Hemingway: "The first draft of anything is poo." He's on the money, and this applies to level design just as much as it does to writing novels. If you really want to make something good, you need to give yourself time to make something first, and then spend even more time repeatedly improving it. This obviously ties in with point number one, about keeping projects small. The first level you make probably won't be your life's masterpiece – but if it's small, you'll be able to start iterating much earlier, and that much faster.

"If you really want to make something good, you need to give yourself time to make something first"

In 2007, Steve made his own two-part level for *Half-Life 2*, called The Terminal, which helped him get his first level design job in the industry.

Level design or environment art?

Level design and environment art sometimes get mixed up because of how much the two disciplines can overlap. Put simply, the latter is generally about making the environments look great, whereas level design is all about how it plays, and the overall player experience. Both involve a lot of thinking about presentation, composition and layout, and ideally complement each other. On the other hand, they can be in tension with each other and cause problems if they're not working together very well.

Creatively, most people lean more towards one of these disciplines than the other. And either is fine, of course. But if you consider yourself a level designer, you have to be focused on the player experience when other people play your game, and how everything (including the environment art and the visuals) serves the goal of helping the player understand and interact with it.

The theory behind first-person hitboxes

Choosing the right hitbox is key to making a great shooter. Here's the difference between them and why they matter

AUTHOR
PATRICK GORDON

Patrick is a research engineer at Hadean, a deep tech startup in Shoreditch, and a former competitive *Counter-Strike* player.

Figure 1: Hitboxes for *CS: GO* players are built from several capsules to closely match the character model, because the emphasis is on accuracy rather than speed of movement.

Almost all modern games simulate physics in some way. From the most basic collision in a roguelike to the complex calculations powering simulations like *Kerbal Space Program*, if you want to build a 3D game, you'll need to make the world feel solid. This is why your game needs hitboxes – the industry term for the physicality of a virtual object.

A hitbox is the representation of a shape that can't overlap with other hitboxes. The world has a hitbox, each player has a hitbox, the scenery, the houses, almost everything you can see and 'touch' in a game has a hitbox. To give the player a sense of realism, they have to be stopped from walking straight through that object, and will often see a physical reaction when two objects connect – bouncing is a common effect of a collision between hitboxes.

Why have we singled out first-person shooters for this feature? Because it's the genre that contains the most varied hitboxes, and where hitboxes have the most tangible impact on the action. The hitboxes you choose have to work hand-in-hand with the shooter you want to make. Do you want your game to feel slow and deliberate, with an emphasis on accuracy, or fast and arcade-like, where twitch reactions determine the winner?

It's useful to understand a little bit of geometry here, since we'll be talking about shapes and lines in three dimensions: spheres, boxes, rays, and segments. You can see these clearly laid out in the diagram on the bottom left.

The two most popular game engines today, Unity and Unreal, both have tools for working with simple capsules and joint articulated hitboxes (the most complex kind we'll be talking about) out of the box. Unreal lets you edit hitboxes of models in the Physics Asset Editor, while Unity gives you the Ragdoll Wizard for complete customisation and Character Controllers for single capsule hitboxes.

PRIMITIVES

'Hitbox' is actually a bit of a misnomer, because they come in more shapes than just boxes. The most common approach to making a hitbox is to use a set of primitives, such as spheres, rays, and more complex objects like capsules, which can be efficiently tested for intersecting with each other one-to-one. Boxes (or cuboids) aren't often used in shooters because they're more computationally expensive to intersect with each other and other primitives.

Axis-alignment and orientation is an important consideration for a hitbox. If a hitbox is axis-aligned, it means the primary axes don't rotate relative to the world/map axes: the 'up' direction on the box will always be the same vector. Boxes, cylinders, and capsules are often axis-aligned.

This will explain some of the terms you'll come across in this article and, more importantly, the parameters you'll need to set to define them.

Name	Diagram	Common Parameterisation
Axis aligned box		Width, height
Oriented box		Width, height, orientation
Ball/sphere/circle		Radius
Ray		Start, direction
Segment		Start, end
Capsule		Radius, segment

^ *Apex Legends* uses segmented trajectories for its weapons, which means its projectiles are all affected by physics.

When it comes to applying a hitbox to a character model, the process typically involves lining up boxes or capsules to the model's joints. If the triangle mesh around the upper arm bone of a player has a radius of roughly 10 cm all the way along the bone, for example, then the hitbox for that bone will have a radius of 10 cm and a length that is the same as the bone (**Figure 1**).

PROJECTILE HITBOXES

Once you've built a player hitbox, how does a non-player object interact with it? There are other primitives to consider here: rays and segments. Rays are straight lines that start at a point in space and go to infinity, while segments are lines with start and end points. Both of these can be used for hitboxes of projectiles. A ray would be used for something that travels with infinite speed and hits its target instantly, whereas a segment might be used for something that travels with a finite speed (**Figure 2**).

If a ray's start point and direction vector are the same as the position and direction of the barrel of a weapon, then the first intersection point along the ray is where the projectile will hit. The ray might intersect with many objects along its path, but you're mainly interested in whatever the ray hits first. The same is true for a segment, except this changes its position each 'tick' (or iteration of the game loop) until it reaches its end point. These two methods are commonly referred to as 'hitscan weapons' and 'projectile weapons'.

First-person shooters frequently use hitscan for most weapons, since developers make the assumption that bullets move fast enough to instantly hit their target. This can be both for gameplay and simulation reasons, since players may expect their shot to strike an object regardless of how fast they or the target is moving. If you plan to build a more realistic shooter, however, you may not want to make this assumption. In this instance, you should segment the trajectory of the projectile, and simulate one segment per tick, giving it a finite speed. The *Battlefield* and *Arma* games are examples of this approach: both simulate projectile drop-off over long distances due to gravity. *Arma* even →

"'Hitbox' is a misnomer, because they come in more shapes than just boxes"

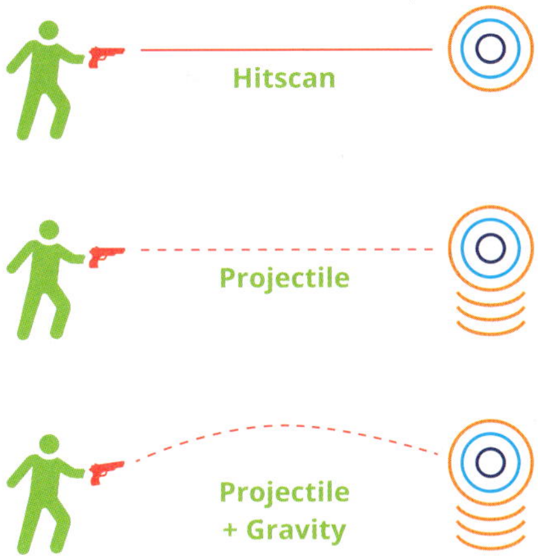

^ **Figure 2:** A comparison of hitscan weapons versus projectile weapons. Unlike hitscan weapons, projectile weapons can also simulate the effect of gravity.

For military shooter *Arma 3*, developer Bohemia Interactive went into obsessive detail over the physics, with projectiles even affected by wind speed.

Figure 3: Segments can be used to approximate the path of a projectile object like a grenade or a bouncing bomb.

simulates the lateral movement due to wind. Dropoff can have even more of a gameplay impact if a projectile's damage decreases the further it flies, as in *Counter-Strike: Global Offensive*.

Grenades are another type of projectile. These have a finite and relatively small velocity, so they're much more affected by gravity. A number of segments are generally used to approximate their path, tracing a perfect parabola that ignores wind resistance (see **Figure 3**).

To add dropoff for low-velocity projectiles, the length of the segment should be velocity * time delta per tick. For each tick, you should also change the direction of the segment according to gravity. Do this by adding g (= 9.81m/s^2) to the downwards velocity each tick (or do it through acceleration by applying a force $F=mg$ each tick, where m is the mass of the projectile – this will cancel out when the force is applied to acceleration).

The main decisions for projectiles come down to how fast the projectile is moving relative to the simulation tickrate, whether gravity and/or wind affects the path, and whether it bounces. There's a fun versus realism trade-off to be made here, though, and it may well be that the realism is part of your game's specific appeal.

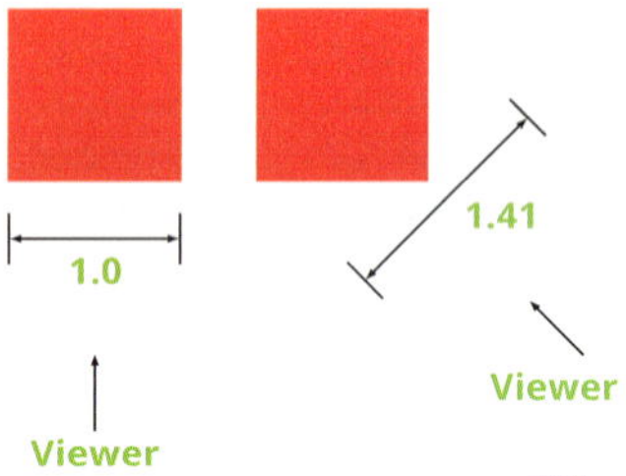

Figure 4: Although Axis-Aligned Bounding Boxes are great for computation speed, they suffer for hit accuracy. Hitboxes change size depending on another player's view, meaning shots that should 'miss' will hit.

EXPLOSIONS AND SPLASH DAMAGE

Low-velocity projectiles often have an area of effect, commonly known as 'splash damage'. This doesn't just occur at one point in space where the ray/segment hits, but radiates outwards. The best way to simulate this effect is to use a sphere or a cylinder (you can also use a spheroid or ellipsoid, although the latter isn't as common because it usually makes sense for the effect to radiate equally in all directions).

This could be as simple as finding all objects within a radius of the collision point and applying an effect. One problem with this method is that thick walls or other objects might not block the effect – think about how FPS players hide behind 'cover' when a grenade is thrown at them – without a very complex calculation. A workaround for this issue is to project rays out from the hit point to the edge of the sphere, and then applying the effect where those rays intersect with objects. This can avoid splash damage effects passing through walls, but the downside is a more expensive computation.

SPEED VS ACCURACY

Before you go ahead and build an approximation of your player model out of capsules and spheres, you'll want to think about gameplay. An interesting decision you

Scenery in *Battlefield* is built from several hitboxes, so destruction can take away the walls, the floors, and so on. In games like *Call of Duty*, walls will usually consist of a single hitbox rather than several.

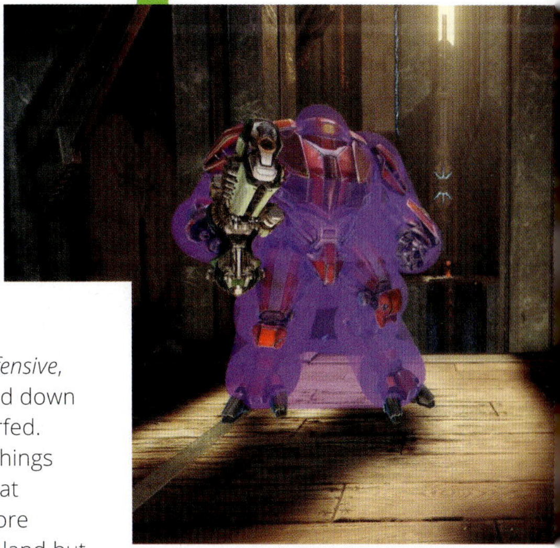

^ **Figure 5:** *Quake Champions* used chunky hitboxes to make characters easier to shoot.

have to make when building a shooter is that the accuracy of hitboxes for players and NPCs is strongly linked to the movement mechanics and speed of your game. The faster a player moves, the harder they are to hit; combining this with 'model tight' hitboxes might make for a game that is either too hard, or one that makes players think the collision detection is bad.

The *Quake* series is a good example of this. Up to and including *Quake 3*, the hitboxes for players were Axis-Aligned Bounding Boxes, containing the whole of the model. The advantage here for id Software was computation speed, but in terms of hit accuracy, it is probably the worst solution. The corners of the box stick out far further than the rendered model of the player, meaning even nearby shots that 'miss' the model would be counted as hits. This method is also directionally dependent, meaning that if you move vertically around another player by 45 degrees, the hittable area could expand by a factor of $\sqrt{2} \approx 1.41$ (**Figure 4**). But this was still great fun for players! Because movement speeds are insane, the hitboxes need to compensate for that slightly.

In *Quake Champions*, there are a couple of interesting differences. Its creators experimented early on with having hitboxes that almost exactly matched the rendered model using a triangle mesh hitbox, but, according to one developer, it turned out to be frustratingly difficult to hit. They then moved to a hitbox that comprised a sphere for the head and capsules for the torso and limbs. This sphere and capsule model was then expanded by about double for the lighter player models, to make players easier to hit and match the players' expectations of what they *should* be able to hit (**Figure 5**).

The developers chose this approach because the *Quake* games are arena shooters with an emphasis on fast movement techniques such as bunny-hopping, so having accurate hitboxes isn't as important as players being able to hit their opponents who are bouncing around the maps at high speed. Consider *Counter-Strike*, and particularly *Counter-Strike: Global Offensive*, where movement speed has been slowed down and bunny-hopping has been hugely nerfed. The slower speed of *CS: GO* means two things happen: the player finds it easier to aim at exact hitboxes, and it becomes much more obvious to the player when a hit doesn't land but 'should' have.

COUNTER-STRIKE

Counter-Strike is a great example of why hitboxes are so important in shooters. Its players are well aware that its hitboxes don't match the rendered models, and there have even been a few hitbox bugs in the game's history, each resulting in a community-led investigation. One of the larger ones was the fast-crouching bug, where the player could stand and crouch quickly, gaining sight of the enemy, but the hitbox would change back to crouching much quicker than the model would, meaning the other player wouldn't be able to hit the crouching player even if they could see the model.

If a player can give away their position by firing a single shot, and this can dramatically alter the outcome of a round, then the player needs to know for sure whether a shot has hit its target. The only way to do this is to ensure the hitbox matches accurately with what they see. Because this accuracy is so important to a slower-paced, every-shot-counts game like *CS: GO*, its developers have spent considerable time fine-tuning its hitboxes. *CS: GO* started with much tighter hitboxes than *CS: Source* or *CS 1.6*. The developers also decided to move from a box model (**Figure 6** overleaf) to a majority sphere and capsule model, and worked to make sure the hitboxes accurately reflected the bones of the character models for all animation poses.

The more complex and accurate the hitbox becomes, however, the more work you make for your netcode. Increasing the number of articulated joints increases both the game's bandwidth, and the chance that internet latency will cause a hitbox to appear out of sync to some players. →

THE QUAKE EFFECT

Fast-moving and competitive, *Quake* kick-started a subgenre of arena shooters, such as *Warsow*, *Reflex Arena*, *Xonotic*, and *OpenArena*. Each tends to closely follow *Quake*'s hitbox design: models are entirely cosmetic, and the player can choose what model to use for other players – every player has exactly the same hitbox, whatever they look like. These design decisions are made specifically for high-level competition – this competitiveness is one of the main drivers of hitbox importance.

Hitboxes in *Counter-Strike: Global Offensive* are smaller because the game emphasises accuracy over speed.

TWEAKING

In Unity and Unreal, you can tweak your hitbox sizes using either the Ragdoll Wizard (Unity) or the Physics Asset Editor (Unreal). Gathering feedback from playtests might be valuable here; your players may tell you that your fast-moving player models with highly accurate hitboxes are just too hard to hit, or that your slow-moving players with large hitboxes feel unfairly vulnerable to attack.

APPLYING HIT EFFECTS

Detecting a hit is only the first part of making a game feel real. The second part is applying a realistic effect to the hit player. In some games, this means different damage is applied, depending on which part of the hitbox was hit. For example, *CS: GO* applies less damage for leg and foot hits than it does for headshots. Headshots are so key to the *Counter-Strike* series that weapons are defined by whether they can kill a helmeted enemy with one headshot or not. The most well-known weapon which can do this is the AK-47, compared to the alternate teams' M4A4 and M4A1-S, which can't 'oneshot'.

Another mechanic that can be applied here is armour penetration and surface penetration. You may want projectiles to affect multiple objects along their trajectory and change the behaviour depending on what they pass through, which is sometimes known as 'wallbanging'. In this case, the hitbox intersection should return all of the objects or surfaces along the ray, not just the first. To implement this in your game, you may want a generic system that can calculate the proper modifier from each surface based on the thickness, angle of penetration, and material.

"The more complex the hitbox becomes, the more work you make for your netcode "

Varying damage by material and position can be done by detecting which part of the hitbox the ray or segment intersected with first, then choosing from a damage table what to apply. Varying by material could be implemented by lowering the damage of a projectile when it has already hit and passed through a thin wooden wall. Your game engine and terrain hitbox will need to detect these collisions and tell you what material an object is made of, then you can look up in a material table how much something penetrates that material, or lower the damage based on the thickness of the wall by detecting and calculating the distance between both the entry and exit points.

Just how weapons will interact with your game's hitboxes is a vital consideration. *Counter-Strike: Global Offensive*'s AK-47 can kill an opponent with one headshot.

DESTRUCTION

Vehicles are another aspect to consider. *Battlefield* has a system where a vehicle has multiple component hitboxes, which have unique effects when they're damaged or destroyed. Short of outright blowing it up, for

^ *Battlefield V*'s vehicles, including its tanks, have multiple hitboxes, allowing for different damage effects depending on where the player shoots.

example, destroying the tracks on one or both sides of a tank may limit its movement or stop it completely. Damaging the turret may disable it, and of course, hitting the players through a hole in the armour will damage them too. These are all possible if your hitboxes are fine-grained and well-matched to the model. Vehicle hitboxes can be quite different from the ones for players/NPCs and the map. Because vehicles have lots of flat surfaces, it makes much more sense to build them from oriented boxes rather than capsules.

Destructible environments can provide a great spectacle for players. In the *Battlefield* series, most structures can be damaged or completely destroyed, while the landscape itself can be destroyed by blowing holes in it. This requires something new in the hitbox system, where hits from a powerful class of weapon can *change* the hitbox of large objects. This could be accomplished by having the structure of a house, say, composed of smaller hitboxes for each individual wall. The wall-sections could either be destroyed in an on/off way, or broken up into even smaller wall-sections on a hit. These details help to immerse the player, but should be balanced carefully so that using buildings for cover isn't completely useless.

Allowing players to create their own cover is one way to balance the destruction aspect. In *Fortnite*, players can make and repair buildings with prefabricated walls and stairs. Players can create buildings taller and larger than anything else in the game, but this is balanced is by making the structures collapse if they cease to be connected to the ground. Other players then have the chance to kill their opponents with fall damage if they climb too high – although this tactic was slightly nerfed by allowing players to use their glider if they were at a high enough altitude.

^ Despite rumours on some corners of the internet, skins don't affect the size of a character's hitbox in *Fortnite*.

CONSIDERATIONS

There are so many decisions to make when developing your game, and there are examples of shooters that have found success with all kinds of different hitboxes. *Fortnite*, *Quake*, *Counter-Strike*, and *Battlefield* are all popular at least in part because of the consideration that went into designing hitboxes for players, NPCs, the map, and objects. By putting the time and thought into your hitboxes, you'll greatly increase the chances of making a successful shooter of your own.

< Most weapons in *Fortnite* are hitscan, but sniper rifles use segmented trajectories to simulate bullets that take a split second to hit their target, and drop off at longer ranges.

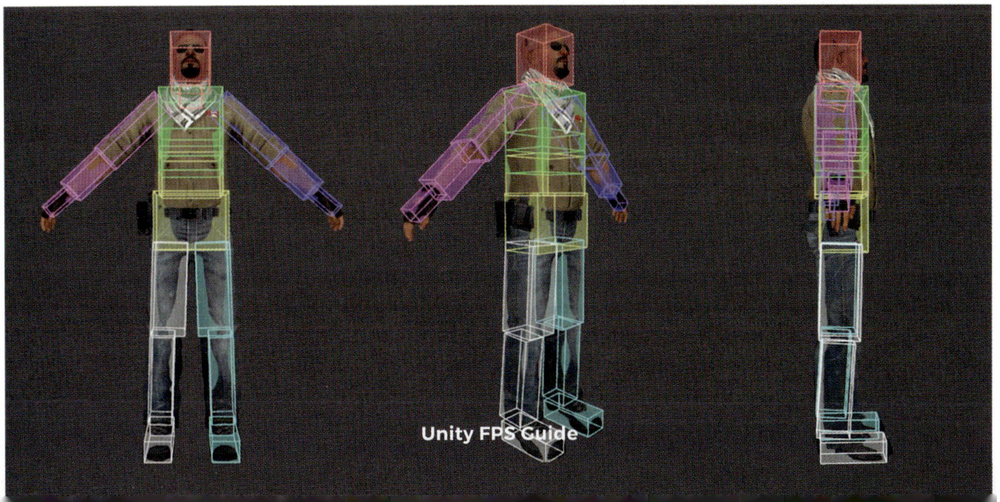

< **Figure 6:** Early builds of *Counter-Strike: Global Offensive* used cuboid hitboxes, before switching to mostly spheres and capsules for greater accuracy.

Level design, from a designer

The thoughts, feelings, and tips on great FPS level design by Blue Manchu's Jon Chey

It's obvious but true: level design is important. You can have all the best coding tricks and ideas in the world, but if your game's stages aren't any fun, people will switch off. Think back to something like *Halo*'s Blood Gulch, *BioShock*'s Fort Frolic, or *Half-Life 2*'s Ravenholm: they're all levels in which the wider game concepts take a back seat to the level design. It could be that they're intricate and smart, they tell a story, or they terrify you, but they all get your attention.

With this in mind, we took a few questions to Jon Chey, founder of Blue Manchu Games and developer on the likes of *Void Bastards*, *BioShock*, and *System Shock 2*. Basically, someone who knows a fair bit about FPS level design. What follows are his thoughts and top tips on the best – and worst – of FPS level design. Enjoy.

Breaking it down to a few parts, what are the essentials of good FPS level design?

Every FPS is different, and each demands a different approach. The number one pillar of good FPS level design is to respect the design goals of your game and support them through your levels. For example, *System Shock 2* is a game that supports a strong narrative, focuses the mood on anxiety and dread, and demands tactical skills as well as navigation and exploration from the player. It also supports revisiting levels multiple times, as well as grinding respawning enemies for resources.

So, good levels for *System Shock 2*:

- Supported the narrative.
- Made sense as 'real' spaces, not just combat arenas.
- Provided the opportunity for exploration and reasons to search spaces for loot.
- Afforded opportunities for interesting combat encounters that weren't always pre-scripted.
- Provided multiple pathways without becoming so complex that the player would get lost (unless that was our goal in a specific place – like in the engineering ducts).

These requirements result in a very different set of design constraints than were applied in, for example, *Tribes: Vengeance*. That being an open-world, team-based shooter with extremely rapid movement, flying, and focus on high-skill long-range shooting.

Of course, there are some principles that generally apply to most shooters. These would be things like:

CHEY'S GAMEOGRAPHY

- **Void Bastards** – 2019
- **Card Hunter** – 2015
- **BioShock** – 2007
- **SWAT 4: The Stetchkov Syndicate** – 2006
- **Freedom Force vs The 3rd Reich** – 2005
- **Tribes: Vengeance** – 2004
- **Freedom Force** – 2002
- **Thief II: The Metal Age** – 2000
- **System Shock 2** – 1999
- **Wall Street Tycoon** – 1999
- **Thief: The Dark Project** – 1998
- **British Open Championship Golf** – 1997
- **Flight Unlimited II** – 1997
- **Terra Nova: Strike Force Centauri** – 1996*

*Five lines of code!

^ *Call of Duty 4: Modern Warfare*'s 'All Ghillied Up' proved that a level doesn't need wall to wall action – just rock-solid design.

- Support the combat skill set you want from your players by providing the right amount of cover, terrain features, etc.
- Be visually interesting without distracting from the key gameplay features of the space.
- Be visually distinctive to aid navigation.
- Respect the performance constraints of your engine!

What are the basic mistakes people make when designing FPS levels? How can they avoid them?

A very common mistake I've seen is designers trying to create levels at a final art quality or focusing on the look of a space before understanding its gameplay. This creates two big problems: 1) the level takes too long to build; 2) the designer or team is reluctant to change it because they've already sunk so much time into it. This is where the process of 'greyboxing' is important – blocking out a space in a functional way so it can be gameplay tested before art polish is required. Of course, greyboxing has its own risks – by focusing on the gameplay, you may end up with a level that is visually boring. Or, you may build a level that doesn't make good use of prefabricated mesh pieces that have already been developed for the game. It's a constant struggle to balance the competing interests of gameplay and art.

There's a related set of challenges around the issues of making levels that feel like real spaces and levels that play well. The dimensions of real spaces often don't work well in games, and vice versa. For example, say you're building a level set in an office cube farm. The corridors between the workstations might be way too small for player or enemy navigation if they're based on real-world dimensions. Often, designers will make the mistake of scaling things too realistically. Or they might make the opposite mistake and create a great gameplay space that looks weird because it's so out of scale with the real-world place it's trying to represent.

THE BEST LEVELS EVER MADE

HALO: BLOOD GULCH

One of the things that makes this perennial favourite one of the best of all time is its design: it's an enclosed arena, but it's styled like a natural, American Midwest environment – and it's done so subtly that at no point do you feel hemmed in. It's also home to some of the finest capture-the-flag-focused multiplayer map design ever seen, a landscape of peaks and troughs, routes to sneak through, and boulders to hide behind; open space to make a run for it in, and the safety of a couple of home bases in which to be ambushed in another surprise attack. It even has enclosed corridor sections for some more traditional FPS action in the midst of a manic multiplayer melee. There's a reason Blood Gulch keeps on coming back for more in the *Halo* series (admittedly under new names each time).

Is there a magic sauce you've applied or seen applied to get around this problem of scaling? How is it something you avoid?

I don't think there's a magic sauce other than 'don't get lazy'. The right answer for any level is probably going to require some thought, and generally relies on prioritising gameplay over realism, using iconic visual elements rather than reproducing everything that might appear in an actual location, and compressing space (e.g. if you're building a level based on the Eiffel Tower, the scale is probably going to be nothing like the actual tower). 'Don't get lazy' isn't just a directive to produce more assets; it's also important not to just fall back on lazy stereotypes – i.e. the abundance of crates in FPS levels from *Doom* to now. I do think that understanding the function of a space you are building (in the game world) is important. →

THE BEST LEVELS EVER MADE

HALF-LIFE 2: RAVENHOLM

You almost don't pay it any attention, walking past a dark corridor on reaching a secret base in the opening hours of *Half-Life 2*. "That's the old passage to Ravenholm," Alyx Vance tells you. "We don't go there any more." This being a video game, the inevitable happens and you end up having to traverse this ex-mining town on your way to take down the Combine forces. And hoo boy, it's a doozy. Ravenholm single-handedly switches *Half-Life 2*'s tone from a smart, action-packed blast, into a panicked traversal of terror. The town is dark, dank, and riddled with headcrab zombies. Within seconds of arriving, you know exactly why Alyx and the resistance don't go there any more, and within minutes you never want to go back there either... except for all the times you replay this, one of the best levels in one of the best games ever made.

If you don't know what the inhabitants of the space use it for or why it exists, you're going to end up building rooms full of crates, and that's boring. If you know that this room is a kitchen or a laundry, you've got a head start on knowing how to decorate it and lay it out. Every good dungeon master knows the same thing.

Where should we look for examples of great FPS level design?

Of course I'm biased, but I think *System Shock 2* and *BioShock* both have a very interesting selection of levels to look at. *BioShock* in particular provides a great deal of lessons about how to weave narrative elements and gameplay together in tight ways. Jordan Thomas's Fort Frolic is rightly acclaimed as a very powerful level amongst many good ones in that game.

How important is writing/narrative? Is it something you'd recommend FPS designers look to?

I wouldn't recommend anyone get into writing or narrative design unless they're going to take it very seriously. Games have often suffered from designers thinking that writing and narrative can be done by someone who has read a lot of books or seen a lot of movies. Yes, some of the games I've worked on are guilty of this. I'm not trying to gatekeep writing, just making the point that it has to be treated as a serious skill set that takes a lot of time, effort, and talent to be good at – just like any other discipline, from programming to QA.

What are the unique factors that matter when designing a large level?

Performance, obviously, but also navigation and connectivity. Do you want your players to be able to navigate the level easily or do you want to challenge their spatial skills? Do you plan to provide them with a map or do you want the level itself to provide all the navigational cues they need? If the latter, you better be sure you design visually distinctive spaces that provide memorable landmarks, and think about how those landmarks reveal themselves from every direction you expect the player to arrive from.

What would you recommend as an approach for each 'type' of design you mention?

Most FPS levels are probably built for ease of navigation, supporting a fast-paced play style. That relies, of course, on fairly simple connectivity and heavy use of recognisable landmarks. Most single-player levels tend to push the player forward without any significant branching choices and with clear imperatives to move forward (a light shining onto the door that leads into the next area, for example).

If you're building a game that wants to challenge navigational skills instead, you're probably looking at much more complex connectivity that rewards players for finding alternate routes. Maybe you want to build in windows where players can look ahead and see what's coming up before they decide how they're going to approach the next combat encounter.

When designing *Void Bastards* levels, which have very free-form gameplay and thus can't be designed as a fixed linear experience, we focused on making each room (module) a small but interesting combat arena, and then built each level so that it had a small number of loops, allowing the player to traverse the level without having to backtrack through already cleared areas. We then sprinkled a bunch of shortcuts, either corridors or crawlspaces, on top of this to provide variety. In addition, varying the connectivity could then create new types of challenges, like dead ends or highly connected sub-spaces.

> **"If you're building a game that wants to challenge navigational skills, you're probably looking at much more complex connectivity that rewards players for finding alternate routes"**

And what are the unique factors that matter when designing a small level?

In *Void Bastards*, we built a level that is literally just two rooms connected together. I love that level because it's really different to our normal-sized ships and provides a nice variation in gameplay – get in and get out in under a minute.

Of course, you wouldn't want to play a level like that too frequently because the choices you can make inside it are pretty limited.

^ *Void Bastards*: a strategy shooter, and much more.

What was the process like to make a two-room level as impactful as an intricately designed, sprawling mass?

Oh, I don't think that level is as impactful as a normal level. What makes it interesting is the contrast with other levels in the game. And that's an important point – games are boring if the experience is flat and repetitive. Each level should have something to say that's different, otherwise why is it in the game at all?

What's the difference between designing for single and multiplayer levels?

It is literally designing two different games, and that's why I think we're finally seeing many shooters not trying to support both. I mean, just look at some of the key differences:

- MP levels designed to be played hundreds or thousands of times; most SP levels designed to be traversed once or twice.
- SP levels support narrative; MP levels are largely combat arenas.
- MP levels generally designed to get players into combat quickly without much travel time; SP levels often support exploration as well as combat.
- Massively different performance constraints.

What are examples of co-op multiplayer needing different design approaches?

It's not an area where I have a lot of experience. Co-op was added to *System Shock 2* after it shipped, which obviously meant that we didn't spend a lot of (or any) time thinking about how it should impact level design. I think that shows in the final product, and not in a good way.

Games with complicated narrative scripting (like *System Shock 2*) obviously introduce a lot of potential problems when you have more than one player running around in the space – for example, we want to lock the player in a room and then have some scripted moment happen. What happens if the other players aren't in the same room?

Are there any tools or pieces of software you'd recommend for use in designing the perfect levels?

Given the 3D nature of FPS levels, I think sketching in 2D has utility, but blocking out in the actual engine quickly becomes more useful. I think the most critical thing is the ability to quickly switch between the editor and running around in the level in the game itself. Nothing beats viewing (and playing) your level in the actual game to understand if you're going in the right direction.

Do you think paper prototyping is useful for FPS design?

It's useful at an early stage to talk about ideas and rough flow. I think it very rapidly becomes insufficient – and potentially misleading, due to the huge difference in representational complexity.

What feature can no good FPS level be without?

Cover. The player needs the ability to not get shot, as well as shoot their enemies.

Outside of building the map, what's another important design factor people might overlook?

Do you include placement of spawn points, loot, and scripting in 'building the map'? Because those things can easily take more time than the raw placement of geometry.

Probably the biggest thing novice level builders might overlook, though, is data gathering, analysis, and using that to drive changes to the level. Obviously, this is true in MP levels, but every SP level can also benefit from seeing how real players interact with it. Sitting behind a player and watching them get lost in your level can be very illuminating.

Is it helpful to consider other genres when working on a first-person shooter?

Yes – particularly these days as new games are often crossing genre boundaries. For example, we describe *Void Bastards* as a 'strategy shooter', but it also contains roguelike elements. So, the rhythm and pacing of roguelike games was an important reference point when thinking about how large and complex our levels should be. When we were mixing RPG elements with an FPS for *System Shock 2*, we drew inspiration from other RPGs. I'm a big believer in genre mixing and being aware of what's going on in the larger game design space.

If you could boil it down to one bit of advice, what would you say to the aspiring FPS designers out there?

Please don't just copy other shooters. I want to experience something different from your game – go to someplace I haven't been before or [where I'll] be challenged by something that I haven't [yet] confronted.

THE BEST LEVELS EVER MADE

BIOSHOCK: FORT FROLIC

BioShock has the player travelling through the undersea world at the behest of one main character or another, until they enter a very separate realm: Fort Frolic. Like the rest of Rapture, this was once a thriving region, presided over by an artist known as Sander Cohen, and home to all the fine art, theatre, and debauchery a person could reasonably crave. After the fall of Rapture, Fort Frolic remained closed off in its own little bubble inside the larger sphere of the city. Cohen's world mixes things up significantly, throwing the player at the mercy of a new character, who tells them to carry out acts which are… *different*, let's say, from the rest of the game. It's terrifying, atmospheric, and brilliant.

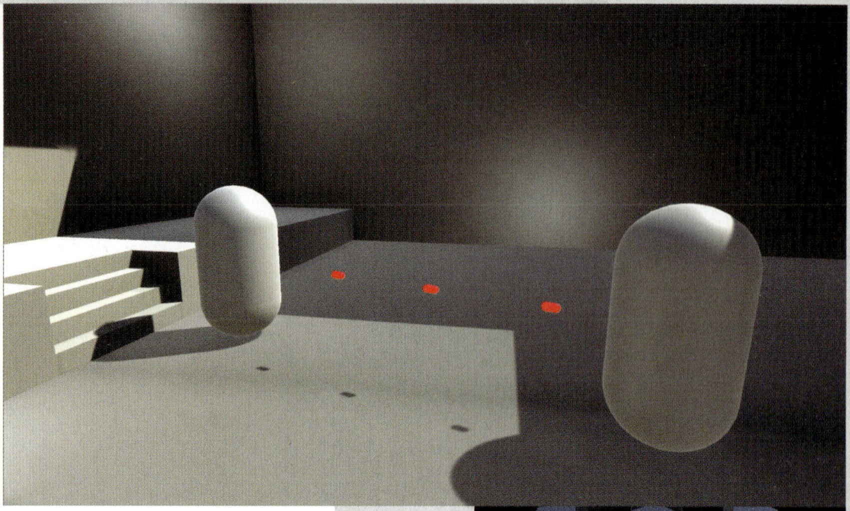

So there you have it: by now, you should have a simple yet fully-functioning shooter up and running in Unity, complete with marauding zombies, a level to explore, and items that top up your health and ammo levels. Better yet, piecing *Zombie Panic* together should have given you a better understanding of Unity, and how you can use it to extend and customise the game almost beyond recognition.

Maybe you don't want to have zombies slowly staggering around the place, and prefer the idea of having smaller, speedier creatures attack the player instead. Maybe you'd prefer to have levels that are more open than our infested castle, with more branching paths and items to collect. Or maybe you want to drop the shooting angle altogether, and have the player laying traps or using stealth and cunning to evade enemies.

As the past 25 years have proved, the first-person shooter is a hugely malleable genre: we've seen fast-paced, arcade-like shooters; other shooters that favour narrative over action; and shooters that emphasise planning and tactics over razor-sharp reactions. With time, practice, and imagination, the design possibilities are almost limitless.

What will you come up with?

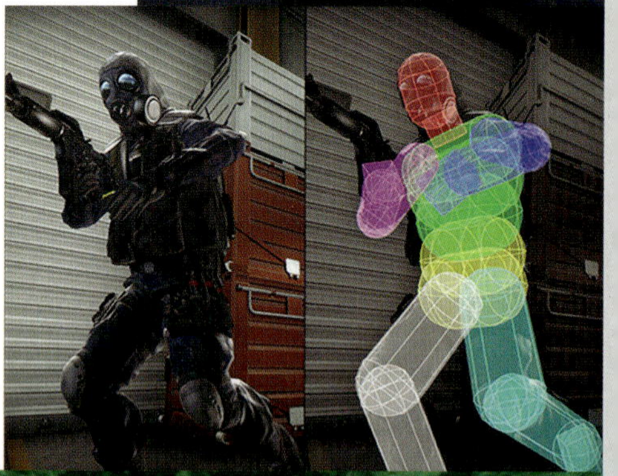